BUSINESS DRIVEN PMO SUCCESS STORIES

Across Industries and Around the World

MARK PRICE PERRY

Copyright © 2013 by Mark Price Perry

ISBN-13: 978-1-60427-076-1

Printed and bound in the U.S.A. Printed on acid-free paper.

10 9 8 7 6 5 4 3 2 1

Library of Congress Cataloging-in-Publication Data

Perry, Mark Price, 1959–
  Business driven PMO success stories: across industries and around the
world/by Mark Price Perry.
     pages cm
  Includes bibliographical references and index.
  ISBN 978-1-60427-076-1 (hardcover: alk. paper) 1. Project
management. 2. Project management—Case studies.
I. Title.
  HD69.P75P472 2012
  658.4'04—dc23

                              2012043502

Phone: (954) 727-9333
Fax: (561) 892-0700
Web: www.jrosspub.com

Dedication

This book is dedicated to the hundreds of executives, PMO managers, and practitioners of project management whom I have had the opportunity to work with and learn from over the last three decades.

I can only hope that I have accurately portrayed the wisdom that you have graciously shared with me.

Contents

Foreword

Over the last 25 years, project management has been indispensable in the successful management of change. In this time, project management has evolved from a skill set exhibited by a few to a profession espoused by a practicing community. Due to its success and unlimited practical application enterprise-wide, project management has further evolved into an essential core competence for all knowledge workers, not just those formally trained and certified, not just those who work within the boundaries of the formal project portfolio of the organization, but all workers who have some kind of a project to deliver.

Project management is ubiquitous. It is all around us. And so too are the benefits of systematically doing a better job of it. Toward that aim, one would think that a project management office (PMO) would be a natural and welcome driver to improvement in the management of projects and a successful, long-lived organization within the enterprise. This has not been the case. As reported by numerous research organizations and industry sources, a majority of PMOs are shut down after two years. Though some PMOs have met with success, most have not.

As there is no shortage of best practices, standards, tools, smart people, and even a practicing community, these things can't be the problem. So then what is? The problem is the wide chasm that exists between theoretical strategies buffeted by knowledge standards and practical application honed through measurable achievement. What is needed is a way to bridge this chasm and reach a balanced PMO perspective on both the purpose of the PMO and the needed behaviors of the PMO to fulfill that purpose.

The book you have in front of you won't by itself hold all the answers that you need in order to find your unique balance—but it will greatly help. It will provide you with what you must first know and do in order to avoid being yet another failed PMO statistic. It will shed light on techniques to ensure that your PMO is driven by business needs and accountable in a manner that can be quantifiably measured. It will also provide you with numerous case examples of PMO success stories, each in a format that articulates the business problem to be addressed by the PMO and how the success of the PMO was achieved.

Most of all, this book is about PMO business acumen, leadership, and the recognition that the practical application of project management and of PMOs spans from the formal project portfolio of the organization to the informal project mix of the business units, and it incorporates both plan driven techniques and the principles of complex adaptive systems. The tested perspectives and experiences of the author and of the many PMO success story contributors provide a bouquet of acumen, leadership, and real-life lessons. With the importance of the PMO only rising and with the PMO failure rate still far too high, this book and the Business Driven PMO book series should be on the bookshelves of all PMO managers.

Bernie Keh
President, BOT International

Acknowledgments

I began researching and writing the Business Driven PMO book series five years ago in 2007. This effort was spurred on by a number of colleagues, who have been the dearest of friends, and by my loving Singaporean "Chinese Tiger Wife," whose lofty goals and unreasonable expectations only increase with time. Collectively, this trusted inner circle of mine not just believed and shared my convictions that the formal project management and PMO community was making a mess of things with respect to PMOs and needed to be steered in a much more business driven and balanced direction with respect to standards of practice and their practical application, but believed that I was worthy of the effort—an effort that would include not just putting words to paper but spreading this message all over the world to a formal project management and PMO community that for the most part was not that open to having their belief system challenged. I have no doubt that this PMO book series and the worldwide tour of speaking engagements that have spanned six continents and over 50 countries would not have come to completion without their encouragement and support, and for that I am very grateful.

I would like to equally acknowledge the many project management and PMO professionals who have come to hear me speak and who have participated in the Business Driven PMO workshop experience. These workshops by design are meant to be highly challenging, provocative, and rich in interaction and idea sharing. Though the maverick provocateur role is not my nature, I have found it to be the most effective way to both shine a bright light on the elephant in the room and to stimulate a reflective discussion and call for action. Much like panning for gold, a bit of agitation is sometimes needed to shed that which is worthless and to discover that which is treasure. Typically, by the end of these workshops that are structured to commence with argumentative dissension and to conclude with Kumbaya celebration, many lasting friendships have been made. And my reward has been not just these friendships that in their own right have been more than I could have ever hoped for, but all that I have learned from others over this journey. With sincere appreciation and humility, I am highly grateful to all of you who have collectively challenged, questioned, helped define, confirm, and temper my perspectives.

Lastly, it would be remiss of me to not acknowledge Drew Gierman, my publisher at J. Ross Publishing, for the continued advice, support, and friendship that you have afforded me over the years with this book series that enabled me to never doubt that it would come to fruition.

About the Author

In 1999, Mark Price Perry founded BOT International, a boutique firm that specializes in PMO setup. As the head of operations, Mr. Perry manages product marketing, services, and support for Processes on Demand (POD), a productized offering for PMO content assets.

Mr. Perry has been with BOT International since its inception and has implemented POD in more than 100 PMOs in North America, Asia Pacific, Europe, and Latin America. Largely as a result of years of experience in PMO setup work with companies and organizations and with talented project management practitioners of all disciplines, Mr. Perry is a servant-leader and subject matter expert in the practical application of project portfolio management (PPM) applications, collaboration platforms, and PMO content assets.

Mr. Perry is the author of two best-selling PMO books, *Business Driven Project Portfolio Management: Conquering the Top 10 Risks That Threaten Success* (2011) and *Business Driven PMO Setup: Practical Insights, Techniques and Case Examples for Ensuring Success* (2009), both published by J. Ross Publishing. Additionally, Mr. Perry is the host of "The PMO Podcast," the leading podcast for PMOs of all shapes and sizes, with over 250 PMO podcast episodes to date. Mr. Perry is the author of the Gantthead blog, "PMO Setup T3—Tips, Tools, and Techniques." He is also the author of BOT International PMO "Tips of the Week," a column that has provided PMO and project management tips for over a decade.

In addition to formal project managers and members of the PMO, Mr. Perry has helped tens of thousands of *informal* and *accidental* project managers apply the knowledge and techniques of the Project Management Institute Project Management Body of Knowledge.

Prior to BOT International, Mr. Perry had a 17-year career with IBM, including positions as the IBM AS/400 Division telecommunications industry manager based in New York, the IBM Asia Pacific AS/400 channels manager based in Tokyo, and the IBM Asia Pacific AS/400 general manager for Southeast Asia and South Asia based in Singapore. Following IBM, Mr. Perry was the vice president and managing director of Singapore-based Saville Systems Asia Pacific, a leading provider of billing and customer care solutions, and vice president of Hong Kong-based Entrust Greater China, a leading provider of identity management and digital security solutions.

Mr. Perry is from the United States and attended the American College in Paris in 1978/1979 and graduated Beta Gamma Sigma from Virginia Tech in 1981. Mr. Perry speaks English and is conversant in Japanese, German, French, and Spanish. Outside of work, Mr. Perry enjoys golf and music and is a volunteer bugler at Bugles Across America, a nonprofit organization dedicated to ensuring that a live rendition of "Taps" is played at the funeral services of American's veterans.

Workshops and seminars by the author on Business Driven PMO Setup and Management using this book, as well as other training and consulting programs on various PMO and PPM topics are available by contacting BOT International via the Internet at www.botinternational.com or toll-free at 1-877-239-3430.

Contributors

Panagiatis Agrapidis
Suhail AlAlmaee and Mounes Rashid Shadid
Juan Arraiza
Marion Blake
Harlan Bridges
Jimmy Char
Luis Crespo
Jennifer Drai
Richard Eichen
Laila Faridoon
Ricardo Ferrero and Kathie Mitchell
Ole Holleufer
Henry Kazalma-Mantey
Wai Mun Koo
Yechie Labay
Vanessa Matsas
Colin Anthony McCall-Peat
Christopher McCourt
Frank R. Myers
John O'Neill
Frank Parth
Henny Portman
Patrick Richard
Andrew Wilson and Karen Krause
Troy Youngnickel
Erhard Zingg and Martin Kuepfer

Preface

I wrote this book and the Business Driven PMO book series for a new generation of PMO managers: a generation that is far more concerned with ensuring the project-related business success of their companies as opposed to defending outdated approaches, a generation that provides accountable leadership that offers no distinction between product of the project failure and project management failure, a generation that views PMOs and project management as indispensable business tools—a means to an end, but never, ever the end unto itself.

This book and the Business Driven PMO book series presents a new paradigm for PMO management. For many this new paradigm will be a welcomed change in perspective, for others it will be a challenge to the current thinking about PMO setup and management and test one's convictions. In either case, I truly believe that if you apply the principles and techniques of these books, you, like many others before you, will have a successful business driven PMO. Additionally, you will do a significantly better job of applying project management and project portfolio management techniques, working with the members of your leadership team, and mentoring and improving the technical project management and leadership skills of not just your project managers but all those involved in the projects of your business.

There are many contributing factors that make setting up and managing a PMO a perilous undertaking. Additionally, it would be a huge mistake to assume that everyone in the organization stands behind, is truly committed to, and wants the PMO to succeed. And setting aside resistances to change and the intentional mischief that must be dealt with, the highest hurdle that most organizations must leap over is not being led astray by all the well-intended but misguided PMO advice that comes not from outside kibitzers but the very institutions, organizations, and sets of people that comprise the formal project management and PMO community.

Fortunately, there are a number of very good PMO books that any organization seeking to set up a PMO would be well advised to read. For years I have recommended some of my favorites, which include *Advanced Project*

Portfolio Management and the PMO by Kendall and Rollins, *The Program Management Office* by Letavec, *Project Portfolio Management* by Levine, and *Taming Change with Portfolio Management* by Durbin and Doerscher. These books are very good in their own right and I highly agree with the thought leadership, principles, and techniques they represent relative to the context of the environment for which they are offered. Yet, as good as these books and others are, there is a reluctance to address the elephant in the room. That is, the practical application of project management and PMOs is stuck in a rut and has been boat anchored by the unintended consequences of a successful industry—an industry that promotes a myopic view of the project-related world that we all live in, an industry that promotes the profession with no accountability for results, and an industry that has created its own jargon and set of terms having forgotten and long lost the ability to speak the language of business. Yes, we have found the enemy and the enemy is us.

Like the two books that preceded it in the Business Driven PMO series, this book seeks to fill a void in the current industry literature. It boldly confronts and challenges both our thinking about project management and PMOs as well as our thinking about our project management institutions. In addition to a presentment of PMO research, studies, findings, and perspectives of the author, this book features the business and PMO management leadership of a blue-ribbon set of PMO managers from all over the world who share their perspectives, their PMO success stories, and their agreement with and endorsement of the Business Driven PMO mantra.

Business Driven PMO Success Stories was written by and with over two dozen contributing authors from the worldwide project management and PMO community. Collectively, the 12 chapters of Part 1 of this book and the PMO manager success story showcase pieces in Part 2 present a tapestry of knowledge for how to ensure a successful PMO. Although there isn't a single approach that is categorically the best or a one-shoe-fits-all-sizes solution or road map for how to set up an effective PMO, there are two distinct differences in philosophies, or mind-sets, for how to go about it all, one that is aligned to general standards of practice and another that is driven by specific needs of the business. This book advises and introduces its reader to the latter.

Business Driven PMO Success Stories offers executives, managers, and all those involved in the projects of the organization the knowledge they need to first determine the purpose of the PMO, their PMO, and to then craft a PMO best suited to the fulfillment of that purpose. In a few hours of reading, you will gain insights from the authors' and contributors' tens of decades of PMO-related experience. For those seeking to set up a new

PMO or to refresh an existing one, this book will start you off on the right track and in the right direction, it will ensure your success, and it will spare you from the execution difficulties and in many cases failures that most organizations needlessly suffer through when setting up and managing their PMOs.

Introduction

In 1981, I entered the workforce after graduating from college and landed a job at the International Business Machines Corporation or IBM as most people call it. I joined the Data Processing Division as a marketing representative in the Dallas Branch Manufacturing Office and embarked upon its 18-month training program. Formally, I learned much about data processing equipment from mainframe to personal computers, industry applications, databases, development tools, networking systems and protocols; this was what we sold to our customers. Informally, I learned much about project management and PMOs; this was what we employed to manage long, complex, and competitive sales cycles and to transform areas of the business.

From my experiences being in PMOs, managing a few PMOs, and having PMOs report up to me or serve me along with other constituents, I have witnessed how PMOs can play a key role in meeting an unmet business need, fulfilling a mandate, achieving a set of defined objectives, and delighting stakeholders as measured by a very real and quantifiable business value. In short, I learned firsthand and have come to passionately believe in how PMOs of all shapes and sizes can be of tremendous benefit to an organization.

Imagine my surprise when in the late 1990s I entered the formal project management and PMO community. I had had two decades of very successful project management and PMO experience, all on the goal-oriented and objective-rich line of business side. In my mind's eye I had a clear perspective on what project management was and more importantly what a PMO was. What I soon discovered within this formal project management and PMO community was a much different perspective. Adorned by its industry associations and standards and certifications, these new PMO perspectives that I soon discovered were far more than disappointing; they were nothing short of shocking and, I might add, disturbing.

Far from the results-oriented, management by objective, delight the customer, respect the individual, and seek continuous improvement culture that I was trained in and understood, I found a myopic and self-serving project management community and view of what a PMO should be. This myopic view was characterized by theoretical PMO models, simplistic strategies absent of any measurable objectives to be achieved or mandate to be fulfilled, and misguided advice for obtaining executive buy-in and selling the PMO by those who have never sold, have never been trained in selling, and who wouldn't recognize a sales best practice from a telephone book. Yet, without any such training in sales or experience in selling, they spoke about *Selling the PMO* and gave advice on how to do it. Really?!

In this formal project management and PMO community, I also observed the exploitative promotion of knowledge-based certifications and all that comes with that in the form of products, consulting services, and training that would violate any sensible code of professional conduct guidelines. Also in plain sight was a view of the PMO that was more loyal to *the profession* and more interested in the establishment of a Center of Excellence or Community of Practice of some kind than it was in being a properly cast and accountable organization, as managed and measured by goals and objectives that served to fulfill a mandate or in the least solve a set of business problems as determined by the leadership team for whom the PMO exists to serve.

Harsh words? I don't think so. Anecdotally, having worked with hundreds of PMOs in over 50 countries across six continents and having seen how these organizations have suffered such similar fates and consequences of a misguided project management and PMO community, I stand behind these words resolutely. And statistically, with generally accepted industry studies and research from multiple sources citing that 25% of PMOs fail within year one, 50% of PMOs fail within year two, and 75% of PMOs fail within three to four years, all permanent PMOs mind you, the only sensible inference that one can make is that within the formal project management and PMO community there is a significant problem with its view of what a PMO is.

The remediation of the industry's incorrect view and poor PMO track record is not to throw out all that has been advanced over the years within the formal project management and PMO community. To the contrary, much of what has been accomplished has served to build a foundation from which greater works can be realized. But, there is a difference between laying bricks and building an architectural work of art. Toward that aim and in the context of a PMO, that difference is the balance that must be struck between *the means to the end* and *the ends to be achieved*. Put another way, until an organization casts the purpose of its PMO in terms of what business problem the PMO is solving and how the PMO will be held accountable, then there can be no sensible discussion of such things as theoretical PMO models, simplistic strategies, and techniques for tricking people into being happy with their PMO.

Perhaps there is no wiser man and stronger advocate of this premise than Mark Langley, the CEO of the Project Management Institute, who not long ago advised attendees of the 2010 Gartner Group PPM and IT Governance Summit that if we continue to speak of project management in terms of such things as scope, time, and cost, then project management will fail us all. Mr. Langley went on to suggest that we need to speak of project management in terms of a new and more contemporary project management triangle, one that has at its three points (1) technical project management per our standards and bodies of knowledge, (2) business acumen, and (3) leadership. And for this, there is no certification.

What Mr. Langley and other project management and PMO experts know all too well is that when PMOs are driven by the needs of the business, they succeed, and when PMOs are driven by other motivations and biases, they are short-lived. This premise is what distinguishes the business driven PMO from other forms of an organization that concerns itself with projects.

The purpose of this book is not intended to be a detailed description of best practices or functions that a PMO could do, as there is no shortage of already published works that present the means to the ends. Rather, this book as the third in the Business Driven PMO series presents a worldwide perspective that highlights PMO success. The first part of the book, Part 1, presents 12 chapters that provide information essential to PMO success that is organized and referred to as PMO Mandate, PMO Business Acumen, and PMO Future. The second part of the book, Part 2, features PMO success stories from all over the world. These stories all follow a common format of first describing the overall business environment, the specific business problems to be addressed by the PMO, the story of the PMO, the achieved success of the PMO, and the aftermath of concluding thoughts and advice. These stories also demonstrate, in practice, the importance of being driven by business needs as opposed to merely rushing into a cookie-cutter PMO model and strategy in advance of real leadership team involvement and support.

If your organization is starting a PMO, this book and its predecessors in the Business Driven PMO series will ensure a PMO success and spare you immeasurable amounts of time, money, and organizational frustration. If you have a PMO that is struggling, this book will help you find the success that you know it is capable of achieving. And if you have the PMO that believes it has already done it all and that has little else to do aside from maintaining its current course and speed, this book will open a world of new perspectives and opportunities.

Lastly, in addition to providing a corrected, balanced, and business driven focus to the formal project management and PMO community perspectives and views on the PMO, this book seeks to make PMO managers aware of, and challenge them to, greater professional and career heights and to provide them with the means with which to reach those heights. Over the years, I have witnessed numerous, highly talented PMO managers promoted to positions of greater rank, responsibility, and remuneration. Always, these promotions were because of the PMO manager's achievement of measurable business results and the leadership team's belief that the PMO manager was the best candidate for further advancement.

Technical project management expertise, business acumen, and leadership are the required fortes of business management, and they are not limited in application to the traditional view of a PMO and placement of a PMO manager. Yet, for many PMO managers, there is an uncomfortable feeling and sentiment that the career path for PMO managers is limited to nonexistent. In one sense, I tend to agree. For the PMOs that are not business driven, it is quite likely that their PMO managers will soon find themselves defending their PMOs and their jobs or looking for new PMO manager positions elsewhere. But in another sense, I quite disagree. PMO managers who are driven by the needs of the business, accountable for the achievement of measurable business results, and who display not just project management competence but business acumen and leadership will find themselves highly competitive and in continual demand. Toward that aim and the success of your PMO, I hope that this book provides compelling insights, actionable ideas, and testaments of worldwide PMO success worthy of your consideration.

Mark Price Perry
Orlando, Florida

At J. Ross Publishing we are committed to providing today's professional with practical, hands-on tools that enhance the learning experience and give readers an opportunity to apply what they have learned. That is why we offer free ancillary materials available for download on this book and all participating Web Added Value™ publications. These online resources may include interactive versions of material that appears in the book or supplemental templates, worksheets, models, plans, case studies, proposals, spreadsheets and assessment tools, among other things. Whenever you see the WAV™ symbol in any of our publications, it means bonus materials accompany the book and are available from the Web Added Value Download Resource Center at www.jrosspub.com.

Downloads available for *Business Driven PMO Success Stories: Across Industries and Around the World* include three PMO planning and management primers to help you establish and manage a business driven PMO:

◆ **A Business Driven PMO Mandate Primer and Template.** For those seeking to avoid the unnecessary mishaps of traditional PMO setup, this primer offers an effective approach and template for establishing a business driven PMO mandate.

◆ **A Business Driven PMO Strategy Primer and Template.** This primer and template guides the user through the process of developing a business driven PMO strategy that will outline the success criteria, action plan, critical success factors, and key needs to ensure the mandate of the PMO is fulfilled.

◆ **A Business Driven PMO Executive Dashboarding Primer.** This primer provides an effective approach and policies for establishing effective PMO executive dashboards.

Part 1

Business Driven PMO Insights and Techniques

Section 1

PMO Mandate

Mandate (noun)—the approval, power, or command to do something.

3

1

Why PMOs Fail

It's a simple question. Why do PMOs fail? Over the years, there has been no shortage of analysis and commentary on this subject. We have all been treated to the research reports that show 25% of PMOs fail within their first year, 50% of PMOs fail by their second year, and 75% of PMOs fail and are closed by their fourth year. And these are permanent PMOs, not temporary program offices that by design will be closed after the program has concluded.

So, given this more than ample amount of analysis of the marked and measured rate of PMO failures, the documented reasons why PMOs fail, and the proposed recommendations for what a PMO should be and do to avoid failure, why has there been such little movement and improvement in the rate of PMO failures over the years? And with respect to PMOs in general, why is the project management community making such a mess of it all? We have tools, we have standards, we have certifications, and we have a lot of really smart people. So what is the problem?

I have my own thoughts and perspectives on why PMOs fail that are based upon more than a decade of asking this specific question to executives to whom the PMO reports, to management and constituents served by the PMO, to IT professionals, to agile software development enthusiasts or agilistas (a term many use to describe the passion and perspectives of this vibrant and growing community) and I have asked this question to the members of the PMO itself such as PMO managers, PMO officers, project managers, business analysts, and a wide variety of others who work in the PMO. But before sharing my thoughts and perspectives on why PMOs fail, let me first suggest that as a community of project management professionals most of us are stuck inside the box in terms of our thinking about PMOs.

Figure 1.1   Stuck inside the box

As depicted in Figure 1.1, being stuck inside the box is not a lot of fun or where you want to be and it is hard to get out. It is akin to being stuck in a rut where the direction and outcome are all but predetermined. In the context of why PMOs fail, the only way we can become unstuck and get out of the box is to think outside the box. After all, it has been the same inside the box thinking about PMOs that has led to the high failure rate and in many cases negative sentiment about PMOs and the project management community as a whole.

For example, did you know that in the agile development community, the term PMO means Pissed Me Off? Other nonflattering terms that I have heard over the years include Pretty Myopic Organization, Pouring Money Overboard, Project Management Overload, Poorly Managed Office, Project Management Orangutans, and on and on.

Thinking outside the box, especially when trying to break a pattern or poor track record or losing streak, is tremendously beneficial. Actually, it is a requirement. Thinking outside the box can reveal new approaches and techniques that are often right before our very eyes and within our grasp. However, for most people, thinking outside the box is not natural, it is very hard to consciously do, and it is very difficult to see even the easiest and most obvious solutions to problems even though they are right in front of us all the time. Don't believe me? Let me prove it to you.

Over the years, I have given PMO presentations and conducted PMO workshops in over 50 countries spanning six continents. When presenting new, outside the box ideas and concepts, I always like to start the presentation with a little exercise to demonstrate how hard it is for us to think outside the box, as well as to demonstrate how natural and prevalent our tendencies are to remain inside our own little box of thinking even when we are specifically asked to step out of it. As no challenge is complete without a reward, I always take a $100 bill out of my wallet and offer it as a reward to the first person who can successfully find the answers to the exercise. Are you ready?

The exercise goes like this. In less than five minutes, using the four numbers (1, 2, 3, and 4) and the two arithmetic operators for plus and equals (+ and =) as shown in Figure 1.2, rearrange all these numbers and operators into three different and correct equations. Each equation must use all four numbers and both operators and use them only once.

This seems simple enough. Did you already think of the answer 1 + 4 = 2 + 3? That is the most common wrong answer that is quickly cited. The equation is correct of course, but the plus sign is used twice. Again, all numbers and operators must be used and used only once. As depicted in Figure 1.3, the three solutions to the exercise are (1) one to the power of two plus three equals four, (2) one to the power of four plus two equals three, and (3) three times four equals twelve. In this last solution, the plus sign is rearranged by rotating it 45 degrees, making it a multiplication sign. Arguably, this last solution is more outside the box than the first two solutions, which merely employed the use of exponential notation.

Rearrange the following numbers and operators into three different and correct equations, using for each equation all of the numbers and operators only once.

$$1\ 2\ 3\ 4 + =$$

Hints:
You know the answers.
If you have kids in fifth grade, they know the answers too.
If you think inside the box, you will not arrive at the answers.
If you think outside the box, you will.

Figure 1.2 Thinking outside the box exercise

$$\text{Solution \#1} \longrightarrow 1^2 + 3 = 4$$

$$\text{Solution \#2} \longrightarrow 1^4 + 2 = 3$$

$$\text{Solution \#3} \longrightarrow 3 \times 4 = 12$$

Figure 1.3   Solutions to the thinking outside the box exercise

The broader point, however, is that all these solutions to the exercise are quite simple, one might even say trivial. But did you arrive at any of these solutions, not to mention all three of them? If you did, then give yourself a pat on the back as you are in very select company. In all the times over the years that I have conducted this little test at various PMO workshops and seminars as an example of how hard it is to think outside the box, only once have I lost my $100 bill to someone who was able to come up with all three answers.

Now, with that exercise behind us, think about all the reasons and rationale for why PMOs fail that have been posited within the project management community over the years as well as the suggestions and advice that are given to avoid PMO failure. The top five reasons for PMO failure that I often read about or hear in presentations are as follows:

1. Lack of executive support
2. Ineffective and overburdensome project management methodologies
3. PMO viewed as template police rather than helpful to the business
4. PMO does not have enough decision-making authority to ensure success
5. Value of the PMO not understood

But are the above reasons really the reasons why PMOs fail or are they merely symptoms of a deeper root cause for PMO failure?

For example, few PMOs magically appear out of thin air. There was obviously executive support for the PMO or it would not have come into existence. Likewise, such things as methodologies and templates are a means to an end, not the end to be achieved, so it is illogical that these things would be a root cause of PMO failure. In a similar vein, what can possibly be meant by not enough decision-making authority? Most people will inherently do what helps them succeed and avoid what doesn't. If the PMO is helping others succeed, then wouldn't people take the appropriate actions without the PMO needing more decision-making authority over them? And more decision-making authority for what aim—to make the business successful or to comply with a PMO strategy and project management methodology that may or may not be effective and appropriate for the organization? When people suggest that the value of the PMO is not understood, do they mean the value of preparing documents and reports or do they mean the value of best addressing specific project-related issues and opportunities that the organization has?

There is a very simple reason why PMOs fail, but it will not be found from inside the box of the traditional thinking about PMOs. Before we get to that very simple reason, let's reflect upon some of the advice that has been given over the years and that has dominated the project management community. Have you heard the term people, process, and tools? Have you read the often suggested road map for setting up a PMO that includes (1) pick a PMO model, (2) list your PMO roles and responsibilities, (3) establish quick wins, and (4) sell the value of the PMO? Have you heard the advice to crawl, walk, run?

All these perspectives and many more are the result of an inside the box way of thinking about the PMO, a perspective that is more focused on the means to the ends of the PMO and what a PMO ought to be in a perfect world, rather than a perspective that is focused on the ends to be achieved by the PMO as driven by needs of the business for which the PMO exists to serve. This causes execution difficulties for the PMO right from its start; PMOs are far too often set up and managed based upon someone's idea of what a PMO ought to be, rather than specific business end results to be achieved.

Take the advice of a well-known and well-intentioned PMO authority who shall go nameless so as not to embarrass this individual. The advice that this individual, like so many others, has given on the role of the PMO includes the following:

- Strategically align the project portfolio to the goals of the organization.
- Develop project, program, and portfolio processes aligned to industry standards.
- Implement a project management information system.
- Develop a training program to certify project managers.

- ◆ Develop a list of PMO services.
- ◆ Conduct project audits.
- ◆ Provide project reporting to management.
- ◆ Conduct regular project management maturity assessments.

That the above list, and other lists like it, is a collection of well-intentioned ideas for a PMO is of no debate. That the above list solves the specific business problems of a given organization would be a gross assumption and an error in business judgment. In layman's terms, it is putting the horse before the cart.

It is put best by one of my dear friends and longtime project management and PMO expert Doc Dochtermann, formerly of the Microsoft Project Portfolio Management (PPM) Solutions team, who rhetorically asks:

If the PMO is the answer, then what was the question?

This pithy and pointed question illustrates a tremendous problem and issue within the formal project management community. There is far too little focus, virtually nonexistent, on what business problem, as determined by the constituents of the PMO, the PMO is actually going to solve for the organization, right now, and what the value of solving that problem is in terms of, and as measured by, PMO end results achieved. It is hard to argue the point that without knowing the problem to be solved, one can't advance a sensible solution. Yet, this is exactly what is advised and happens, time and time again, within the formal project management community. And this is the reason why PMOs fail with such speed and regularity and, I might add, lose the support of executives and annoy others along the way.

2

PMO Survey Findings

When I entered the formal project management and PMO community over a decade ago and after 20 years of experience, all of which was in the field lines of business of the company, I was quite surprised to see, hear, and learn how different the formal project management community's view of a PMO was as compared and contrasted to the view that I and my line of business colleagues had about our PMOs and PMOs in general. For the first few years of my entrance into the formal project management and PMO community, I just assumed that the differences in our PMO views were simply because of the interactions that I was having with specific individuals at various project management conferences, seminars, and events and that these individuals, though they presented a common view as a subset group, could not possibly represent the collective view of the formal project management community as a full and broader group of PMO professionals. After discussions with my colleagues at BOT International, we decided to conduct a survey for the purposes of determining if there are any inferences that can be made, based upon research data, from the different views of what a PMO is and what a PMO should do.

The year was 2007. Using Student's t-distribution analysis techniques, we structured our initial survey to ask a set of questions to a very homogeneous group of 25 IT PMOs at companies with similar fundamentals such as revenue, income, number of employees, etc. Obviously, there are many other kinds of PMOs, and IT PMOs should not be viewed as the only or best or most important type. In fact, one could argue that too much of what is presented within the project management community about PMOs comes from a slanted, IT PMO perspective. Nonetheless, IT PMOs are perhaps the most homogeneous of the lot and it was necessary to have a homogeneous sample size; otherwise differences in the data might be attributable merely to differences in the PMO types contained within the sample.

One section of the survey concerned itself with the focus and perceived value of the PMO as shown in Figure 2.1. We asked the following questions:

◆ Does your PMO have measurable objectives? By measurable objectives, we mean measurable performance objectives for a given report period from which the PMO is held accountable. This is not to be confused with key performance indicators.

◆ What is the top area of focus of the PMO? This question was intentionally open-ended so that the answers provided would best reflect the top focus of the PMO and not the closest fit of the multiple choice answers provided. Also, using an open-ended question prevented the potential bias of selecting from a predetermined list of answers.

Survey Questions to Determine the Perceived Focus and Value of the PMO	
Survey Question	**Response**
Does the PMO have measurable objectives? (Yes/No)	
Top area of focus of the PMO? (Open-Ended)	
PMO self-assessment of performance? (A-F Grade)	
CIO assessment of PMO performance? (A-F Grade)	
How Important is it to sell the PMO? (Very Important to Very Unimportant)	

Figure 2.1   PMO survey questions

◆ What is the PMO manager self-assessment of the performance of the PMO? The answer to this question was in the form of a grade, much like a school grade, where A is outstanding (honorable distinction), B is above average (honor roll), C is average (not bad), D is below average (needs improvement), and F is failing (not passing and not acceptable).

◆ What is the CIO assessment of the performance of the PMO? By design, these were all IT PMOs that reported to the CIO, so the grade would be coming from that titled position. The grading scale was the same as described above.

◆ How important is it to sell the value of the PMO? The answers to this question included very important, important, unimportant, and very unimportant.

The answers to these questions are shown in Figure 2.2.

What can be inferred from the answers to these survey questions? At first glance, one might conclude that PMOs are organizations that are not held accountable, their top area of focus is concerned with project management methodology, they are performing quite well as self-assessed and

Survey Questions to Determine the Perceived Focus and Value of the PMO	
Survey Question	**Response**
Does the PMO have measurable objectives? (Yes/No)	No
Top area of focus of the PMO? (Open-Ended)	Methodology
PMO self-assessment of performance? (A-F Grade)	B
CIO assessment of PMO performance? (A-F Grade)	B–
How Important is it to sell the PMO? (Very Important to Very Unimportant)	Very Important

Figure 2.2 Answers to PMO survey questions

Survey Questions to Determine the Perceived Focus and Value of the PMO		
Survey Question	**Business Driven PMOs (8) Response**	**Theory Driven PMOs (17) Response**
Does the PMO have measurable objectives? (Yes/No)	Yes	No
Top area of focus of the PMO? (Open-Ended)	Speed	Methodology
PMO self-assessment of performance? (A-F Grade)	C+	A–
CIO assessment of PMO performance? (A-F Grade)	A–	C–
How Important is it to sell the PMO? (Very Important to Very Unimportant)	Very Unimportant	Very Important

Figure 2.3 PMO survey analysis

assessed by the executive to whom they report, and it is not just important but very important for the PMO to engage in *Selling the PMO* activities to ensure that others throughout the organization understand the value of the PMO. Overall, one might tend to think that this would seem to be a good reflection of the state of the PMO in terms of focus and value; not a bad picture.

After peeling the onion back and taking a second, more detailed look at the data, a quite different picture came into view. As shown in Figure 2.3, a further analysis of the answers to the survey questions revealed two distinct statistical modes. One of these groups we classified as business driven PMOs and the other we classified as theory driven PMOs.

The analysis of this simple survey was quite revealing and suggested that there were, in essence, two very distinct types of PMOs in terms of perceived focus and value; in subsequent telephone interviews with all the participants, this distinction further crystallized and manifested itself.

Of the business driven PMOs, these organizations were all driven by very clear mandates and these mandates were ensured by specific goals and objectives for which the PMO was held accountable. This was clear not to just the PMO but to those served by the PMO, as in most cases the mandate and objectives were set not by the PMO but by those served by the PMO. The top area of focus of the business driven PMOs was speed. When asked what speed was being referred to, such as the speed of selecting new projects, speed of project management activities, speed of delivering projects, speed of making decisions, and speed of identifying and resolving issues, the answer was yes to all the above. It was interesting that the PMO managers of the business driven PMOs gave themselves very modest grades (C+) while at the same time their immediate bosses, the CIOs, were extremely satisfied with the PMO and gave it high marks (A−). And neither the PMO managers nor the CIOs of the business driven PMOs felt that ever so recommended tactic and advice of *Selling the PMO* was needed and rated that as very unimportant.

By way of comparison and contrast, the theory driven PMOs had no performance objectives in place. Their top area of focus was project management methodology, all of which was aligned to the Project Management Institute's *A Guide to the Project Management Body of Knowledge* (*PMBOK® Guide*). These PMO managers graded themselves rather high (A−), yet the executives to whom they reported graded these PMOs at a much lower, marginally acceptable level (C−). The PMO managers and CIOs of these theory-oriented PMOs all felt that it was quite important to engage in *Selling the PMO* activities. With no clear mandate, no performance objectives, inward focus on project management methodology, and a marginal level of performance, it is not beyond the realm of possibility that the constituents of these PMOs are not particularly thrilled with their PMOs. Of course, the conclusion that the PMO should go about engaging in *Selling the PMO* activities and campaigns is woefully misguided, and that is a topic for the next chapter of this book.

This PMO research is interesting and insightful for a number of reasons. First, given the very high rate of PMO failure, this research helps to reveal foundational reasons for that failure. Few organizations can have a marked, measured, and sustained success without a compelling mandate for the organization, mechanisms to measure fulfillment of that mandate, a focus on what is most important, a tempered perspective on achievement, and a satisfaction of end customers through effective plans, strategies, and tactics. The PMO is not immune to these basic management premises, yet in far too many PMOs these basic business management tenets are absent.

The PMO failure rate as discussed in the previous chapter is often cited as 25% by the first year, 50% by the second year, and 75% by the fourth year. This 2007 PMO survey revealed that 17 out of 25 (68%) of PMOs are set up with no measurable performance objectives. Using small sample size statistical methods and reasonable margins of error, these findings can

2012 Survey Questions to Determine the Perceived Focus and Value of the PMO		
Survey Question	**Business Driven PMOs (28) Response**	**Theory Driven PMOs (52) Response**
Does the PMO have measurable objectives? (Yes/No)	Yes	No
Top area of focus of the PMO? (Open-Ended)	Agility	Methodology
PMO self-assessment of performance? (A-F Grade)	C+	A–
CIO assessment of PMO performance? (A-F Grade)	A–	D+
How Important is it to sell the PMO? (Very Important to Very Unimportant)	Very Unimportant	Very Important

Figure 2.4   PMO survey analysis (2012)

be extrapolated to the broader PMO community. In light of this, can it be a surprise to anyone that the PMO failure rate is so high? And wouldn't it be interesting and insightful to see if there has been any change in the last five years in the perceived focus and value of the PMO per these exact same questions? Well, that is just what we did. In 2012, we surveyed 80 PMOs and asked them the exact same questions. As before, we kept the survey homogeneous and limited participation to just IT PMOs so that differences in responses could be studied and attributed to something other than differences in PMO types.

As shown in Figure 2.4, there are a few subtle differences in the data from five years ago, but the overall results are just about the same.

Overall, from 2007 to 2012, the percent of business driven PMOs went up from 32% to 35% and the percent of theory driven PMOs went down from 68% to 65%. However, this is within the statistical margin of error, so it would be incorrect to suggest that a marked level of improvement has been made.

It is interesting to note that for the business driven PMOs, the top area of focus changed from speed to agility. In subsequent phone interviews, this distinction was attributed to a focus on being both concerned with speed in terms of total cycle time and flexibility or nimbleness in terms of having and demonstrating the ability to adapt to different program and project situations and needs. This combination of speed and flexibility was what the survey group meant by agility. This did not mean Agile in terms of Agile software development, but rather just what the word agile implies: quick and nimble.

Aside from the change in top area of focus from speed to agility, the remaining responses of the business driven PMOs showed no changes from 2007 to 2012. The PMO self-assessment of performance was still a C+ (slightly better than average), the CIO assessment of PMO performance was still an A− (just about outstanding), and the response on how important it is for the PMO to sell itself still came back as very unimportant.

For the theory driven PMOs, there was insignificant change in the responses between the 2007 and 2012 surveys. The overall percent of theory driven PMOs went down from 68% to 65% from 2007 to 2012. Again, this was within the statistical margin of error so it would be incorrect to conclude that improvement had been achieved. The top focus area of the theory driven PMOs was still methodology and the PMO self-assessment was still an A− (quite confident); however, the CIO assessment of PMO performance dropped from C− (not quite average) to D+ (needs improvement). And again, the PMO managers and CIOs of the theory driven PMOs still responded that the activity of *Selling the PMO* was very important.

In terms of what can be inferred from the data of these two PMO surveys, 2007 and 2012, the key observation is that there are clearly two kinds of PMOs from a business management perspective. We can debate about whether or not the two labels, business driven PMOs and theory driven PMOs, are the most appropriate labels to assign. But what is not debatable is that there is a clear and measurable difference and distinction between these two types of PMOs.

Another aspect of the 2012 PMO research that we conducted was to obtain survey response information from the heads of other functional groups to add further depth and clarity to the topic of the perceived focus and value of the PMO. Two of these questions that we asked the vice presidents of marketing, sales, services, and the CFO were:

1. Should a PMO have measurable objectives?
2. Should a PMO engage in *Selling the PMO* activities?

The response scale for both questions was as follows:

- Strongly agree
- Agree
- No opinion

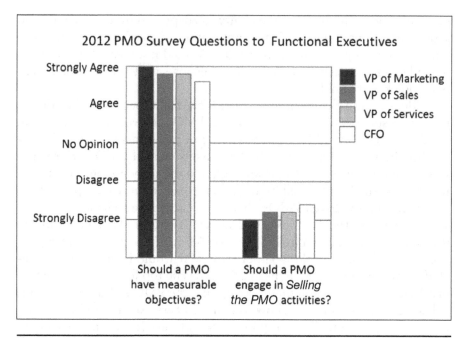

Figure 2.5   Functional executive responses (2012)

◆ Disagree
◆ Strongly disagree

As shown in Figure 2.5, it is quite clear that the heads of these other functional groups strongly agree with the idea that PMOs should have measurable performance objectives in place, and they strongly disagree with the idea that *Selling the PMO* is an appropriate activity for the PMO to engage in.

We asked these functional heads these two questions in particular for two reasons. First, since joining the formal project management and PMO community over a decade ago, we have been a bit dumbfounded at the resistance to the idea that PMOs should have measurable performance objectives in place, much like any other business unit or organization within the enterprise. In all of our collective line of business PMO experiences as members of PMOs, as heads of PMOs, as executives to whom the PMO reported, and as members of the leadership team for whom PMOs existed to serve, these PMOs always had performance objectives. How else could it be determined that the mandate of the PMO had been fulfilled? How else could the business plan and strategy of the PMO, including budget and head count, be approved, evaluated, and managed?

Secondly, this ill-conceived idea of *Selling the PMO* that has been and continues to be espoused within the formal project management and PMO community has always been a source of bewilderment to us. Setting aside for a moment that most PMO managers have no training in selling, have never had a professional role as a salesperson, and would not recognize the leading sales best practices (SPIN, RADAR, TAS, GTM, COS, and MDM) or a Miller Heiman *Blue Sheet* from a telephone book, who thinks this is a good idea to do? As a PMO manager, I never did this. But more importantly, as an executive to whom the PMO reported and in executive roles in which I was a constituent of the PMO, I can't imagine in my high-performance business environments and rich management by objective company cultures how a PMO manager could do this but once and not be severely reprimanded, not to mention lose professional credibility with the leadership team.

It was refreshing and a validation to see that the PMO survey responses of these leadership team members were consistent with the business driven PMO. Perhaps if more of these functional executives participated in the formal project management and PMO community, we would have fewer theory driven PMOs. In Chapter 5, Techniques for Establishing a PMO Mandate, it will be shown that PMOs that are set up correctly do not need to engage in *Selling the PMO* activities and conversely those PMOs that are prone to adopting *Selling the PMO* activities choose to do so because the PMO was not set up correctly in the first place.

Lastly, in working with hundreds of PMOs over the last decade, I have seen a very consistent pattern of evolution among the theory driven PMOs. Very predictably, a PMO is set up much along the lines of a theory driven PMO. By that, I mean that the PMO was set up with no real mandate, no performance objectives in support of that mandate, and a focus on project management methodology and *people, process,* and *tools* kinds of cookie-cutter strategies. Like clockwork, by the end of the first year there is disillusionment with the PMO and a feeling that despite all the efforts of the PMO team, not much has improved. In fact, it is unclear among the ranks of the leadership team whether the PMO should even be continued.

Predictably, the leadership team is not ready to abandon the PMO, but they are ready to replace that first PMO manager. So, the second PMO manager in the early life of the PMO arrives. How is that second PMO manager different from the first? What does the second PMO manager do that is different from what the first PMO manager did? What I have seen over and over is that the second PMO manager is markedly different from the first PMO manager: higher in real or perceived rank, much more of an alpha personality type, more competitive, more of a go-getter, and much more intolerant to the perception of failure. In terms of strategy, what does the second PMO manager do differently from the first? Not much different is done in terms of strategy, but in terms of tactics the second PMO manager engages in *Selling the PMO* activities to promote the PMO internally, make friends, and achieve buy-in to the PMO by others.

This pleases the PMO team and provides them a temporary sense of comfort and security. But soon enough the PMO hype and jazz wear thin, and by the end of the honeymoon period of the second PMO manager, usually the second year of the PMO, the leadership once again expresses concerns and doubts about the value of the PMO. It is at this point in time that one of two outcomes occurs. About half of the time, the PMO is shut down. It may or may not rise from the ashes at a later point in time. And the other half of the time the PMO is continued and another change is made in the position of the PMO manager.

This time, the discussions of the PMO that are commenced are not in the language of the formal project management and PMO community in terms of PMO models; cookie-cutter *people*, *process*, and *tools* strategies; PMBOK methodology; project management training and certifications; and such things. Rather, the discussions of the PMO are conducted and carried out in the language of business. What specific problems does our business have which a PMO of some kind can meet? What is the value to the business of having those specific problems resolved? Based upon the desire of the business to have the PMO solve those specific problems, what shall be the mandate of the PMO and how should the PMO be measured?

Almost always, from this construct of the PMO based upon the language of business, not the babble of the formal project management and PMO community, the third attempt of the PMO meets with success.

3

Project Management Community Mind-set All Wrong

For quite some time, I have advocated that the formal project management community mind-set is all wrong with respect to the PMO as an organizational entity of some kind within a business setting such as a commercial for-profit firm, a governmental institution, or a nonprofit organization. In my two previous books, *Business Driven Project Portfolio Management* (2011) and *Business Driven PMO Setup* (2009), as well as numerous white papers that I have submitted and presentations and workshops that I have conducted, I have shared my observation that the formal project management community focus in terms of PMOs is entirely too centered upon the *means* (PMO models, methodology, tools, training, and technical project management techniques) to the end and not focused enough on the ends to be achieved in terms of the specific business problems, the business need that the PMO exists to address and meet, and the benefits to the business of having met those needs.

Some of my business driven PMO colleagues suggest that those who weigh in and shape the formal project management community do not have the requisite training, executive development, and experience in business management, financial management, and organizational development and leadership to understand and speak the language of business. As a consequence, the formal project management community has invented and has adopted its own jargon and language. Now, after so many years and as a matter of self-determination and preservation, it stays within this comfort zone, chooses to focus on that which exists in this alternative world, and ignores and has a blind spot for that which is outside of it. One unintended consequence of many is a disconnection between business professionals and project management professionals (PMPs) in terms of perspectives, behaviors, and language. Simply put, business people don't speak project management and project management people don't speak business.

Not long ago I had the pleasure to meet Harvey Levine, who is the author of a very good book on project portfolio management (PPM). Harvey was attending one of my PMO workshops, and I must admit, upon learning that he was in attendance I was quite nervous having him in the audience. It wasn't so much because Harvey is a recognized subject matter expert and guru in project management, PPM, and the management of the PMO and that I have far more to learn from him than the other way around. Nor was it because he has written dozens of white papers and a few very good books on the subject and is often credited as the early pioneer in what is now commonly referred to as PPM. All of that did weigh in, mind you, but what made me just a little bit anxious was the fact Harvey was a Project Management Institute (PMI®) Fellow, a past President and Chair of PMI from 1983 to 1986, and he was instrumental in establishing PMI's certification program. And in the next three hours I was going to present provocative material and engage the audience in workshop exercises that would reveal and prove, with one real-life business case example after another, that the formal project management community mind-set with respect to the PMO is all wrong and that there is far too much focus on knowledge and certifications and far too little focus on the practical application of project management and end results achieved.

In short, PMI was the mother, the formal project management and PMO community was her child, and I was calling her baby ugly. This was what made me just a bit apprehensive and overly careful in my choice of words throughout my Business Driven PMO Setup and Management workshop. Imagine my surprise when, after the workshop concluded, Harvey commented that the workshop was spot-on and addressed the core, fundamental problems and issues that threatened the success of PPM as a management practice and the implementation of a PMO as a business driven, goal-oriented, organizational entity. Imagine further my surprise when Harvey Levine mentioned to me that, after discussions with PMI leadership about strategy and direction, he withdrew his membership in PMI over concerns that PMI was becoming too commercialized in terms of revenues, certifications, and products and losing its way and losing its place

Figure 3.1   Mind-set all wrong: a call for balance

as a trusted industry standards organization for the advancement of project management standards and best practices.

So what exactly is it about the mind-set of the formal project management and PMO community that is all wrong? Many people advocate, and I agree, that it is the unbalanced focus between the means to the ends and the ends to be achieved, as depicted in Figure 3.1.

This unbalanced view is the myopic, all-consuming focus on such things as PMO models, project management methodologies, tools, training and certifications, and technical project management know-how without the accompanying focus on what these things are intended, or even can achieve, for the organization. In layman's terms, it is putting the horse before the cart. When this happens, as it far too often does, you inevitably have a runaway freight train of well-intended ideas that result in a calamity of mishaps, errors, and organizational frustrations. Why? Because the ideas for the practical application of project management and the setup of the PMO are not based upon the end results achieved of solving specific business problems and meeting specific business needs; hence, they seldom do!

Let's examine a few examples of the formal project management and PMO community mind-set. The following five points represent the perspectives and mind-sets of very well-known people in the formal project management and PMO community who often present at the conferences and events of the community. Naturally, I will not disclose the names of these people as I have no desire to publicly embarrass anyone; my only aim is to reveal what I believe are incorrect views that contribute significantly to PMO execution difficulties and in many cases PMO failures. For each of these points regularly advocated within the formal project management and PMO community, I will provide a counterpoint.

- ◆ Point 1: PMO placement in the organization
  - • The PMO should report to the CEO or COO and it should be enterprise in scope. If not, the PMO will not have the full view of the projects of the organization, it will not be able to strategically align the projects to the strategy of the company, and it will not have the power to get things done.
- ◆ Counterpoint 1: PMO placement in the organization
  - • Although there can be tremendous value in an enterprise PMO that reports to a CEO or COO, the enterprise PMO is but one of many types of PMOs. Not every PMO needs to be an enterprise PMO and not every PMO needs to report to the CEO or COO. This mind-set overlooks the tremendous value that PMOs can provide to the many different constituents in the many different places within the organization from lines of business to divisions, departments, and functional teams. Where a PMO should be placed and who it should report to should be driven by needs of the business, not a narrow view and predetermined mind-set of what a PMO should be.
- ◆ Point 2: Considerations for setting up a PMO
  - • Unless an organization has a lot of projects and named project managers, you don't need a PMO. Establishing a large PMO with complex methodologies and tools would be overkill.
- ◆ Counterpoint 2: Considerations for setting up a PMO
  - • Why does a PMO have to be a large PMO with complex methodologies and tools? The mere fact that the organization does not have a lot of projects is likely to mean that there will be a wide variety in the project management skill of those who have some kind of project to manage. It is not just named project managers who have the formal title of project manager who manage projects. In such organizations a one-person PMO, or even a virtual PMO in which the responsibility of setting up and managing the PMO is an assigned duty of a functional manager, can be of tremendous

value. By standing up and making available tempered guidance that is easy to access, promotes skill development through learning as you do, *and* is based upon the business need for how to manage projects, significant improvement in the management and delivery of these project efforts can be realized.

♦ Point 3: Project management methodology
  • The purpose of a project management methodology is to apply the standards and practices for project management that are contained in the PMI Guide to the PMBOK.
♦ Counterpoint 3: Project management methodology
  • The purpose of a project management methodology is not to apply the standards and practices for project management that are contained in the PMBOK. The purpose of the project management methodology is to ensure a consistent and repeatable outcome whether based upon one standard in particular, multiple standards collectively, or parts of both standards and emerging best practices yet to become a standard. It is important to note that the PMBOK is a project management body of knowledge, not a methodology. As a body of knowledge, it does not provide contextual guidance for projects of different types and sizes. It also does not provide guidance for the PMO and project-related work that takes place before initiating a project and after closing it. As a body of knowledge for plan driven projects, the PMBOK fails to provide any guidance with respect to other approaches for the management of projects and project-related work such as those contained in the contemporary field of study referred to as complex adaptive systems. Organizations that seek to merely apply the PMBOK as a project management methodology will fail.
♦ Point 4: Project management training and certification
  • PMOs should develop an ongoing project management training program that seeks to certify all project managers and provide basic project management training to all employees in the organization.
♦ Counterpoint 4: Project management training and certification
  • For most businesses and organizations it is not possible, practical, or affordable to train all employees in project management. Training strategies, including certification of project managers, should be driven by business need, not a mind-set that every project manager should get a PMP and every employee should learn basics in project management. Though well intended,

strong advocates of project management with such views actually do project management a disservice as this mind-set can result in a misplaced focus. Rather than developing business driven strategies for training related to specific areas of need, the purpose of training is measured in terms of certifications for project management staff and attendance in basic project management training for all others. Rather than viewing the PMO as a business unit that has accountability just like other business units in the organization, the PMO is viewed as a center of excellence. Rather than being viewed as a needed organization that ensures the project-based success of the company, the PMO is viewed as bureaucratic overhead staff that makes work for other people.

♦ Point 5: Technical project management approaches
  • If you are not using earned value management (EVM), then you are not reporting project performance accurately or managing the project properly.
♦ Counterpoint 5: Technical project management approaches
  • EVM is not appropriate for all projects. Although EVM might be suitable for plan driven projects with fixed requirements such as building a parking garage, where, with the possible exception of weather and the time it takes to get building permits, all that is needed to know such as materials (concrete, wood, steel) and resources (workers) is knowable, EVM may not be required or even possible for other projects. This is especially the case for projects where requirements are not knowable, not to mention small projects, where the project is over before such time as earned value techniques can be sensibly applied. Use of techniques like EVM should be a matter of PMO policy, not mandatory for every project, and projects should not be viewed as improperly managed just because EVM was not used.

It would not be hard to go on and on with these points and counterpoints. If such mind-sets were those of just a few misguided project management and PMO enthusiasts, they could be dismissed. Regrettably, these mind-sets are commonplace and continually perpetuated within the formal project management and PMO community. But how do our executive and leadership teams feel about all of this? Do they also share the view that the formal project management and PMO community mind-set is all wrong in these matters?

As part of our 2012 PMO survey, we asked the functional executives of the 80 companies in the survey if they agreed with the mind-set of

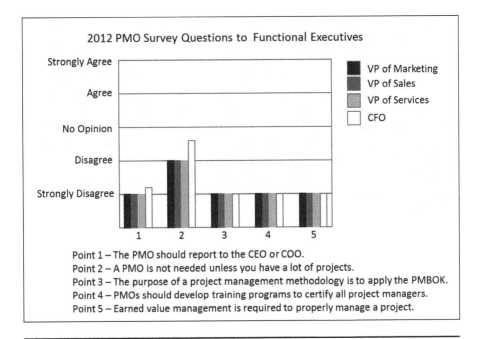

Figure 3.2 Degree of leadership team agreement

the formal project management and PMO community as represented by the five views just given on (1) PMO placement, (2) considerations for having a PMO, (3) project management methodology, (4) project management training and certification, and (5) technical project management approaches. As shown in Figure 3.2, it is quite clear that the members of the leadership team do not agree with the views of the formal project management and PMO community.

The point of bringing to the attention of the formal project management and PMO community that their mind-set toward project management and the PMO is all wrong is not intended to unfairly criticize the community, nor is it to suggest that all the advances in project management that have been attained should now be summarily dismissed. To the contrary, the point is to shed a rather bright light on what we all know as a public secret. There needs to be more business focus and accountability for business results within the project management community.

The PMO is not a country club. With rare exceptions, for most businesses the PMO is not a Community of Practice and the PMO is not a Center of Excellence. The idea that at Level 5 of PMO maturity the PMO becomes a Project Management Center of Excellence is nothing but mis-guided folly. Being good at what we do merely gives us the opportunity to play the game, and that should never be confused with the final score.

The sooner the formal project management and PMO community rec-ognizes that it has a mind-set problem, the sooner it can then not just learn how to speak the language of business but embrace it in their views, convictions, and business driven strategies for the practical application of project management and effective use of PMOs. At that point we will have a balance between the means to the ends and the ends to be achieved with respect to project management and PMOs. This, I truly believe, will be fol-lowed by a significant improvement in the performance and track record of PMOs.

4

Case Study Example
of PMO Failure

There are many ways for a PMO to fail and examples of PMO failure are not too hard to find. As always, there are many contributing factors that lead to execution difficulties of any organization. Some suggest that the more a business unit that is supportive in nature spans multiple functional organizations that each operates in its own silo with differing objectives and motivations, the more that support business unit is likely to encounter resistances to its plans and strategies and sometimes resistances to its existence. Few business units fit that description better than a PMO. Others suggest that the more a business unit is supportive in nature and contributing to but not directly in the value chain of the enterprise, the more likely that business unit is to be perceived as overhead, whether in fact it is or not, and a leading candidate for restructure or closure in the face of organizational downsizing and budgetary cutbacks. As most PMOs inherently contribute to but are not in the value chain of the enterprise, there is some merit to this premise as a rationale for the conditions that contribute to PMO failures.

These insights and others offer a perspective on some of the institutional factors that make it so challenging for even the best of PMOs to have and sustain success, but the reason for PMO failure, especially first-time PMOs, is much simpler. There is a very common theme and reason why most first-time PMOs struggle and 25% of them fail in their first year. And there is a villain, a culprit that can be clearly identified and blamed for this PMO failure track record without any sensible disagreement.

There is no better case study example of PMO failure than the company that I first wrote about in *Business Driven PMO Setup* (2009). It offers a didactic allegory for anyone wishing to understand why so many PMOs fail and why the rate of PMO failures has not diminished over the years. Additionally, having presented this story to C-level executives, project management and PMO practitioners, and agile development professionals in PMO seminars, workshops, and executive breakfasts all over the world, the moral of this story has been validated by thousands of PMOs across six continents and in over 40 countries.

This case study example of PMO failure is a story about a small, high-growth company. This company had a few hundred employees, and under the leadership of its CEO and management team it had enjoyed tremendous success. The CEO of this high-growth company recognized that all the entrepreneurial behaviors, risk taking, and seat-of-the-pants decision making that had worked so well in the past would not be scalable into the future as a management strategy. In fact, the CEO was already witnessing organizational growth frustrations and the inability to keep up with the market demand. Success was breeding success, and the more the company enjoyed success, the more it found new opportunities to pursue, opportunities that to this company were projects. Consider the following:

- Large high-value customers were demanding ever-increasing levels of support to better manage enterprise implementation projects.
- New customers and business partners were seeking to adopt the technology of the company and the number of potential project opportunities to pursue had doubled over the last year.
- Product management had a rich product development plan and three-year statement of direction that also contained a significant increase in the number of proposed research and development projects.
- A number of internal infrastructure projects in support of the growth of the company had gradually found their way to the doorstep of the IT director and were queued up for approval by the management team.

The entire management team continually expressed concern to the CEO that there were too many projects under way and too many project opportunities, really good ones at that, to pursue. However, no one had a solution or good recommendation to address the project-related business problems the company was now facing.

In response to the project-related business problems that had been weighing on the CEO's mind for quite some time, the CEO presented the idea of a PMO to his leadership team in response to their current set of needs. The idea of a PMO was met enthusiastically by the entire leadership team. Did everyone on the leadership team have the same view of what the PMO would actually do? Did the leadership team even have a common view of the business problems to be addressed by the PMO? Of course they didn't.

The Vice President of Sales wanted the PMO to help him make the revenue plan. In particular, the head of sales wanted to sell and perform more billable project engagements. He also wanted to perform more discretionary, nonbillable customer projects such as specification studies, solution prototypes, and proof of concepts.

The Vice President of Professional Services wanted the PMO to help him make his billable utilization targets. Specifically, the head of professional services wanted the sales teams to use more project management discipline in their approach to sizing customer requirements and proposing firm commitments for price and delivery. Also, the head of professional services wanted to ensure that no professional services resources would be used for nonbillable work.

The Vice President of Business Development wanted the PMO to help him achieve his business development goals and objectives. Toward that aim, the head of business development wanted the strategic business partner projects such as developing a long-term original equipment manufacturer relationship to have the same level of importance and support, as measured by budget and resources, as the projects that immediately produced revenue for the company.

The Manager of Product Development wanted the PMO to help him with the problems that threatened the release date integrity of the product road map. Among other issues, he wanted to prevent the temporary assignment of his best developers to high-priority sales opportunities for which custom development was required to win the business, according to the VP of Sales, who organizationally had the power to conscript the development staff.

The CFO wanted the PMO to help him with the preparation and management of the forecasts and formal projections of revenue. In particular, project-based revenue needed to be better identified and planned. As a small private company, this had been managed haphazardly, but as a firm with the prospects of going public or being acquired, a revenue recognition policy was no longer a luxury; it was a necessity.

The CEO wanted all these things and more, including the ability to double the size of his company, not to mention to beautify it for its suitors. It did not take long for the CEO and the leadership team to interview a number of candidates for the new position of PMO manager at this company. A number of candidates stood out, and as a management team they had arrived at a short list of the final two. Candidate number one was a certified project management professional (PMP), had years of PMO experience, and had been a PMO manager at three other companies where he had set up new PMOs, rolled out project management methodologies, and implemented project management systems. Candidate number two was not certified and had never been a PMO manager, but he had 20 years of technology and software development company experience, having had management positions in sales, marketing, business development, and professional services at a number of firms very similar in shape, size, and growth stage to the CEO's very company.

Who did they hire, candidate number one or candidate number two? Who would you hire? Although each of the two candidates possessed strengths, experiences, and qualities that were highly appreciated by all the management team, as a group, they felt the wisest choice would be candidate number one. After all, this was the first time the company would have a PMO and none of the existing management team had any previous PMO experience. Who could be better than a certified PMP and experienced PMO manager to establish and lead their PMO?

Candidate number one was hired. In week one, each leadership team member met with the new PMO manager and in week two the PMO manager presented his PMO strategy. What was that strategy? You already know. It was those three words that are responsible for more PMO failures than any three words in the English language: people, process, and tools. As shown in Figure 4.1, the PMO manager's strategy called for the setup of a coaching model PMO focused on the following:

◆ People: A small team of project managers would report to the PMO. They would provide project consulting and mentoring. The business units would continue to own and be responsible for their projects. The PMO was not looking to build a fiefdom.

◆ Process: A methodology for the management of projects would be developed and made available. It would be aligned to the *PMBOK® Guide*.

◆ Tools: A vendor evaluation of project management systems would be made and a best-fit solution would be implemented. As the PMO manager had experience using Microsoft Project Server at three other companies, he had a preference for Project Server but was willing to consider other vendor offerings.

◆ Training: A training plan would be developed. A number of project managers would be selected for training and certification. Training in project management basics and tool usage would be provided to everyone.

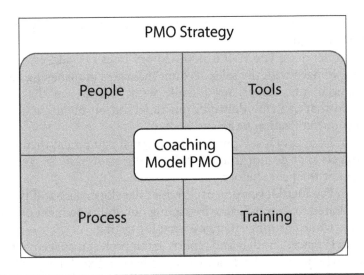

Figure 4.1   PMO strategy

Though there were questions about the PMO manager's strategy, the common view of the leadership team was that they should yield to the expert. After all, he, not they, knows what a PMO is and does. Hence, they should let him go about his craft.

By the end of the first month, the PMO had been staffed. By the end of the second month, demonstrations had been concluded and a decision was made to implement Project Server. By the end of the third month, a detailed project management methodology aligned to each of the PM-BOK processes had been developed and placed on the PMO SharePoint team site for all to access and use. Through the fourth, fifth, and sixth months, the PMO manager drove the training plan, sending a selection of project managers to PMP certification training and training others himself in project management basics, tool usage, and the methodology.

By chance, have you seen this movie before? Do you know how it ends? Are the business needs that led to the consideration of having a PMO being met? Are the executives for whom the PMO exists to serve delighted with the PMO, their PMO? And how about the PMO manager; is he up for a leadership award or cash bonus? Or is his job at risk? And is the PMO as an organizational entity within the company at risk of being closed down?

By the end of these six months, the honeymoon period, everyone was unhappy and to some degree frustrated with the PMO. Sentiments included the following:

- From Sales: Takes too long to get new projects under way. We won't make our quotas.
- From Services: The PMO methodology does not address the problem we have with the sales account managers in managing customer requirements and pricing billable work. We are on the hook for scope that can't be delivered on time and on budget and we will miss our utilization targets to boot.
- From Business Development: Our original equipment manufacturer projects that do not immediately produce revenue are getting less support than ever before.
- From Product Development: Product developers are still being requisitioned to support sales, impacting our ability to meet our release dates while ensuring adequate time for testing.
- From Finance: The data and reports in our project management system are no better than the data we used to have in Excel. They still cannot be used for forecasting project revenues and revenue recognition.

In the next staff meeting, these sentiments and more were expressed by the management team. Their patience with the PMO was waning. In response to their questions and concerns, the PMO manager advised that most of their problems and issues were outside the scope of a coaching model PMO. This statement and the discussions that followed were bewildering to the management team. Soon thereafter, support for the PMO began to fade away.

Over the next six months, the business went on and the PMO manager went about his coaching model strategy. The project managers of the PMO for the most part engaged in fighting one project fire after another. The project management system, Project Server, was never fully deployed or used effectively. The training program all but stopped, with the only noticeable training activity being already experienced project managers going to project management certification training, and this was only for personal reasons, to get a PMP, and not by any stretch of the imagination to manage projects differently at work.

In hindsight and based upon your PMO experiences, whether you have been in a PMO or served by a PMO, using the school grading system of A through F, how would you grade this PMO manager in terms of (1) strategy, (2) effort, (3) results, and (4) overall satisfaction? As you reflect upon your answers, have a look at Figure 4.2, which shows the grades of attendees at the Business Driven PMO workshops that I have conducted over the last five years, which are broken down by leadership team and PMO team responses.

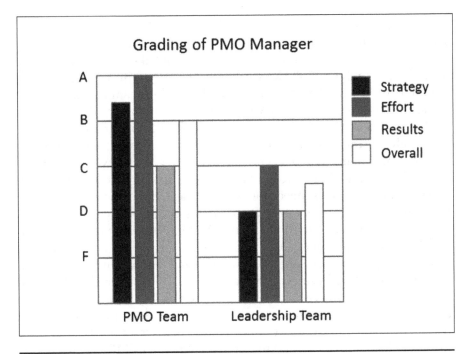

Figure 4.2   Workshop grading of PMO manager

It is hard to miss the glaring difference in how the PMO manager was graded by these two groups. The PMO team as represented by PMO managers, project managers, and project management consultants gave the PMO manager high marks for his PMO strategy and his efforts in executing that strategy. And despite a complete lack of results, the PMO team still awarded the PMO manager very good grades for everything else. It should be noted that within this PMO team peer group, there were some who offered much harsher grades and there were some who offered exceptional grades, giving the PMO manager an A grade across the board.

By way of comparison, the leadership team as represented by C-level executives and functional management outside of the PMO gave the PMO manager marginal grades, with only the effort category assessed as satisfactory, a C grade. It should be noted that the grade for effort was often a source of debate among the leadership team members. Virtually all the leadership team members felt that the effort of the PMO manager was actually quite minimal. How much effort could the PMO manager have expended in developing a strategy for the PMO after only two weeks on the job? Was there really a great deal of effort behind that PMO strategy or was it a cookie-cutter strategy that had simply been touched up? Though the leadership team as a peer group felt that the effort of the PMO manager was actually quite minimal and nothing to be praised for, they did recognize that there was a considerable effort expended by many others, who were the ones who did all the work. Balancing the effort of others with the effort of just the PMO manager, the leadership team as a peer group tended to settle on giving the PMO manager a C grade for effort.

During this workshop exercise in which the PMO manager is graded, almost always there is the sentiment among the PMO team peer group that the PMO manager did a good job. Their view is that even if the PMO is at risk of being closed after a year because it does not fundamentally meet any of the business needs for which it was created and exists to serve, the PMO can adjust its strategy at that point in time and carry on. This is a view that is not unique to the United States. PMO managers and certified PMPs from just about every country and region of the world have echoed this premise. Imagine their surprise and defensiveness when I tell them that any other business unit manager in a company, such as the head of marketing, sales, business development, services, or finance, who set up and managed a business unit in such a manner would at minimum be put on performance improvement notice and in many cases fired outright for managerial incompetence, and so too it should be for PMO managers.

Can you imagine the head of any of these other business units with such a mind-set and strategy for setting up and managing their organization? People, process, tools—and while we are at it why don't we conduct a maturity assessment and develop a plan to become a Level 5 Center of Excellence? Can you imagine a conversation between the CEO and Vice President of Sales in which when asked by the CEO how the new sales organization had been performing over its first six months, the head of sales responds by telling the CEO that they staffed a team, developed a methodology, and implemented a sales tool—so far so good? Such a conversation between the CEO and VP of Sales, or any other business unit head, would never take place. Yet, in the formal project management and PMO community such a conversation, regrettably, is business as usual and the prevailing mind-set for how to set up and manage a PMO.

Is it possible that I am being overly critical? Admittedly, the first two decades of my business and PMO experience were all in the field lines of business where we were managed by objectives and inherently self-motivated and driven to develop business driven plans and strategies to achieve those objectives, both by way of performance-based incentive compensation and a company culture that tied promotion and advancement to end results achieved. Effort was a condition of employment, knowledge and the ability to learn over one's career were expected, and the idea of re-warding or promoting an individual based upon effort and knowledge was nonexistent. What do others think? What do you think?

To ascertain whether or not the mind-set of the formal project management and PMO community is shared by members of the leadership team, we included this case study example of PMO failure with the survey group in our 2012 PMO survey and asked the members of the leadership team, including the PMO manager, to grade the PMO manager in the case study example on his (1) strategy, (2) effort, (3) results, and (4) overall satisfaction, just like in the PMO workshops. We were keen to find out how members of the leadership team viewed the performance of the PMO manager. Would they be lenient and suggest that after a year of poor results the PMO can adjust and carry on? Or would they hold the PMO to a higher standard of accountability, one that would be commensurate with most any other business unit in an organization?

As shown in Figure 4.3, the grading of the PMO manager in the case study by the survey group differed significantly between the leadership team members and the PMO managers in the survey group.

A few observations stand out. First, the members of the leadership team have a different view of how well the PMO manager in the case study example performed. The grades that they gave were not just significantly

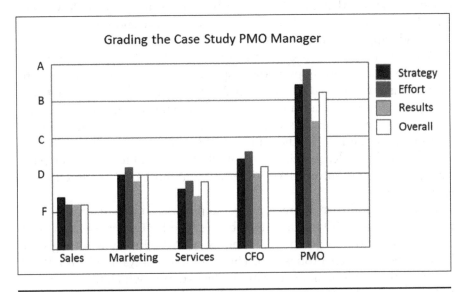

Figure 4.3 Survey group grading of PMO manager

lower than the grades that the PMO managers in the group gave, but none of the grades were even passing. Clearly, the idea of a people, process, and tools strategy that showed no evidence of being directly focused on, or even tangentially aligned to, the business needs for which the PMO was created did not resonate. Second, unlike the leadership team members of the survey group, the PMO managers gave very high marks—honor roll—for the strategy, effort, and overall satisfaction of the PMO in the case study. It is hard to believe that a group of people, all of whom belong to a professional association and most of whom have a certification from that association, could have such a misguided view and assessment. And third, the grades that the members of the leadership team gave as part of this PMO survey were quite similar to grades that leadership team participants in the Business Driven PMO workshops had given.

In the various PMO workshops that I have conducted worldwide, almost always, after the discussions of grading the PMO manager in this case study example come to an orderly close, more than half of the participants admit that they have just done, or are planning to do, exactly what the PMO manager in the case study did. Of those first-year PMO managers already in the process of executing their people, process, and tools strategy for the PMO, they all readily admit that things have not gone well and the support for the PMO by the leadership team that was once strong is now much less enthusiastic. The remaining workshop attendees share with the rest of the group that they have been brought in to fix their PMOs and that the case study example is all but a carbon copy and mirror image of what had happened in their PMOs.

Who's to blame for this? That is a question that I enjoy asking when conducting such workshops as the responses that I get are rarely close to the real answer. Who would you blame? If you blamed the leadership team, then you are not alone as most of the workshop participants placed blame with the leadership team as well. After all, the leadership team hired the PMO manager and they either approved his strategy or tacitly sat by as it was executed. The leadership team got what they paid for, right? So many times, one or more of my PMO workshop attendees have uttered those exact words.

Every now and then, a brave person steps forward and offers the point of view that the PMO manager is to blame. The PMO manager knows, or should know, how to go about setting up a PMO. Rarely is setting up a PMO a cookie-cutter proposition. There are many ways in which a PMO can meet the needs of an organization. The extent to which this is successfully done, or not, is the responsibility of the PMO manager. If you blamed the PMO manager, then consider yourself in this humble and honorable company.

I have a different view of who is to blame for two reasons. First, PMOs all over the world have embarked upon a very similar strategy and approach as this case study example of PMO failure for setting up their PMOs. With that much worldwide failure, whether measured in PMO execution difficulties or PMO closures, the blame for this cannot be assigned to any individual such as a PMO manager or his/her boss or leadership team. And second, few PMO managers come to the table with a clean slate of strategies and ideas for how to set up and manage a PMO; rather they come with books and years of presentations and white papers on the subject. In fact, most PMO managers continually seek out advice and expend money, time, and effort to learn and stay on top of the leading approaches advocated in the formal project management and PMO community for ensuring PMO success.

Hence, the blame for this can only be assigned institutionally. Therefore, it is only right and fair that those institutions (project management industry associations, trusted governmental authorities, leading research firms, best-in-class project portfolio management vendors, renowned consulting firms, educational institutions, reputable training organizations, leading professional, social, and online communities, etc.) that weigh in, advocate, and shape the practicing project management and PMO community and that take credit for its successes must also be the ones that step up and accept responsibility for its failures. Simply put, it is from these institutions that the cookie-cutter people, process, and tools PMO strategies have emanated. Though the motivations from one institution to the next for these strategies might be different, the results are typically the same.

Web Added Value™

5

Techniques for Establishing
a PMO Mandate

Picking up from the case study example of PMO failure presented in Chapter 4, at the end of the first year of the PMO, the PMO manager resigned. The CEO still believed in the promise of the PMO and tried to convince the PMO manager to stay on, but the PMO manager felt that he had done all he could do and that perhaps the company wasn't ready for a PMO.

When the CEO announced to his leadership team that the PMO manager had resigned, there was a heated discussion. It wasn't about hiring a new PMO manager; it was about whether or not the PMO should be continued. Half of the leadership team wanted to disband the PMO altogether. They weren't seeing the benefits of having a PMO, their project-related business needs and issues only got worse because of it, and many of their professional associates in their executive networks had told them that a PMO would be a big mistake for a small, innovative and agile, high-growth company.

The other half of the leadership team, including the CEO, wanted to carry on with the PMO. Sure, it had pursued a path that was not particularly useful for the company, but the company still had a myriad of project-related business problems and issues that were preventing it from sustaining its high growth rate and fulfilling its potential as a bigger and even more successful company. Although the team could not agree on the future of the PMO, there was one thing they could agree on: they hired the wrong candidate. In hindsight, they should have hired the other short-listed candidate that they liked, the one with the business experience.

As it so happened, the CEO contacted that other candidate and explained all that had transpired in the first year of the PMO. The CEO also offered him the PMO manager job, which was accepted on the spot. There were continued concerns by the leadership team over the decision to continue the PMO, but those concerns were quickly put to rest. Where the first PMO manager went about setting up the PMO adhering to the traditional *people, process, tools* approach and mind-set as posited each and every day within the formal project management and PMO community, the second PMO manager went about the role of PMO manager in a vastly different manner.

After the customary pleasantries and welcome to the team discussions, the second PMO manager called a meeting with the leadership team to prioritize and agree upon the key, top problems to be addressed by the PMO. Using the Nemawashi technique made popular by the Toyota Way management system, the second PMO manager met with each of the leadership team members prior to the meeting to ensure their understanding of the meeting, to give them an opportunity to discuss any questions or issues that they had, and most importantly to help them envision in each of their own minds exactly what they wanted the PMO to do for the business. Toward that aim, the second PMO manager prepared a one-page business planning template, as shown in Figure 5.1, which was required to be completed by all parties before the leadership team meeting could take place.

Business Planning Template

I. Problems to Be Solved

The top three problems that our company faces are:

1. _____
2. _____
3. _____

II. Vision

The vision of the PMO is to _____

III. Mission

The mission of the PMO is to _____

IV. Goals and Objectives

The goals and measurable objectives of the PMO are:

Goals	Objectives (how much by when)
1. _____	1. _____
2. _____	2. _____
3. _____	3. _____

Figure 5.1   Business planning template

After each of the leadership team members had participated in the Nemawashi process with the PMO manager, a half-day planning meeting of the entire leadership team was then scheduled. Naturally, the chance of all leadership team members having the same views of what the PMO should concern itself with per their one-page business planning summaries was all but nil. In fact, the discussions were passionate and at times heated. Throughout the planning meeting the PMO manager made it clear that the PMO was their PMO, not his. He was just the humble servant-leader who served at the pleasure of the leadership team. If the leadership team felt there was no need for a PMO, his service to them would no longer be needed.

The idea that there was no need for the PMO was not on anyone's mind. To the contrary, each of the leadership team members had an abundance of ideas, many even good, for how the PMO could be of value to the company and of value to their respective functional business units. In fact, the discussions and enthusiasm for the PMO were right back where they started after the CEO announced his idea to have a PMO, before they had hired that first PMO manager. By the end of the half-day planning meeting, the leadership team had reached agreement on the top three problems to be solved by the PMO and based upon this mandate the vision, mission, and goals and objectives of the PMO. This is depicted in Figure 5.2 and it became the PMO mandate for the next 12 months.

Business Planning Summary

I. Problems to Be Solved

    The top three problems that our company faces are:
1. Poor forecasting and manangement of project-based revenue
2. Not enough capacity to perform more projects
3. Lack of visibility into all of the projects of the company

II. Vision

    The vision of the PMO is to be an enabling and facilitating organizatoin that is focused on, and accountable for, the project-based success of the company

III. Mission

    The mission of the PMO is to develop and execute annual plans and strategies that solve the top project-related problems faced by the company

IV. Goals and Objectives

    The goals and measurable objectives of the PMO are:

Goals	Objectives (how much by when)
1. Improve project revenue managment	1. Reduce forecasting margin of error to 5%
2. Increase project capacity	2. 100% increase by year end
3. Provide holistic view of all projects	3. Effective reporting in place within 90 days

---

Figure 5.2 Business planning summary

The PMO manager also asked the leadership team to quantify the value of fulfilling this mandate, their mandate, as this would, in essence, represent the value of the PMO and serve as both the committed focus of the PMO and the reason for having the PMO at this point in time. The leadership team members each had slightly different views on this value, and the CFO took the lead in establishing a best-effort view and assessment of this value. It was significant. From this point of unanimous consensus for the PMO, the PMO manager developed and executed an effective PMO strategy that fulfilled the leadership team's mandate for the PMO, their PMO.

The details of the strategy and what happened next are written about at length in Chapter 2 of *Business Driven PMO Setup* (2009) so I will not repeat the entire story. I will offer that the leadership team noticed and commented to the CEO just how different the two PMO managers had been. I would also offer that the second PMO manager did have a *people, process,* and *tools* component to his PMO business plan. Of course, they were components of the strategy, not the purpose of the PMO. More importantly, the *people, process,* and *tools* component of the strategy was related to the fulfillment of the PMO mandate. Hence, the people within the PMO were used differently, the process was fitted to meet the needs of the business, not to adhere to each distinct process of the PMI Guide to the PMBOK, and the tool (Microsoft Project Server) was resurrected and successfully used in a manner that directly supported the project and resource management needs of the business as expressed in PMO objectives.

This is a good place to take a pause and revisit that *Selling the PMO* advice that is so often advocated by those in the formal project management and PMO community. When a PMO is set up using time-tested management techniques like Nemawashi of the Toyota Way and other generally accepted management systems and philosophies, is there a need to sell the PMO? After that second PMO manager concluded the leadership team meetings in which they told him what they want the PMO, their PMO, to do, is it necessary for the PMO manager to go back and sell those people on the PMO? Really? I think not. Sure, the PMO manager needs to report progress, fulfill the mandate, and for each business planning cycle (such as annually) recast the PMO mandate with the leadership team, just like all the other line of business units and functional departments. But this is not selling. A good business driven PMO management rule of thumb is that a PMO that has a need to sell itself with its leadership team has not been set up properly and is already off the track.

Getting back to that second PMO manager in the story, he did one more thing quite well that regrettably the formal project management and PMO community continues to get wrong. The PMO manager used key performance indicators (KPIs) to serve as measures of progress toward the fulfillment of the PMO mandate. For each PMO objective, three KPIs were established, tracked, reported, and managed. Most PMOs today use KPIs, but they use them incorrectly. That is, most PMOs view and establish KPIs based upon the knowledge areas of the PMBOK. In fact, there is an abundance of PMO consultants who make a living out of helping PMOs with assessments, metrics, and plans for improvement. These consultants arrive on the scene, perform a gap analysis, and report their findings and recommendations, which are always the same. They tell you that (1) you are at Level 1.xx of maturity for each of the knowledge areas of the PMBOK, (2) you need to be at Level 3 of maturity, and (3) in six months to one year we can help you get there with our project management training and consulting.

Set aside for a moment the time, cost, and quality of such an effort. Until such time as the PMO has a proper PMO mandate (ends to be achieved), how can it know which capabilities (means to the ends) need to be improved in order to fulfill the goals and objectives of the PMO? It can't. This will be discussed further in Section 3 of this book on PMO maturity, but to summarize, KPIs for the PMO are measures of progress toward PMO objectives, not knowledge areas of the PMBOK or any other standard.

I have always been a strong advocate of the business driven approach to PMO setup and management, and I highly encourage PMOs to adopt the same kinds of business planning and business management techniques that the heads of other business units within their own companies employ. Often, in various workshops and seminars, my words of encouragement can sound provocative and even blasphemous to those in the formal project management and PMO community. For example, when discussing techniques for establishing a PMO mandate I usually ask the audience for a show of hands of those PMOs that have a PMO charter. Typically, about half of the attendees raise their hands. I then advise that for all those that have a PMO charter, do your company a service and throw it away. And for those that do not have a PMO charter, don't create one. This always agitates a few folks and provokes a few sneers, but the rest of the audience is prone to sit up with raised eyebrows.

Next, I wait for a moment of silence and then state unequivocally that there is no such thing as a PMO charter. As proof I offer three facts. First, the PMO is not a project; it is a business unit. Therefore, it should be managed like any other business unit with a proper business plan. Sometime back, within the formal project management and PMO community, people started talking about setting up a PMO as if the PMO was a project. With this kind of mind-set, it's no surprise that as a business unit the track record of PMO failure is so high. If you can show me a vice president of sales with a sales management charter, or a vice president of marketing with a marketing management charter, or a vice president of just about any other business unit with a charter for their business, then I will consider changing my position. Until such time, I will continue to plead with the formal project management and PMO community to at least try to speak the language of business.

Second, what the formal project management and PMO community refer to as a PMO charter is almost always a document that is prepared by someone within the PMO, usually the PMO manager or a consultant working on behalf of the PMO manager, and somewhere in the PMO charter document there is a signature page. It is here, the signature page of the PMO charter, where you will find the names of some of the members of the leadership team and sufficient space allocated for their dated signatures. That such a document can be prepared and signed is of no debate. But did each member of the leadership team who signed the PMO charter actually read it? Did they really agree with it? Is the PMO charter their PMO mandate? Did each member of the leadership team at least contribute materially to the PMO charter, their charter, in terms of the specific problems to the solved by the PMO, the vision, the mission, and the goals and measurable objectives for which the PMO will be held accountable? Assuming the leadership team had no meaningful input to the PMO charter, was it at least vetted by more than one member of the leadership team? If one of the answers to these questions would be no, the idea of a PMO charter would be tenuous. The fact is in most organizations the answers to all these questions would be no; hence, as a mere practical reality there is no such thing as a PMO charter.

Third, let's judge the tree (the PMO charter) by the fruit it bears. One example of the fruit that the tree bears is the PMO research on the rate of PMO failure. These PMOs had PMO charters. Another example of the fruit that the tree bears is an anecdotal one. In over a decade of work with hundreds of PMOs of all shapes and sizes, I have only seen three PMO charters that have met what I believe is an acceptable standard of business management and planning. Hence, the sooner the formal project management and PMO community drops the term PMO charter from its vernacular and adopts the language and practices of business management, the better off PMOs will all be.

If you are like the many PMO practitioners I have worked with over the years, then you are likely having one of two thoughts after reading these

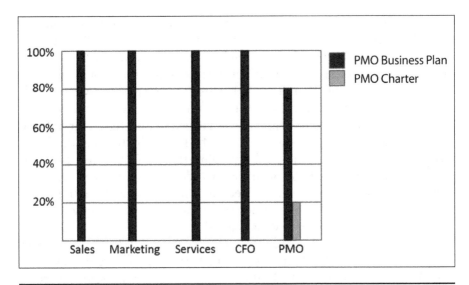

Figure 5.3   PMO charter versus PMO business plan

last few pages. You are either simpatico with my prose and are thinking that it is about time that the formal project management and PMO community becomes more business focused and balanced, or you are taking umbrage at my words and are feeling both irritated and maybe just a bit defensive as I have challenged the business acumen of your profession.

But what do business people think? More specifically, what does your leadership team think? Would they prefer a PMO charter that is prepared by the PMO manager or a consultant and is routed around for leadership team review and signoff, with some degree of leadership team involvement of course? Or would they prefer a PMO business plan and strategy that is developed by the PMO manager after receiving input from the leadership team for what they want the PMO to do by way of a properly prepared and unanimously agreed to PMO mandate that clearly states the top problems the PMO is to solve, the vision and mission of the PMO, and the goals and measurable objectives for which the PMO is to be held accountable?

PMO charter versus PMO business plan; what does the leadership team prefer? We asked this question to members of the leadership team in our 2012 PMO survey of 80 organizations. Figure 5.3 graphically depicts their responses.

Each and every one of the members of the leadership team preferred the PMO business plan over the PMO charter. Not one of these executives wished to have a PMO charter for their PMOs. It is interesting to note that even the PMO managers preferred the PMO business plan and by a wide margin: 80% in favor of the PMO business plan to 20% in favor of the PMO charter. In subsequent telephone interviews with the PMO managers who preferred the PMO charter over the PMO business plan, 8 out of these 16 (50%) indicated that their PMO charters were developed collaboratively with the leadership team and the development of the charter process and the charter itself was viewed as effective. Four of these 16 (25%) PMO managers who preferred the PMO charter over the PMO business plan cited that they did not think the PMO business plan approach would work in their organizations. The remaining 4 of these 16 (25%) PMO managers who preferred the PMO charter over the PMO business plan said that they did not think measureable objectives at the PMO level could be effectively established.

Accepting at face value the PMO charter versus PMO business plan perspectives of the PMO managers, which there is no reason not to, I would suggest that the eight PMO managers (10%) who said that their PMO charters were collaboratively developed with the leadership team and were effective, in essence, had PMO business plans. Hence, I would be inclined to place them in the camp of those who prefer a PMO business plan over a PMO charter document. This would, in effect, increase the number of PMO managers who prefer a PMO business plan over a PMO charter to 72 out of 80, or 90%. Using Student's t-distribution statistical analysis techniques for small sample sizes and a reasonable margin of error, it can be concluded that the members of the leadership team of most businesses, and even the PMO managers themselves, would prefer a PMO business plan over a PMO charter.

If you happen to be one of those PMO managers, like the 10% of the above survey, who has an effective PMO charter that was collaboratively developed with the leadership team, then you are in very good company. It is highly likely that your PMO is not just meeting the business needs of your company but playing a key role in its success, and my hat is off to you. I would be the last person to recommend changing what is working well. However, if you are in the process of setting up a new PMO or revitalizing an existing one and you don't have a PMO charter in place or one that you are happy with, I would urge you to throw the very idea of a PMO charter out of the window. I can't imagine any PMO not being well served by a PMO business plan, and I have seen and can imagine hundreds of PMOs being poorly served by a PMO charter.

Section 2

PMO Business Acumen

Acumen (noun)—the ability to make good judgments and quick decisions.

6

Project Acumen

Without a doubt, the most profound revelation that I have had in working with the formal project management and PMO community is how poor the project acumen is of many of its certified project management professionals (PMPs) and members; not all of course but far too many. Poor project acumen is manifested in many ways. Let's start with the project management triangle, also referred to as the project management triple constraint or by some as the iron triangle.

I first learned of the project management triangle over 30 years ago in Phase I of the IBM Data Processing Division training program. Of course, the class instructor didn't refer to it as the project management triangle; he called it the Pick Two Triangle. As shown in Figure 6.1, he drew a triangle on a flip chart and labeled the three points of the triangle as good, cheap, and fast, and then he said, "Pick two." In the context of developing an application, he went on to explain the following:

- If you want the product to be good and cheap, it won't be fast.
- If you want the product to be good and fast, it won't be cheap.
- And if you want the product to be cheap and fast, it won't be good.

The utility of the Pick Two Triangle was that it helped to reveal biases and it enabled clearer communications, more effective planning, and better decision making.

Where one customer might have a requirement and preference for a solution that can be delivered fast and is good, with cost not being as important in the scheme of things, another customer might have a strong bias for a solution that is cheap and good, with fast delivery not being as important. Recognizing these biases is essential for understanding what is

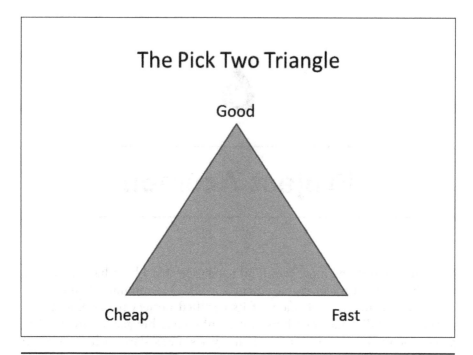

Figure 6.1   The Pick Two Triangle

required to satisfy the customer. Or put another way, failure to recognize these biases could easily result in a very dissatisfied customer.

In the formal project management and PMO community, the concept of the project management triangle with scope, time, and cost at its points is very often misunderstood and misapplied. I have seen this all over the world, whether exhibited by project management professionals who are trained and certified by PMI or project management professionals who are trained and certified in the PRINCE2® standard of the United Kingdom Office of Government Commerce of Her Majesty's Treasury.

There is no better example of this misapplication of the project management triangle than a simple exercise that we do in our Business Driven PMO workshops. Consider the following two projects depicted in Figure 6.2.

Which project manager did a better job? As you study the various graphical indicators, I would like you to further consider that these two projects are the exact same project in terms of scope, phases, and tasks. For purposes of this comparison, assume that one project is being managed by a project manager in one division of a company and the other project is being managed by a project manager in another.

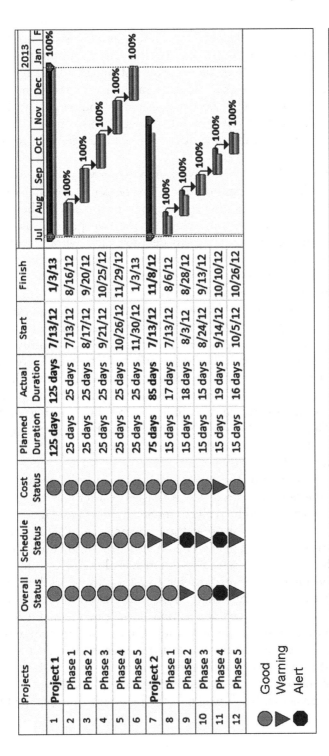

	Projects	Overall Status	Schedule Status	Cost Status	Planned Duration	Actual Duration	Start	Finish
1	**Project 1**				**125 days**	**125 days**	**7/13/12**	**1/3/13**
2	Phase 1				25 days	25 days	7/13/12	8/16/12
3	Phase 2				25 days	25 days	8/17/12	9/20/12
4	Phase 3				25 days	25 days	9/21/12	10/25/12
5	Phase 4				25 days	25 days	10/26/12	11/29/12
6	Phase 5				25 days	25 days	11/30/12	1/3/13
7	**Project 2**				**75 days**	**85 days**	**7/13/12**	**11/8/12**
8	Phase 1				15 days	17 days	7/13/12	8/6/12
9	Phase 2				15 days	18 days	8/3/12	8/28/12
10	Phase 3				15 days	15 days	8/24/12	9/13/12
11	Phase 4				15 days	19 days	9/14/12	10/10/12
12	Phase 5				15 days	16 days	10/5/12	10/26/12

Good
Warning
Alert

Figure 6.2   Which project manager did a better job?

Additionally, I would like you to assume that all the data are trustworthy and correct and that the product of the project, in both projects, met the expectations of the stakeholders. And just to add a little fun, I would like to add to the scenario that the corporate executive team has $10,000 to award as a bonus to the project manager who you judge was the better project manager of the two. Who did you pick? Did you pick the project manager for project number one or the project manager for project number two?

In the Business Driven PMO workshop, when we do this exercise we split the workshop attendees into small, five-person teams and we ask that each of the team members discuss with their peers each of their perspectives and rationale for selecting which of the two project managers did a better job and to arrive at a team decision onto whom to award the $10,000. We then have a team captain from each team present a summary of the team discussions and their final vote.

Almost always, the team discussions and conclusions are that the first project manager was the better project manager and did a better job, as indicated by each phase of the project that finished right on time and as indicated by nothing but "good" indicators in the scope, time, cost, and overall status columns. No, it did not go unnoticed that the second project manager finished earlier than the first project manager, but the second project manager missed the schedule for all the phases of his project and also experienced cost overruns, as indicated by the "warning" and "alert" indicators. The overall status of the project, which was an average of the assessments for scope, time, and cost, also had a mixture of "good," "warning," and "alert" indicators.

Every so often, one of the workshop teams votes for project manager number two because the project was finished earlier and the product of the project benefits could be realized sooner. As shown in Figure 6.3, however, by a large margin most project management and PMO professionals who have participated in the exercise all over the world voted with strong conviction for the project manager who managed the first project.

Before revealing the correct answer, I first ask the workshop attendees which project finished late. What would your answer be? Every now and then, we have a manager of application development in the room who will share with us some of the principles of agile development and defend the position that it was the first project that finished late. Just look at the calendar. But for the most part, the preponderance of workshop attendees all agree that the second project finished late as evidenced by the schedule, which shows an actual finish well past the baseline of the planned finish.

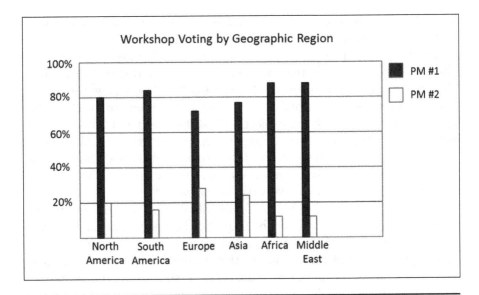

Figure 6.3 Workshop voting by geographic region

I then ask the workshop attendees which of the two projects finished later. Surprisingly, quite a few PMPs and PMO managers can't bring themselves to say that the first project finished later. Though it is a clear calendar fact, the mere admission that a poorer managed project crossed the finish line first tends to serve as a blemish on an otherwise perfectly managed project.

At this point in this exercise I reveal that these two identical projects are TTM projects. Naturally, no one has an idea what TTM is. I then explain that TTM is a very well-known business term and it means time to market. With this explanation, some eyebrows are raised and others are furrowed.

I then reveal that the two project managers had two completely different approaches to the management of this exact same project. In the case of the first project manager, his primary concern was successfully managing the project in terms of ensuring that there were nothing but "good" indicators for the project measures of scope, time, cost, and overall satisfaction. When he asked his five project leads for each phase how much time their phase would take, his sole motivation was ensuring that the schedule for the phase would be met. So when the project manager was told by each project lead that their phase would take about 20 days, he replied, "If I give you 25, can you promise to complete your phase on time no matter what?" Hence, the project manager added buffer to the project and went about what he thought was good project management.

The second project manager, on the other hand, asked the sponsor of the project for more information about the project and in particular about the project biases of the sponsor. He drew the Pick Two Triangle and asked, "Good, cheap, or fast—which two are most important to you?" To this question, the sponsor of the project replied that good and fast were most important, and upon further probing by the project manager, the sponsor shared that as soon as the product of the project, in this case a new website ordering system, went live, there would be an expected $50,000 per day of net new revenues, each and every day of the week.

The sponsor added that he most assuredly wanted the project manager to make every effort to deliver the project as fast as possible and to eradicate any slack or student syndrome tendencies from the project, such as waiting until the last minute to get things done. The sponsor also added that he did not want the project manager to be so concerned over meeting the initial cost and time estimates, which he viewed as imperfect anyway, that he lost sight of the purpose of the project. The sponsor further punctuated his point by saying that if in the project status reports he sees nothing but "good" indicators for schedule status, then he would be more than a little bit unhappy, as that would be a telltale sign that the project manager didn't listen and didn't get it.

The project manager repeated back in his own words all that he had just heard from the sponsor. Just to make sure they had a meeting of the minds, the project manager once again confirmed that the sponsor wanted his TTM project to be very aggressively scheduled and that if some project misses in terms of tasks and phases did not meet their very aggressive schedule, it would not only be tolerated but welcomed. He also confirmed that after all was said and done, task schedule misses, if any, would not be viewed after the fact as a reflection of poor project management by the project manager, but rather as a reflection that the project manager had listened to and understood what the sponsor wanted. The sponsor offered a broad smile and handshake as they had communicated well and reached a meeting of the minds.

Later during meetings with the project leads, the project manager asked each of them how much time would be needed to complete their tasks and phases. When they responded that it would be about 20 days, unlike the first project manager who applied the technique of buffering and asked if they could do it in 25, the second project manager applied the technique of negative buffering and negotiated with them for more aggressive estimates. In fact, he negotiated the estimates down from 20 to 15 days. The project manager, of course, anticipated that most if not all these aggressive estimates might not be achieved, and that was addressed in his risk management plan.

The end result was that the second project manager delivered the TTM project 40 man-days earlier and 57 calendar days earlier than the first project manager and had delivered to the sponsor a net additional revenue amount of almost $3 million to the delight of the stakeholders.

At this point in the Business Driven PMO workshop I ask, "Would anyone like to change their vote on which project manager did a better job from project manager number one to project manager number two?" You would think that everyone would say yes and change their vote, but you would be wrong. To my surprise, over the years of conducting these Business Driven PMO workshops with countless project managers, most with PMP certifications mind you, they answer with the following:

◆ Project manager number one was still a better project manager because he delivered his project on time.
◆ Project manager number one was still a better project manager because he created a less stressful project environment for the project leads.
◆ Project manager number one was still a better project manager because he effectively used buffers to ensure that every project measure (scope, time, cost, and overall) was met, thus alleviating undue stress and worry of the sponsor and stakeholders.
◆ Project manager number one was still a better project manager because the product of the project benefit was still delivered successfully and the same benefits would be realized anyway just a few months later.
◆ Project manager number one was still a better project manager because you can't have two sets of books for the project—an aggressive schedule that you know can't be made and the real schedule in your mind.

Although I try my best to be professional in the face of such attitudes that are so often on display within the formal project management and PMO community, I nearly lost my temper in one such Business Driven PMO workshop. I was in the middle of a workshop tour with stops in eight different cities throughout Australia and New Zealand. In the beautiful city of Perth, during this part of the workshop one of the PMO managers in attendance adamantly insisted that project manager number one was the better project manager. He offered up by way of defense that it is the project manager's and the PMO's job to negotiate with the sponsor dates that can be met, not to play games with the schedule. And in the case of the first project manager, the stakeholders had agreed to his schedule and that schedule was met perfectly. You can only imagine how this conversation carried on. In the end, we agreed to disagree.

As part of our 2012 PMO survey, we added this workshop example to the survey for the purposes of learning from the leadership team members who participated in the survey which project manager they felt was the better project manager. Would the survey responses from these members of the leadership team echo the prevailing sentiment of those in the formal project management and PMO community or would they have a different perspective? As shown in Figure 6.4, the leadership team members of 80 organizations in the survey unanimously responded that project manager number two was the better project manager.

Not a single member of the leadership team voted for the first project manager. They all recognized that project management techniques are a means to an end; they are not the ends unto themselves. There could be countless projects for which positive buffering would be an effective technique, but this was not one of them.

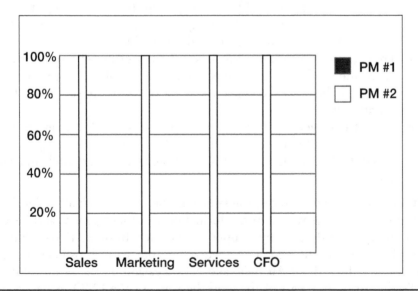

Figure 6.4 Leadership team view of better project manager

This brings us back to the discussion of that project management triangle. What many in the formal project management and PMO community have gotten wrong all these years is that the project management triangle of scope, time, and cost is intended to identify project biases and help us better communicate, plan, and manage project-related work that can have many competing interests, constraints, and complexities. The elements of the project management triangle (scope, time, and cost) were never intended, and should not be used, as project status indicators with a mindset that any project with status indicators other than good is by default a poorly managed project.

This incorrect mind-set needs to be corrected and many people advocate, as do I, that the formal project management and PMO community needs to be much more business driven in all that it does. Take the technique of buffering as an example. You can read about buffering in the current version of the PMI *PMBOK® Guide* in the Time Management Knowledge Area, and just about every certified PMP knows about buffering or at least they think they do. I would venture to say that all of us have experience in using buffers to add contingency to our schedules in order to ensure stakeholders' needs are met with respect to a schedule that is not overrun. But how many of us project management practitioners have used negative buffering or have even heard about it for that matter? Have you?

Negative buffering is actually used quite often. It can be a very effective technique to use in many different kinds of projects, especially TTM projects, commonly referred to as go-to-market projects and product-to-market projects.

Not too long ago I had the pleasure of spending some time with the International Facility Management Association, based in Houston, Texas. In discussions with their highly talented PMO manager, Jennifer Drai, and their exceptional COO, Michael Moss, they shared with me a number of business driven PMO techniques that are in their repertoire, including negative buffering. As Mr. Moss told me, "I've never called it negative buffering, but I have done it for years!"

PMO gurus like Steve Rollins and Gerald Kendall have advocated for years their Delivery Now PMO model that is steeped in business driven techniques, such as intentionally taking actions that might jeopardize the baseline project schedule and budget in order to deliver the product of the project and realize its benefits earlier. Can you imagine the shock and resistance that some may have at the very idea of letting those project management triangle elements go astray? Might it be a good idea to intentionally miss the project budget in order to enjoy a project benefit that is an order of magnitude greater? Is it worth a project cost overrun of $100,000 to finish a project earlier and achieve a project benefit of $10 million? Conversely, is it so critical and important to not miss the project schedule that we are willing to schedule the project with months of project buffer and forgo millions of dollars of benefits? The answer as always is that it depends upon the business context of the project, but not the arbitrary and misguided belief that scope, time, and cost measures must all be met.

Seasoned experts in complex program management and business-critical projects like Tom Atkins, President of the Tramore Group, and his team specialize in applying the science and art of project management in order to achieve the desired results of the sponsor. They, like many other leaders in the domain of complex program management, recognize that the science of project management as embodied by technical project management standards and best practices is not enough. Also required is the art of project management, which to the Tramore Group is represented by good judgment borne out of experience, business acumen, and superior communication.

Perhaps I am expecting too much out of the formal project management and PMO community both in terms of behaviors exhibited by its project managers and the type of knowledge that is presented in its standards. For example, our leading industry association for project management, the Project Management Institute, has a standard for project management and this standard has a knowledge area specifically for time. It's called Project Time Management, but nowhere to be found in it is the essential knowledge about time that all project managers must know. Sure, most project managers likely understand the concept of the time value of money, but do they understand the far more important concept of the money value of time?

As a case in point, earlier this year I was working with an investment firm that specializes in identifying small businesses and helping their clients purchase them. At the time of the initial confirmation of fit between an identified small business and their client, what we may refer to as a *deal* they refer to as a project, and they have lots of them. Imagine how critical the money value of time is in these projects.

When businesses are seeking to acquire a particular kind of company, the mathematics of the acquisition is vastly different for the first few as compared to the last few. Also important is the business cycle. At the peak of a business cycle when large companies are cash rich, there is a much higher demand for and interest in acquisitions of small businesses. This is referred to as a seller's market and it results in a premium of the acquisition price of up to 130% of enterprise value or more. Conversely, at the bottom of a business cycle when large companies may not have cash on hand at all, there is a much lower demand for and interest in these acquisitions. This is referred to as a buyer's market and it results in a discount of the acquisition price of 70% of enterprise value or less. Take a $10M small business with an enterprise value of $30M; poorly managing time in this mergers and acquisitions project could result in an $18M loss. That's quite a project time management error.

Is it reasonable to expect that a certified project manager know more about the time value of money and the money value of time? Should the concepts of the time value of money and the money value of time be contained in the Project Time Management Knowledge Area of our standard? Or is it good enough to continue to view project management through the multicolored lenses of scope, time, and cost?

Perhaps it is best said by Mark Langley, President and CEO of the Project Management Institute, who at the 2011 Gartner Group Project Portfolio Management and IT Governance Summit gave his opinion about the project management triangle. When asked about whether or not project management standards and certifications, and in particular the PMBOK, are meeting the complex and adaptive needs of today's businesses, Mr. Langley responded that technical project management per our standards and certifications continues to contribute significantly to today's businesses. He sagely advised, however, that technical project management is at best 30–40% of what is required for business success. He concluded by showing an updated view of the project management triangle, one that had technical project management, business acumen, and leadership at its three points, and by saying that if all we talk about is scope, time, and cost, then project management as we know it will fail us all. At the end of Mr. Langley's comments, he was given loud and lasting applause by an audience of several hundred large-company CIOs, a group not easily impressed. There is no better example of the need for business driven project acumen than the wise words of Mr. Langley.

7

Portfolio Acumen

Over the years, I have presented and written about the challenges of portfolio management. In my last book, *Business Driven Project Portfolio Management: Conquering the Top 10 Risks That Threaten Success* (2011), I worked with the leading providers of project portfolio management (PPM) solutions to research, study, and understand the top risks associated with portfolio management and how organizations mitigate these risks. Over the course of this collaborative work, I gained a newfound respect and appreciation for the knowledge and practical insights that these firms have and provide to us all. I also came to appreciate that although portfolio management as a concept and best practice is quite easy to understand, as a leadership team management activity it is tremendously difficult to do well.

Most organizations doing portfolio management do so in a business driven manner, as it is almost always specific business needs that drive the interest and agreement of the leadership team in doing portfolio management in the first place. If the need for portfolio management is clear and present, executives tend to be willing to give it a try. If not, rarely will a portfolio management initiative advance.

When a portfolio management initiative does advance, however, there are a number of perspectives within the formal project management community that tend to get in the way of success. As part of our 2012 PMO survey, we selected three of these perspectives that were shown to be highly problematic from past research and we were keen to revisit them. The three perspectives that we selected were (1) views on the definition of portfolio management, (2) views on why and where to do portfolio management within an organization, and (3) views on portfolio management techniques. Collectively, these views represent examples of portfolio acumen and reveal the degree to which many PMOs have and exhibit it and others struggle.

Many PPM experts like Terry Doerscher, coauthor of an excellent book about portfolio management, *Taming Change with Portfolio Management* (2010), advise that portfolio management is all about managing alignments in the complex and ever-present business world of change. This may seem a bit unframed to some, but there is much more to it than meets the eye, and that is what I like most about it. It is when we try to make the definition of portfolio management too precise or mathematically linear that we invite execution difficulties and at times unrealistic expectations.

Take the case of the common view of the definition of portfolio management as expressed by the analogy that portfolio management allows an organization to manage its projects much like the way an investor would manage stocks and bonds. This view has been perpetuated so often within the formal project management and PMO community that it is taken as gospel. Well-intended but misguided vendors, consultants, and PMO managers use this analogy with executives and the leadership team in attempts to explain, and often sell the case for, portfolio management. And there is nothing quite as beautiful as a good portfolio management demo with carefully populated demo data. If only our real project portfolio data could produce such beautiful and usable charts, graphs, and reports.

But setting aside all of that, it is just not helpful or accurate to suggest that you can manage a portfolio of projects like you can one of stocks and bonds. For one thing, the project investments are not at all like financial investments. Projects have no liquidity. You can't invest in a project portfolio and then in a few months, well before any of the projects have completed and their benefits achieved, take your returns off the table and reinvest them elsewhere. For another, and even more importantly, the fundamental environments of managing a project portfolio and that of a financial portfolio are vastly different.

When the financial portfolio manager advises making a change in the portfolio to optimize its return and to minimize its risk, that advice is received with much appreciation and seldom any resistance. The client of the financial portfolio manager is all too eager to make the change. But when the project portfolio manager advises making a change in the project portfolio to optimize its return and to minimize its risk, such as a recommendation to kill a few projects and to commence a few others, that advice is received much differently and in some cases may initiate not just questioning of the data but heated discussions and turf battles among the leadership team all too eager to defend existing projects or advance new ones.

Also, in terms of the actual work effort, it would not be beyond one's imagination to envision a financial portfolio manager sitting alone and undisturbed in his office monitoring the daily market movements and fluctuations using a wide variety of financial analysis and modeling tools. With little need for collaboration with others and little concern over the sentiment that changes in the portfolio components might bring about, the financial portfolio manager is able to effectively manage the portfolio. Does the project portfolio manager work in a similar way? Of course not; the project portfolio manager has a portfolio of components that are anything but inanimate. Changes to project portfolio components represent changes to people, both good and bad. This is an added dimension that makes PPM all the more difficult to do. Simply put, the human element is different.

Arguably, the best authority on the subject would be Dr. Harry Markowitz, the winner of the Nobel Memorial Prize in Economic Sciences for his work in Modern Portfolio Theory. When asked over a decade ago in an interview with gantthead, the leading online community for IT project managers with over 500,000 members (now found at projectmanagement. com), about the notion of managing a project portfolio like one would manage a financial portfolio, he was dismissive of the idea. He expressed concern over the idea and advised that projects are not like financial investments. Funds can be finely subdivided among many liquid assets in a financial portfolio; the same cannot be said of project portfolios.

So, if the leading expert in portfolio theory suggests that it is not a good idea to talk about managing a project portfolio like you would a financial portfolio, perhaps we should take heed of that advice. Aside from questionable marketing buzz and hype that such an analogy by PPM vendors and consultants may foster, the end result is likely to be an unrealistic expectation for how PPM really works in the confines of today's increasingly complex and adaptive businesses. Figure 7.1 shows the results of one of the 2012 PMO survey questions about the degree to which a project portfolio can be managed similarly to a financial portfolio.

There is a marked difference of opinion on this between PMO managers and CFOs. Again, this is yet another example of the formal project management and PMO community not speaking the language of business or speaking it incorrectly.

Another area of dubious portfolio acumen is the view on why and where to do portfolio management within an organization. Far too often within the formal project management and PMO community there is a view that

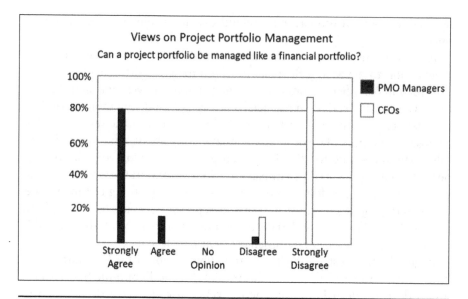

Figure 7.1   Views on PPM

portfolio management must be done at the CEO level of an organization and that every project of the organization must be contained within the portfolio management system. This is problematic for two reasons. First, not all CEOs are ready to have, or need, a portfolio management function reporting directly to them. It would be a pity to miss an opportunity to do portfolio management in an area of the business that has an immediate and pressing need, such as new product development, operations, or IT, because of the misguided belief that unless it is done at the CEO level, it is not portfolio management. So why bother?

Secondly, portfolio management is not about putting every project that exists in the organization into a common PPM system, subjecting them to a common process, and managing them at the highest levels of the organization. For most large organizations this would be impossible. For smaller organizations, though it might be possible, it would never be done. Can you imagine the effort to put all the projects in every department of an organization, such as marketing, sales, services, engineering, finance, accounting, legal, HR, and research and development into one tool and manage them via a single project management process? To what end would this serve?

This view is often the result of a mind-set that as an organization has more projects, it should engage in portfolio management to better align and manage all the projects. But in fact, projects are not a driver of portfolio management; rather, it is the other way around: portfolio management is a driver of projects. Hence, to achieve the goals of an organization, whatever that organization may be, an optimal mix and sequence of projects is identified, and within the governing framework of the organization the project portfolio is managed.

A good example of this was presented a few years back at the IQPC PMO Summit in Miami, Florida. The project portfolio manager of the strategic PMO of a worldwide restaurant chain shared how they selected and managed their strategic projects, all 15 of them. These were very large projects mind you, but they were solely the project investments that were driven by the PPM activities of the strategic PMO. Were there other projects in existence within the various divisions and departments of this worldwide business? Of course. Was there a mind-set at this company that every project within these divisions and departments needs to be part of the PPM being done at the CEO level by the strategic PMO? Of course not. There were quite a few attendees at this presentation who had their perspectives about PPM challenged and, I might add, corrected.

The last example of many about portfolio acumen that is needed to call attention to concerns itself with portfolio management techniques and in particular the evaluation of portfolio components. Consider the following two projects, Project A and Project B:

◆ Project A has a cost of $500K and a benefit of $2M.
◆ Project B has a cost of $500K and a benefit of $5M.

Which project would you select? All things being equal, one might be inclined to select Project B. But all things are never equal, so we need to take a closer look at the key project characteristics of these two projects and assess in a methodical way which project is the more deserving project.

Now take a glance at Figure 7.2, which provides further information about these two projects or portfolio components, as said in the practicing domain. Before reading further, first decide for yourself which of the two projects you would select as the more deserving project; for the purpose of this exercise consider that all information that is needed is represented in this graphic. All other information about the projects is either the same or of little consequence.

This happens to be one of the exercises that we do in the Business Driven PMO workshop. In a typical workshop of 20 attendees, the participants are divided up into 4 teams of 5 people and given about 15 minutes to discuss their views and opinions and to make a project selection. Over the last few years of doing this exercise in workshops all over the world,

	Cost	Total Benefit	Time to Benefit	Project Duration	Risk	Project Description
			Evaluation of Portfolio Components Which project would you select? (Business is good, revenues exceeding plan, NEBT = 20%)			
			Key Project Characteristics			
A	$500k	$2m	< 6 months Recurring annually	6 months	Low	This project will improve the supply chain and will result in reduced operating costs.
B	$500k	$5m	< 6 months Recurring annually	6 months	Low	This project will enhance a current product line and will result in additional sales revenue.

Figure 7.2   Evaluation of portfolio components

there has been an even split of answers given by the workshop teams, with half of the teams selecting Project A and the other half of the teams opting for Project B. The reasons regularly cited were as follows:

♦ Teams that selected Project B: Since the benefit of Project B was larger than the benefit of Project A and they both had the same cost, then Project B was the more deserving project.

♦ Teams that selected Project A: Since revenues were exceeding plan, it would be better to reduce operating costs at this point in time and therefore select Project A.

Both of these perspectives reveal a very common mistake that almost all PMOs make with respect to PPM techniques and in this case the evaluation of portfolio components. That mistake is not translating the two projects, which each have different benefit dollar types, into a common currency.

In order to translate the two projects into a common currency, the benefit amount needs to be restated into a common type of benefit, such as a revenue benefit or a cost benefit. Otherwise, the comparison of benefit amounts would be like comparing apples to oranges. For example, at a 20% net earnings before tax (NEBT), $1 of revenue is the equivalent of 20 cents of earnings. Similarly, $1 of expense would be the equivalent of $5 of revenue. As shown in Figure 7.3, the restated project benefits as a common currency revenue equivalent reveals that Project A is the more desirable of the two.

	Cost	Total Benefit	Common Currency Revenue Equivalent	Time to Benefit	Project Duration	Risk	Project Description
A	$500k	$2m	$10m	< 6 months Recurring annually	6 months	Low	This project will improve the supply chain and will result in reduced operating costs.
B	$500k	$5m	$5m	< 6 months Recurring annually	6 months	Low	This project will enhance a current product line and will result in additional sales revenue.

Evaluation of Portfolio Components

Translating benefits into common currency
(Business is good, revenues exceeding plan, NEBT = 20%)

Key Project Characteristics

Figure 7.3 Translating benefits into common currency

It is tremendously important to understand the difference between types of benefit dollars. As profitability measures such as NEBT are decreased, the multiplier of the common currency is increased. For example, at a 10% NEBT, $1 of a cost benefit would be the equivalent of $10 of a revenue benefit.

Without understanding a few accounting principles, one might easily make the mistake of evaluating a project portfolio assuming that all dollar benefits are in essence the same. In fact, this is exactly what the PMI *Standard for Portfolio Management* does. Throughout Chapter 4 of the PMI standard, most notably in Section 4.3–Evaluate Components, a number of PPM evaluation techniques are provided such as (1) the scoring model comprising weighted key criteria, (2) the graphical comparison based on two criteria, (3) the single-criterion prioritization model, and (4) the multiple-criteria weighted ranking. However, in none of these portfolio management evaluation techniques, and in fact nowhere in the PMI *Standard for Portfolio Management*, is the importance explained of establishing a common currency between revenue dollar and cost dollar benefit types for the portfolio, nor is any kind of technique for how to do it presented.

This is a flagrant example of the lack of business acumen, in this case portfolio acumen, that is so pervasive in the formal project management and PMO community. One does not need to look any further than the very standards our industry has from which training is conducted, certifications are administered, and well-intended practitioners are doing what they know but don't quite really know what they are doing. One can do all the multiple-criteria weighted ranking that he or she wants to, but without translating benefits such as increased revenues and reduced costs into a common currency, the results will be flawed and the project portfolio will not have been evaluated properly.

The presence or lack of portfolio acumen manifests itself in many ways. The three ways that we just touched upon—the views on the definition of portfolio management, the views on why and where to do portfolio management within an organization, and the views on portfolio management techniques—are by no means an exhaustive list. In order to meet the complex and adaptive needs of businesses today, the formal project management and PMO community must step outside its box and venture well outside of its own knowledge-based domain and comfort zone. Not all, but far too many practitioners are learning and developing a project management speak that they use with their leadership and management team, one that is not all that intelligible and in many cases not all that correct.

8

Dashboard Acumen

For most PMOs, effective dashboards are essential to the success of the PMO. Effective dashboards can be helpful in many ways, from ensuring a common focus on what is deemed most important to providing valuable and timely insights, supported by best available data, on what has been achieved, what will be achieved, and all the risks, key issues, and help needed in order to deliver what has been committed to. Yet despite their promise, many PMOs struggle with the concept and purpose of dashboards and others don't take the time to do them at all. Over the years, when working with organizations to help them with their PMO dashboards, I have used the terms concept, purpose, and mind-set to help all involved arrive at a common view of what PMO dashboards are and can be for their organizations. Collectively, these three terms serve as a good basis for understanding and improving dashboard acumen.

Let's start with the concept of PMO dashboards. Most people view a dashboard as some kind of an instrument panel, such as the panel facing the driver of a car or the pilot of an aircraft. As conditions in the car or aircraft change, so too does the dashboard and in real time. The dashboard provides visual information as well as a wide variety of buttons and knobs that when manipulated perform an action such as rolling down a window, turning on the air-conditioner, playing music, or displaying further levels and amounts of information. Every now and then, I am reminded that the actual origin of the word dashboard comes from the days of horse-drawn carriages; the dashboard is the piece of wood fixed at the front of the carriage that protects the driver from mud and debris dashed up by the wheels and horse's hooves. In many ways, this definition of a dashboard would be much better for a PMO to draw upon because, for most PMOs, the idea of a dashboard being helpful, as opposed to a real-time contraption of some kind, would contribute to more effective and realistic dashboards.

Technically, most people view a PMO dashboard as some kind of graphical presentment of information that is contained within the database of a project portfolio management (PPM) tool of some kind, such as CA Clarity, HP PPM, Microsoft Project Server, or any of the other fine vendor offerings. Hence, a dashboard provides a quicker and simpler way to understand, at a summary level, the data contained within the tool. And a well-designed dashboard provides the information that the users, typically the leadership team, want for review and decision making. This technical view of a dashboard represents what I like to call an application dashboard. Yes, it is a dashboard. And if you have a PPM application, you should by all means take full advantage of that application's ability to dashboard, in a sensible manner, the information that is contained within its database.

The application dashboard, though helpful in its own right, is not the only approach or kind of dashboard, and this is where many organizations unnecessarily struggle. Another view of a dashboard is the view of a PMO dashboard as one of the content assets of the PMO. Every PMO, whether it knowingly seeks to establish and manage it or not, has a PMO architecture that includes such things as a PPM tool or capability, whether a spreadsheet or a vendor application; a collaboration platform of some kind, whether a network file share, mapped drive, or something like Microsoft SharePoint; a set of desktop tools that may include a few special purpose tools helpful to project managers like scheduling, drawing, and brainstorming tools; and a wide variety of PMO content assets that comprise all the nonapplication kinds of things that exist in every organization that manages projects, such as processes, policies, guidance, templates, learning resources, subject matter expert knowledge, and executive dashboards; yes, dashboards.

Many people, especially application administrators, scoff at the idea that a dashboard is content. To these people, a dashboard is a visual representation of live, real-time, 24-7 data. It is a way of understanding the data at a high level with just a glance and at a deeper level with a few drill-down clicks. In a PMO dashboard context, this application dashboard view is misguided for a number of reasons and leads to the setup of very ineffective dashboards. In a PMO context, consider time, usage, users, and information:

♦ Time. How often do project managers update their project status reports? Every minute? Once an hour? Three times a day? Daily? You get the idea. For most PMOs, it is considered a resounding success if we can get our project managers to enter their time and project data and update their status reports by 5:00 p.m. on the last day of the week. So, if the period of time by which data and information are entered and updated is once a week, just how live, real time, and 24-7 is that application dashboard? It's not. For most PMOs, not all of course, the term real-time dashboard should be banned from use. In addition to not being possible and meaningless, it promotes a misconception and view of what a PMO dashboard is or should be that only an application administrator would have.

◆ Usage. You use the dashboard of a car every time you drive, but do executives use their PMO dashboards in the same way? Do executives look at PMO dashboards with great frequency, such as multiple times a day? Or is it more likely that executives view the PMO dashboards on a periodic basis, such as the intervals of time associated with the governance or review process of the PMO? If the preponderance of executives look at the dashboard once a month and specifically want the context of the data to be monthly, then what need does a real-time PMO dashboard, assuming that there could be such a thing, fulfill? For most organizations and their executives, not all of course, there is no such need.

◆ Users. For most PMOs, there is a wide variety of constituents for whom the PMO exists to serve. One could argue that at a high level, a PMO would be well served to make available what it has and what it does to just about all the constituents it serves. How likely is it that all the constituents have a username and password for the PPM application? Whether a traditional installed application or Software-as-a-Service (SaaS), cloud-based subscription offering of some kind, it would be very unlikely that all the constituents of the PMO would even have access to the tool as a mere matter of cost. If these constituents don't have access to the application, they don't have access to the dashboard of the application. Hence, the application dashboard is of limited use as a mere matter of the fact that its users are inherently limited.

◆ Information. Executives want a dashboard that helps them with their meetings, reviews, discussions, and decision making. Toward that aim, the data that are contained within the PPM tool of the organization are but one source of data. It is a very important and foundational source of data, but there are other sources of data, information, and relationships that are needed to make the PMO dashboard intelligent, useful, and usable. As business conditions change, as different kinds of opportunities and risks present themselves, as motivations and interests of the leadership team change, the PMO dashboard needs to be supportive of this by way of alerts, advisements, and interpretation of both the data that are contained within the PPM tool and all the knowledge and expertise surrounding those data related to the business environment in which the projects live.

By all means, the application dashboard can be of use in many ways, especially in the narrow context of the data that the application is configured to collect and make use of and in the context of those people in the organization who have access to use the application. However, in a broader context, PMO dashboards are content, not application function keys that when pressed produce a graphic of some kind. This, the concept of a PMO dashboard, is very helpful to understand and to arrive at a common approach for implementation and use.

Next we have the purpose of the dashboard. How can a PMO have an effective dashboard without first having a discussion and clear understanding of what the purpose of the PMO dashboard is? It can't. Yet it happens all the time. The PMO prepares a dashboard that lists all the projects; provides information on the projects for scope, time, and cost; and shows green, yellow, and red icons to depict the status of the project. Is this a dashboard or a fancy report, to no discredit of fancy reports; there is a need for those too.

Imagine for just a moment the dashboard that a vice president of sales has. Is that dashboard likely to be a list of sales opportunities, which by the way are also called projects, or is it likely to be a graphic representation of key measurements such as sales to date, forecast, pipeline, profitability, customer satisfaction, and other important and time-sensitive information such as major wins, major losses, and competitor alerts? Almost always, it is the latter. Similar, and perhaps a better example, is the difference between the dashboards of a professional services PMO compared to most internal IT PMOs. The dashboards of professional services PMOs are much more like those of sales organizations in that they show information related to the achievement of their goals and objectives. By way of contrast, the dashboards of most IT PMOs are lists of projects that show project data and status indicators.

To ensure that they meet the intended need, PMOs need to first establish the purpose of the dashboard. Is the purpose of the PMO dashboard to show the leadership team the status of all the projects of the PMO? Is it to show the status of the PMO's performance in terms of the achievement of the goals and measurable objectives for which the PMO is held accountable? Is the purpose of the dashboard to provide the leadership team with specific report period data to facilitate management reviews, discussions, and decision making? Is the purpose of the PMO dashboard to meet all these kinds of needs? All these views could be valid for a given organization and its PMO. By way of PMO policy, the purpose of the dashboard needs to be established and reviewed and refined continually to ensure that the approach taken for the PMO dashboard is appropriate and meets the needs of the business.

Discussions of the concept and purpose of PMO dashboards lead right into and reveal the mind-set that people have about PMO dashboards. Though there are many different views and approaches for PMO dashboards, over the years working with PMOs on this very issue, I have seen two distinct mind-sets. One mind-set is the supportive mind-set and the other is the transactional mind-set, and here is how they are different. The supportive mind-set has a view that PMO dashboards are in essence management tools that facilitate decision making, strategic alignment, and functional teamwork. The transactional mind-set has a view that the PMO dashboards are for monitoring the elements. There is no better depiction of these mind-sets and who has them than the following research survey that we conducted on this subject a few years ago.

In 2009, we studied 25 PMOs for the specific purpose of better understanding organizational perspectives on PMO dashboards, understanding the challenges associated with PMO dashboards, and arriving at an inference from the data. The format of the survey was a set of open-ended questions with a telephone review of the answers. There were no multiple choice questions by design as we were seeking unstructured responses, not answers from a predetermined list. As we were seeking as much of a homogeneous sample size as possible, the criteria for participating in the survey were that the PMO had to have a PPM tool, a PMO team site or equivalent, and a framework of PMO content assets such as processes, templates, and supporting information in place. In short, the participants were established PMOs, well past their initial setup, and with leadership team developed and approved standard operating procedures in place.

As shown in Figure 8.1, we asked four categories of participants in each of these 25 organizations three simple, open-ended questions related to PMO dashboards: (1) describe three positive attributes of PMO dashboards, (2) describe one negative attribute of PMO dashboards, and (3) describe how the dashboard should be done. Just to restate, we were simply seeking commentary from these participants to understand the differing mind-sets, if any, on what they liked in their PMO dashboards, what they disliked, and how they thought it should be done.

In group 1, the executive team, their three PMO dashboard likes were (1) supportive of decision making, (2) simplicity, and (3) contextual. Their

---

PMO Dashboard Study
25 Organizations
100 Participants

Participants:
- Executive team
- PMO team
- Functional management team
- PPM application support team

Questions:
1. Describe three positive attributes of PMO dashboards
2. Describe one negative attribute of PMO dashboards
3. Describe how the dashboard should be done

Figure 8.1   PMO dashboard study

one PMO dashboard dislike was too much data. Their response for how it should be done was monthly. The commentary of the executive team included:

◆ I want the dashboard to be self-explanatory to all involved.
◆ I want the dashboard to support decision making.
  • Formal quarterly decision making
  • Regular monthly review of issues and action required
◆ I prefer multiple simple dashboards that provide a context.
◆ I don't want to have to relearn or be told what the data mean.
◆ I don't want to see overly detailed status.
◆ I don't want to see a long list of projects.
◆ I don't want one complex dashboard that doesn't provide a context.

In group 2, the PMO team, their three PMO dashboard likes were (1) strategic alignment, (2) comprehensive, and (3) graphical. Their one PMO dashboard dislike was too much complexity. Their response for how it should be done was monthly. The commentary of the PMO team included:

◆ I want the dashboard to show alignment of the project portfolio to the needs of the business.
◆ I want the dashboard to provide the executive team with a context to the projects of the portfolio.
◆ I want the dashboard to facilitate supply/demand management.
◆ I want the dashboard to accurately reflect the status of the portfolio.
◆ I want the dashboard to be graphical and intuitive.
◆ I want the dashboard to be comprehensive, yet easy to understand.
◆ I don't want the dashboard to be difficult to prepare.

In group 3, the functional management team, their three PMO dashboard likes were (1) supports teamwork, (2) graphical, and (3) intuitive. Their one PMO dashboard dislike was too much data. Their response for how it should be done was monthly. The commentary of the functional management team included:

◆ I want the dashboard to foster teamwork.
  • Resource allocation
  • Early warning signals
  • Project rescue
  • Project termination
◆ I want the dashboard to be graphic and easy to understand.
◆ I want the dashboard to provide a monthly assessment of the project portfolio and a call to action, if required.
◆ I don't want the dashboard to be too detailed.

In group 4, the PPM application support team, their three PMO dashboard likes were (1) real time, (2) automatic roll up of data, and (3) drill-downs. Their one PMO dashboard dislike was manual preparation. Their response for how it should be done was in real time. The commentary of the PPM application support team included:

◆ I want the dashboard to provide real-time views of the project portfolio data.
◆ I want the dashboard to provide drill-downs to project details and project status reports.
◆ I want the dashboard to provide different views based upon the role and permissions of the user.
◆ I want the dashboard to provide automobile-like graphical indicators and controls (fuel, speed, oil pressure, etc.).

- ◆ I want the dashboard to be fully automated.
- ◆ I do not want the dashboard to require manual preparation.

As summarized in Figure 8.2, the perspectives of these four groups of participants show a difference in mind-set between the executive, PMO, and functional management teams and that of the PPM application support teams.

The participants from the executive, PMO, and functional management teams all had a PMO dashboard mind-set that was of the supportive type. The people in these groups viewed the PMO dashboard as a management tool, a means to an end. In sharp comparison, the participants from the PPM application support team all had a PMO dashboard mind-set that was of the transactional type. The people in this group viewed the PMO dashboard as a database driven display. Here the importance wasn't placed upon whether or not the dashboard was actually useful, but whether or not the dashboard was fully automated, requiring no manual intervention. It is important to note that it is this group of people who typically are the ones who prepare the dashboard.

In our 2012 PMO survey, we also asked a structured question about PMO dashboards to determine if these observed differences in supportive versus transactional perspectives between executive, PMO, and functional management and PPM application support were still noticeable. The question we asked of these groups at the 80 participating companies was whether they viewed the PMO dashboard as a real-time, 24-7, automated, visual display of PPM data or a semi-manually, periodically prepared,

PMO Dashboard Study Summary of Responses				
	Executive Team	PMO Team	Functional Management	PPM Application Support Team
Likes	Supports decisions Contextual Simple	Strategic alignment Graphical Comprehensive	Supports teamwork Graphical Intuitive	Real time Automatic roll up Drill downs
Dislikes	Too much data	Too much complexity	Too much data	Manual preparation
How to	Quarterly reviews Monthly updates	Monthly	Monthly	On demand

Figure 8.2 PMO dashboard study responses

contextual graphic. As shown in Figure 8.3, these differences in perspectives about PMO dashboards among management and technical support are very present.

To avoid the common mistakes often made when preparing PMO dashboards, for most organizations it can be very helpful to establish the supportive mind-set and the view that PMO dashboards are not limited to PPM reporting or application dashboards and typically PMO dashboards are not transactional, real-time displays of data. To help garner support for that view, in the event of resistance from the technical support teams, it can be very helpful to ensure that they understand that executives do not want and are not asking for a dashboard that is updated in real time. Executives understand that project managers do not enter data and update information in real time. Executives want form over substance. Efficiency in preparation is important, but it is secondary to effectiveness of what is prepared.

In so many ways, the more that a PMO is driven by the needs of the business in all that it does, the more successful it will be. PMO dashboards are not an exception to this premise. Perhaps dashboarding should be a reserved word with only one possible meaning, but it is not and PMO dashboarding will likely mean different things to different people for a long time to come. As PMO practitioners we should expect different points of

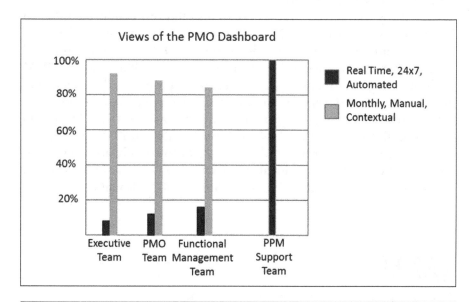

Figure 8.3 Views of PMO dashboard

view and differences of opinion on what the purpose of a PMO dashboard is and how it should be prepared.

Many people advocate, and I agree, that a PMO dashboard provides a filter, context, and a call to action for the constituents of the PMO. By way of PMO dashboard policy, what is highly important is filtered out by what is not. We all have heard the adage *if everything is important, then nothing is important*. Whether we are dashboarding progress against the PMO mandate, the status of the projects of the PMO, or both as well as other things, not everything is of equal importance. In addition to providing a filter of what is most important, the context of whatever data are on hand is what serves to make the dashboard intelligent and actionable. Many leadership teams want the PMO dashboard to have not just the filter and context, but also the working advice of the PMO in terms of a call to action or recommendation for their review and decision making.

There are many examples of good PMO dashboards, but that is not the point. In fact, I have purposely not shown an example, because far too often there can be a tendency to view a sampling of PMO dashboards and quickly turn all attention away from the need of the business and toward the latest graphical design. It is not that good design is of no importance; to the contrary, it is, but good design of the dashboard can only come after the purpose of the dashboard has been agreed to. Otherwise, to what aim is that good design contributing?

It is always a valuable use of time and effort to conduct your own PMO dashboard survey to determine the needs to be satisfied by the PMO. Be mindful that these needs for the PMO dashboard are those of the management and leadership team served by the PMO, not the PPM application support team. Expect to encounter views and mind-sets of the PMO dashboard from the support team that are more focused on efficiency than effectiveness and that are more concerned with form than substance. But once you establish a common view on PMO dashboarding, a unanimous consensus on the purpose of the dashboard, and a supportive rather than transactional mind-set for what a dashboard is and how to do it, the more effective your PMO dashboards will be.

9

Methodology Acumen

Every PMO has a project management methodology of some kind. Some PMOs have excellent project management methodologies and realize the benefits of a defined and documented approach for managing projects. It should be noted that a defined and documented methodology should not be confused with or assumed to be an overly detailed and bureaucratic one. Others have methodologies that were very good at a point in time, but that have become dated and not reflective of how projects and project-related work should be managed. And of course there are those organizations that for a wide variety of reasons have struggled with their project management methodologies from the very start of the PMO.

One might think that in the broader scheme of the challenges that PMOs face, establishing an effective project management methodology would be a fairly easy task. One would be wrong, and there is a big difference between having a methodology in SharePoint and having a methodology in practice. Much like acumen in any other domain, methodology acumen can be easily spotted. In the context of the PMO, it appears when an organization has an understanding of what exactly a methodology is, a clear and unanimous view on the purpose of the methodology, and an effective strategy for the initial setup, use, and ongoing improvement of the methodology, their methodology.

Let's start with the understanding of what exactly a project management methodology is. I write about this at length in *Business Driven PMO Setup* (2009) and quote a well-known authority within the formal project management and PMO community who has the misguided view that a project management methodology is a methodology that is developed to apply the standards of practice contained in PMI's *A Guide to the Project*

Management Body of Knowledge (*PMBOK® Guide*). Is that really what a project management methodology is?

Most dictionaries define a methodology as the methods and principles that are used when doing a particular kind of work. If we add the words project management in front of methodology, the definition of a project management methodology would be the methods and principles that are used when doing project management work. In a PMO context, the project management methodology needs to be PMO-grade in quality and usability. It needs to be relevant to not just projects of different types and sizes but various and sometimes unique review and decision-making processes. The methodology needs to address tools and platforms that are used in support of the management of projects. It also must address the activities that take place before the project is queued up for its initiation as well as the activities that take place after the project has been closed out. In short, the definition of a PMO-grade project management methodology would be the sum of all methods and principles that are used when managing the projects and project-related work of the PMO.

To some, this all might sound like much ado about nothing, but for most PMOs there is no greater mistake in methodology development than to think that a methodology is developed in order to apply what is contained in the PMBOK. Perhaps a better and more business driven view would be that a project management methodology is a consistent and repeatable approach for the management of projects, whether based upon one standard, multiple standards, parts of standards, principles of the practicing community, or expert judgment; a methodology is a means to an end. The end in question should be the best approach for the management of projects for your organization, not the mere juxtaposition of the latest standard into an epistle.

As part of the 2012 PMO survey, we asked the participants a few questions about project management methodology as well. Two of the questions were in the form of degree of agreement with statements. The two statements regarding what a project management methodology *is* were:

◆ A methodology is developed to apply the standards of practice contained in the PMBOK.
◆ A methodology is developed to ensure a consistent and repeatable outcome.

As shown in Figure 9.1, there are considerable differences of opinion in what a project management methodology is.

The survey results clearly show a consensus position and view that a project management methodology is developed to ensure a consistent and

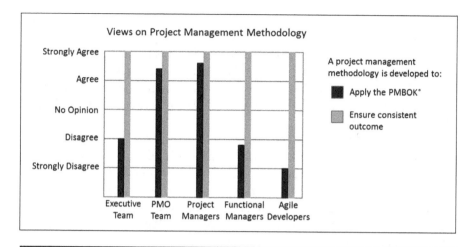

Figure 9.1 Views on project management methodology

repeatable outcome. Although there is also a strong view among PMO managers and project managers that a project management methodology is developed to apply the principles of the PMBOK, this view is not shared by the executive team and functional managers and it is rejected altogether by the agile developers.

These survey results probably do not come as a surprise to most people who are in or served by PMOs. But what does come as a surprise is the fact that most project management methodologies are developed without any effort or attention to first ensuring a shared vision and perspective on what the methodology actually is. Common sense would dictate that the more we all agree on what the project management methodology is, the more likely it is that we will develop a good one that serves the needs of all involved in project-related work. Conversely, the less we all agree, the less likely it will be of use and practical value.

This all leads to the next component of methodology acumen, which is a clear, concise, and unanimous view on the purpose of the methodology. For many PMOs, especially new PMOs, the purpose of a methodology is often taken for granted to be doing a better job of project management from the highly shaded lens of a particular standard such as the PMBOK or the United Kingdom Office of Government Commerce of Her Majesty's Treasury Projects in a Controlled Environment (PRINCE2®). This often results in project management methodologies that are aligned to a particular standard, but that are not necessarily driven by or aligned to the needs of the business.

Consider the following. Does a business need to improve, by way of definition and documentation, every aspect of how projects are to be managed in accordance with a particular standard? Or is it more likely the case that businesses have specific needs related to the management of projects within the context of their own specific environment and sets of business issues directly related to that environment? For most businesses and their PMOs, it is the latter.

In Section 1 of this book, we discussed a real-life company whose leadership team decided that they wanted to have a PMO. As this was the first PMO the company ever had, they hired an experienced PMO manager, or I should say a manager with prior PMO experience, to set things up. The PMO manager rushed right in and among other things developed and made available the project management methodology that was patterned after the then current version of the PMBOK.

Did the PMO manager take the time to first understand the project-related needs of the business as well as the various perspectives of the leadership team on the specific project problems and issues that they had for which the PMO was conceived and funded to address? Would it even make a difference to first gather these needs in order to ensure that the to be developed project management methodology in fact addressed them? Though the first of the two PMO managers that this company hired was oblivious to them because he didn't take the time to ask about them, the project-related needs of the leadership team included some of the following:

- The VP of Sales had a need to do more billable projects in order to meet the services revenue component of his business plan.
- The VP of Professional Services had a need to prevent the sales executives from materially changing the proposed scope, schedule, and budget of billable professional services implementation projects as part of winning the business resulting in implementation projects, now owned by professional services, for which unachievable expectations for scope, schedule, and budget had been contractually agreed to.
- The VP of Business Development needed to be provided with discretionary resources in support of long-term business development initiatives for which no immediate revenue would be recognized, resulting in few if any resources being made available.
- The Manager of Product Development needed to put a stop to the informal practice of the sales executives committing product engineers to custom product development projects because the core

features of the product were not sufficient to win the business over rivals. This compromised the schedule integrity of the established product development plan.

◆ The CFO needed to improve the timeliness and accuracy of the quarterly revenue forecasts, especially services revenue recognition, which was largely driven by billable professional services implementation projects.

◆ The CIO had a need to increase the project capacity and to shorten the cycle times of the internal projects of the company, which included large-scale and complex transformation projects, midsize infrastructure projects, and a large number of smaller and simpler run-of-the mill IT projects.

◆ The CEO and for that matter the senior leadership team had a need and desire to have a holistic and comprehensive view of all the projects and project opportunities of the company in order to ensure that the best possible projects were being selected and were being delivered as fast as possible, all other things considered, such as budget, scope, risks, quality, and benefit delivery.

Given business needs like this as a backdrop, is it possible to develop and roll out a project management methodology that is merely aligned to a given standard such as the PMBOK and have any chance for real success?

In the real-life case study example, the project management methodology that the first PMO manager developed, though it is aligned to the then current version of the PMBOK, ended up being a complete failure. As a means to an end, it fundamentally did not meet that end. Just imagine all the nuances from project management processes that provide both structure and flexibility within structure to accommodate projects of different types and sizes, to guidance for what is mandatory to do and what is optional, to checklists to ensure awareness and understanding of organizational constraints and areas of compliance, to subject matter expert knowledge and past project information that may be helpful to consider, and to advisements on tools and techniques that may be used or even mandatory for certain aspects of the project. If a project management methodology does not fundamentally address or at least take these organizational nuances into consideration, then it will likely be of very little value. In fact, such a project methodology may even cause more harm than good.

In developing project management methodologies, the formal project management and PMO community needs to initially set the various standards' documents and bodies of knowledge to the side. My agile friends, due to years of frustration with their PMOs, would suggest that they should be thrown away. I would not go that far, but the PMO managers from whom I have had the opportunity to learn over the years who have had highly effective PMOs and highly useful project management methodologies all started the development of their project management methodology by first asking about and understanding the top project-management-related problems and needs that the organization had. Cast from the perspective of specific business needs, these methodologies that were developed provided not only a best practice for the management of projects, but a highly tailored approach and useful set of guidance that helped all involved with the projects of the PMO effectively work together toward a successful outcome.

Intuitively, one would think that just about every PMO manager would go about developing their project management methodology in this manner. Again, one would be wrong. As shown in Figure 9.2, there are noted differences in views on how a project management methodology should be developed between the PMO team and project managers who represent the formal project management and PMO community and the rest of the business.

When asked about how a project management methodology should be primarily developed, the PMO team and project managers felt strongly that the methodology should comply, and be kept compliant, to project management standards such as the PMBOK. To the PMO team and project managers, customizing the methodology to meet specific business needs was not viewed as important to do or necessary, and it was believed that a general purpose methodology could be used as is for any project.

This view was not shared by the executive team, functional managers, and agile developers, who all strongly believed that a project management

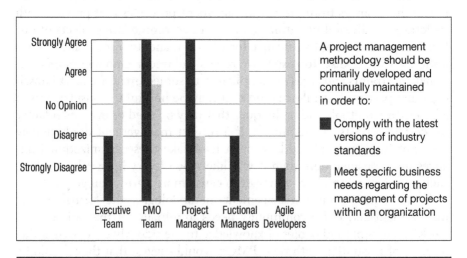

Figure 9.2 Views on project management methodology customization

methodology should be primarily developed and continually maintained in order to meet specific business needs regarding the management of projects. Additionally, this group of responders did not share the same conviction of the PMO team and project managers that the methodology needs to be developed to be compliant, and then continually kept compliant, to an industry standard.

Imagine an organization that has a tremendous need for stakeholder communication, but cost in terms of a perfect project budget is not that essential or even expected. Or what about an organization for which time is precious, yet other aspects of the project are secondary by a large order of magnitude? And what about an organization for which exceeding the project budget is highly problematic, yet other deviations are acceptable? And what about organizations that might have unique people issues, volatile market considerations, highly likely risk events, or the absence of all these things? Is it possible that a general purpose project management methodology would be suitable for all these organizations?

For most organizations the answer is no; a general purpose project management methodology would not be suitable. Unless it is developed and customized to meet the specific project-related needs that the organization has, a general purpose project management methodology would likely be of nominal value for some projects and an impediment to others.

The last component of methodology acumen is an effective strategy for the initial setup, use, and ongoing improvement of the project management methodology. Toward that aim, the following three steps will guaranty success.

Step 1: Immediately forbid the use of the term project management methodology. Project management methodology is an old, stale, and outdated term and view of what is needed by today's PMOs. Since most people outside the formal project management and PMO community don't like the term anyway because of bad past experiences with overly burdensome and ineffective project management methodologies, it is unlikely that there will be any resistance to its abolishment.

Step 2: Develop your own term that describes not just your project management methodology but all the nonapplication kinds of things that every organization that manages projects has. The approach for project management, methodology, is but one member of this family. For years I have advocated the use of the term PMO content assets as it helps to foster that notion that PMOs have a great deal of nonapplication kinds of things such as processes, policies, guidance, templates, executive dashboards, learning resources, training materials, subject matter expert knowledge, past project archives, lessons learned, reviews of highly successful projects, reviews of failed projects, frequently asked questions, glossary of terms, and supporting information of all kinds that is amassed over time. What people in the formal project management and PMO community call a project management methodology is but a very small component of the total content assets of the PMO. In addition to advocating the term PMO content assets, I have also advocated the term process for describing the approach for managing the project. Hence, by way of project type policy, which is also an example of a PMO content asset, a particular project management process, which could be one of many that the PMO has, that is most appropriate for the project is selected and followed.

Step 3: Implement or develop an easy to set up and maintain way for your users to access, find, and intuitively use the content assets of the PMO. I highly recommend HTML-based frameworks for the management and use of PMO content assets. Much like a website, an HTML-based, PMO content asset framework provides users with an intuitive ability to access, find, and use the content assets of the PMO. Project management processes can be followed with minimal effort as compared to the alternative of lengthy project management methodology documents, typically in a document or PDF format, which are unwieldy to use and limited in their ability to render supporting information and guidance. An HTML-based, PMO content asset framework is also highly desirable by those responsible for developing, maintaining, and continually improving upon the content assets of the PMO as it is not limited in its ability to render many different types of PMO content, from HTML pages, to visual process workflows, to executive dashboard graphics, to project management templates, to multimedia learning resources, and other supporting information whether in HTML format or another file type.

Without an HTML-based, PMO content asset framework, a great deal of PMO content is very likely to become orphaned over time. With no home or suitable place to be housed and nourished, the content assets of the PMO become outdated over time or in many cases lost. In this case, rather than a state of organization and continuous improvement, the content assets of the PMO are left in a state of disarray and entropy.

Much like a very simple website, a PMO content asset framework is not very hard to design and build with nothing more than a simple HTML editor. Also, there are a number of HTML-based, PMO content asset products that can be purchased, implemented, and customized, sparing the PMO considerable time and money, not to mention the potential for getting additional content assets that might otherwise have been initially overlooked. Figures 9.3 through 9.8 show a few screen shot examples of

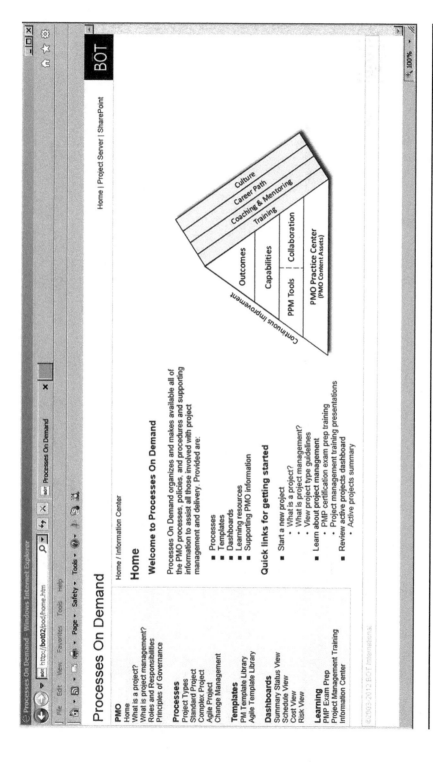

Figure 9.3 PMO content asset framework example

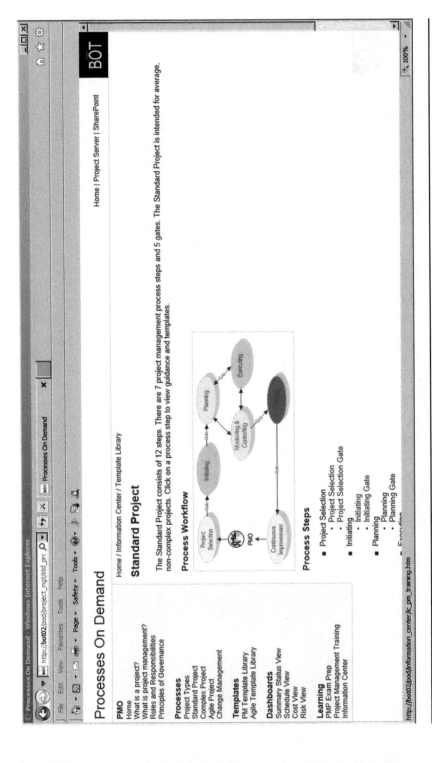

Figure 9.4 PMO content asset framework example—process workflow

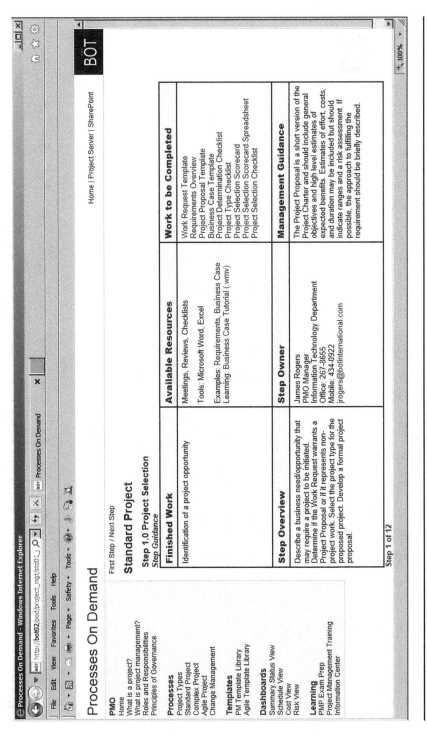

Figure 9.5 PMO content asset framework example—process step guidance

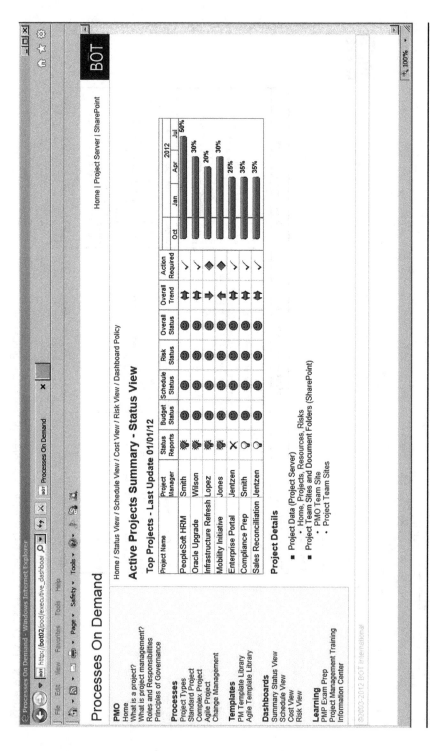

Figure 9.6 PMO content asset framework example—executive dashboard summary status

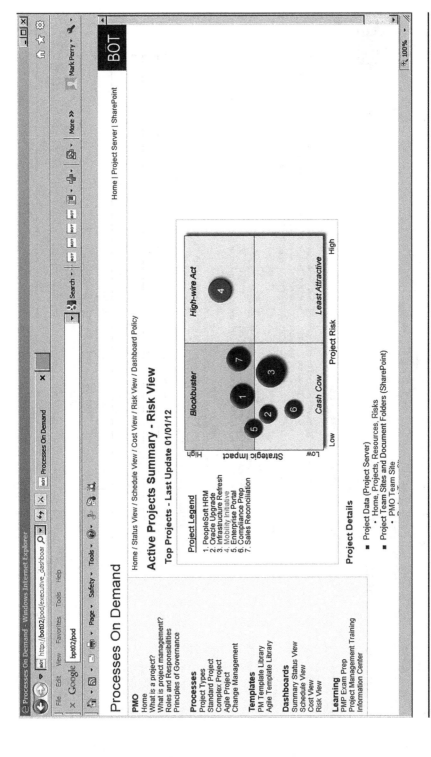

Figure 9.7 PMO content asset framework example—executive dashboard risk status

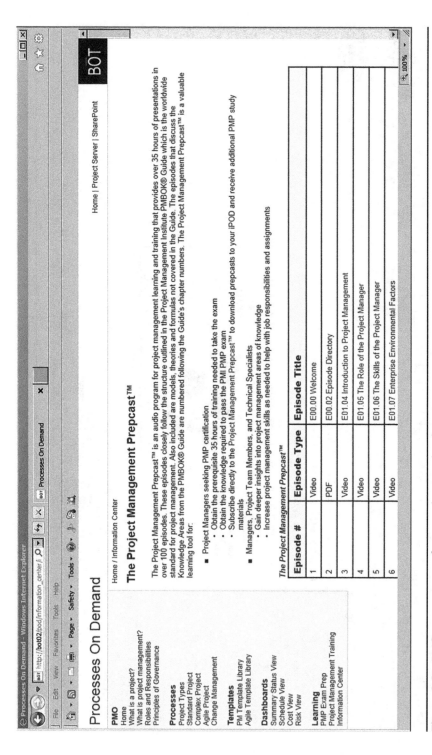

Figure 9.8   PMO content asset framework example—learning resources

an HTML-based, PMO content asset framework called Processes On Demand that is designed to be customized, rebranded, and used by organizations of all shapes and sizes.

In addition to Processes On Demand, there are many other PMO content asset product offerings that can be purchased and quickly set up and customized as an alternative to the PMO having to develop its content assets and all the supporting administrator and user documentation from scratch. The following is a short list of a few of the many offerings that have been in the PMO marketplace for several years:

◆ Processes on Demand by BOT International. Processes on Demand is a rebrandable PMO content asset offering that provides processes, templates, dashboards, learning resources, and supporting PMO information to help ensure the integrity of projects, the effective use of tools, and the successful management of the PMO.

◆ Project Management Community of Practice (PMCOP^{SM}) by PM Solutions. PMCOP^{SM} is a proprietary project management methodology that contains hundreds of forms, templates, and practices.

◆ Unified Project Management Methodology (UPMM™) by IIL. UPMM™ is a software suite of knowledge management tools that provides a complete project management methodology, templates, and guidance that can be purchased and used by individuals, small groups, and enterprises.

◆ Gantthead Project Headway by gantthead. Gantthead Project Headway provides an online project management methodology, guidance, and set of templates, forms, and checklists.

◆ TenStep® Project Management Process by TenStep. The TenStep® Project Management Process provides a step-by-step approach for the management of projects, complete with guidance, templates, forms, and checklists.

◆ Method123, owned and operated by Jason Westland, provides a project management kit of templates, methodology, and guidance.

Whether purchased and customized, developed from scratch, or simply amassed over time, content assets exist in every organization that has projects to manage. For those who struggle with the term, just imagine all the nonapplication kinds of things that abound in even the smallest of PMOs. Another way to grasp the concept of PMO content assets is to think of all the things that do not come with project management applications, platforms, and tools. As an example, and to no discredit to Microsoft, Project Server and SharePoint are excellent vendor products, but where in Project

Server does it tell you how to manage a project and how to manage a PMO, and where in SharePoint does it tell you where to store your project documents or to archive the artifacts of closed projects?

Those PMOs that have taken the time, and sometimes bother, to collaboratively develop a best-in-class project management methodology that is both aligned to generally accepted best practices and honed to meet specific business needs and project challenges deserve credit for their methodology acumen, as there is far more to developing effective approaches for the management of projects and the management of PMOs than meets the eye. For those who have struggled with their project management methodologies and for whom the mere word methodology evokes a negative connotation about both the approach for project management and the sentiment for the PMO in general, an alternative approach is the PMO content asset approach. In this approach, we discard the word methodology from our vocabulary, we seek a clear and unanimous view on the purpose of defining and documenting what we seek to do, and we develop a strategy for the effective use and ongoing improvement of all those non-application kinds of things that would otherwise become outdated and irrelevant to the organization or lost altogether.

10

Maturity Acumen

Many people such as research analysts, executives, functional managers, developers, and operational staff share the view that the formal project management and PMO community too often displays a myopic tendency to only see the world through the shaded lenses of its own standards. The end result of this as perceived by these people is an industry environment in which the resulting certifications and membership revenues not only represent a large, viable business concern for the industry standards organization worthy of being protected and defended, but that also creates an extended ecology of organizations and individuals that practice within the community. These practitioners soon develop and exhibit an unintended but very real bias for their own best practices and approaches which is accompanied by a large blind spot and high degree of resistance for the best practices and approaches of others. This impacts maturity acumen in a number of ways, some helpful and others not, both of which are worthy of review.

Let's start with the helpful ways in which PMO maturity acumen has been impacted by the formal project management and PMO community. First, the various industry standards for project, program, and portfolio management in and of themselves have contributed significantly to the development and ongoing improvement of how projects are managed within an organization. These foundational works have given organizations of all shapes and sizes the ability to speak a common language, define and use a common approach, and continually seek improvement through both objective and subjective measurable means. As noted project portfolio management (PPM) expert Terry Doerscher advises, "Even a poor process is likely to be better than no process at all." What Terry Doerscher and other

PMO and PPM experts recognize is that the mere effort to define and follow a process and get it right is not only better than the alternative of no process, but when done with sincerity of purpose it also spawns an inherent self-correcting aftereffect. That is, areas of work that were problematic before now become more visible as a defined process and easier to discuss, diagnose, and correct. Hence, just the presence of standards within the formal project management and PMO community provides organizations with the ways and means to codify their best practices, whether initially suitable or not, and then to collaboratively arrive at the most appropriate approach and set of guidance for the organization.

Second, in addition to the various industry standards for project, program, and portfolio management, we also have standards for maturity that come to us in the form of maturity models. What is a maturity model? It is a framework that can be used to identify and establish capabilities. Typically, maturity models include methods to facilitate assessment, methods to identify deficiencies, and representations of paths for improvement.

There is no shortage of maturity models. Within the industry the two leading models are the Project Management Institute's maturity model known as OPM3® and the U.K. Office of Government Commerce's maturity model known as P3M3™. Naturally, there are countless other maturity models that have been developed over the years to help organizations improve their project, program, and portfolio management capabilities by research firms like Gartner and Forrester Research, all the leading PPM tool providers, and too many to count consulting firms and training organizations. Hence, for organizations seeking to improve their capabilities, achieve more predictable and consistent outcomes, and to attain higher levels of maturity, there are many alternatives from which to choose. For all of this, and so much more, we owe a debt of gratitude to our industry standards organizations, namely the Project Management Institute and the U.K. Office of Government Commerce.

Third, PMO maturity acumen has been positively impacted by the formal project management and PMO community because of the sheer number of subject matter experts the industry has created and enabled. These professionals, like John Schlichter, Ginger Levin, Claudia Baca, and many others, have deep domain knowledge in organizational project management maturity, experience with the preferred toolset of the practice called the OPM3 Product Suite, and years of business experience that provides them a tempered perspective for the practical application of the maturity model standard. In fact, one could posit that it is the certified professionals who represent the product of the standard. This is because of the fact that if you are not certified, you can't use the OPM3 Product Suite, and until you have had the requisite training and experience, the results that you are able to achieve with it would be quite limited.

Cast in this light, the certified practitioner is the product of the standard, and it is the certified practitioner, whether an external consultant or internal staff, who represents the opportunity for organizations to systematically improve their level of maturity. Hence, what you are buying and the benefit of what you are receiving is in all practical reality the certified practitioner, not the standard. Anecdotally, in my years of experience working with PMOs that have invested in a maturity initiative of some kind provided by a certified consultant, decision makers within these organizations have shared with me that the return on investment is compelling. As shown in Figure 10.1, the return on investment for maturity consulting as assessed by those paying for the service, in terms of perceived benefit to actual cost, ranges from 40 to 1 to 100 to 1 or more. Simply put, the cost of utilizing the services of a certified OPM3 consultant pale in comparison to the hard dollar benefits realized.

Foundational standards, models for maturity, and exceptionally talented practitioners who are worth their weight in gold—these are the helpful ways in which the formal project management and PMO community has impacted maturity acumen.

Now let's turn our attention to some of the unintended consequences of the formal project management and PMO community, in terms of

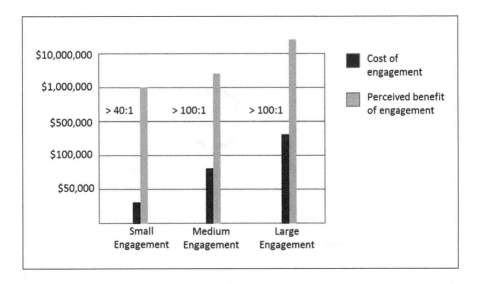

Figure 10.1 Maturity consulting return on investment

maturity acumen, for which the impact and value to organizations seeking to mature have been much less commendable. In this corner we have two villains that are each true forces of wrongdoing, some would say evil. The first villain is the collective set of people who in practice misuse maturity models. In this camp, the leading culprits are all the vendor firms, consulting practices, and individuals for whom a maturity model represents a billable service of some kind. Not all these folks are bad apples and none of them intend to be, but far too many of them are bad apples simply because of the manner in which they sell and perform their billable services for maturity engagements. Before reading further, have a look at Figures 10.2 and 10.3 and study them for just a moment.

How many times have you directly participated in or heard about a maturity initiative in which consultants explain their approach of first conducting a gap analysis to determine the current state of maturity (as compared to the desired state) and then creating an improvement plan of training and methodology development to reach that desired state? And how many times have you seen a radar-chart-style graphical illustration of the gap analysis somewhat similar to Figures 10.2 and 10.3? Setting aside the efficacy of the approach taken to arrive at a numeric value of the current level of capability for each of the assessed areas, how many times have

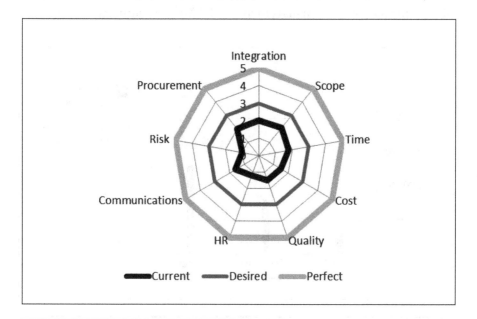

Figure 10.2 PPM gap analysis based upon project management standard

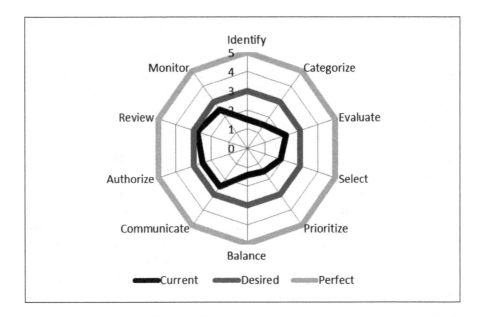

Figure 10.3 PPM gap analysis based upon portfolio management standard

you seen the recommended maturity level of each of the areas assessed to be anything other than the number three?

What follows next of course is much like watching the rerun of a movie that you have seen many times before; the ending is always the same. In the context of maturity consulting such as this, the ending is almost assuredly going to be a recommendation for further consulting in the form of project management training, methodology development, and if the consulting firm is also a tool reseller and implementer, then we will have some of that as well. That this is happening every day within the formal project management and PMO community is very hard to deny. The foundational standards of the practicing community are intended to be used as a means to an end. Hence solutions, in this case billable consulting, are advanced to achieve an end. To the client, the end is solving a problem; to the provider, the end is making a sale as well as, of course, satisfying a client need and hopefully developing a long-term mutually beneficial relationship.

To the extent that the providers of maturity consulting perform their duties as bona fide subject matter experts and trusted advocates of the profession, and that customers of such consulting are well informed and know exactly what they need and are getting, then there is absolutely nothing wrong with this picture. However, when this is not the case and providers of consulting are exploitatively using the tapestry of industry standards to push their billable services wherever possible, and customers of such consulting are duped into lengthy and costly engagements for whatever legitimate pretense and reasons they may have had in the first place, then we have a problem. In this case, consulting firms have not properly applied the standards of the practicing industry, customer needs have not been met, and in many cases the formal project management and PMO community has been left with a black eye and tarnished reputation in the eyes of management. This is poor maturity acumen and the unintended consequence of the collective set of people who, in practice, misuse maturity models.

The other villain is the collective set of people who are so myopic in their views of organizational project management—not the standard but rather the totality of all project management that exists and is undertaken throughout the organization—that their use of maturity models is limited to a small subset of the overall domain. I can give no better example of this than a memorable meeting that I had at the Gartner PPM and IT Governance Summit with a PMO manager and his boss, who was the CIO of the company.

I was invited to give a short fast-track-style presentation on the top risks that threaten the success of PPM and to also conduct a number of 30-minute, one-on-one meetings with attendees of the summit who wanted to have a private consultation or chat of some kind. Gartner has a highly talented team of consultants that do this exceptionally well, such as Matt Light, Michael Hanford, Daniel Stang, Donna Fitzgerald, Audrey Apfel, and many others, so it was an honor and pleasure to be invited, as an outsider, to join them in conducting these private meetings.

At the appointed time, a young and energetic PMO manager arrived at my consultation table along with his boss, the CIO, who was a silver-haired gentleman wearing an expensive-looking suit, yellow power tie with matching pocket handkerchief, and highly polished Florsheim shoes. After the customary exchange of business cards and pleasantries, I asked the two gentlemen what they would like to talk about. The CIO looked over and deferred to his young PMO manager, who responded that they are a highly effective and very mature PMO, Level 5, and just wanted to stop by to stay abreast of the latest PMO and PPM trends in the industry. The PMO manager added that over the last five years they had staffed the PMO with great people, they had developed their project management methodology aligned to the PMBOK, they implemented the leading PPM tool on the market, and all the project managers in the PMO had achieved their project management professional (PMP). They had also conducted a maturity assessment that led to some minor touch-up work in a few areas of their project management methodology. The young PMO manager wrapped up his opening salvo by saying that the PMO had done all there was to do.

After the dust settled, I asked the young PMO manager if before we went further into a conversation about all of that people, process, and tools stuff, which could be quite tedious, he could first tell me the purpose of the PMO in terms of its mandate or in terms of the business problem for which the PMO existed to serve. This produced a blank stare by the PMO manager and I happened to notice a wry smile by the CIO. The PMO manager could not provide an adequate answer to this relatively simple question.

Next, since it was unclear to me what the purpose of the PMO was and since the PMO manager couldn't tell me, I asked the PMO manager if he could tell me or describe to me the mission statement of the PMO as well as the vision statement for the PMO. This would shed light on what the PMO mandate was and whether that mandate was codified. Again, another blank stare by the PMO manager and I noticed that the wry smile of the CIO was growing a bit wider.

Still trying to ascertain what the business purpose of this organization that calls itself a PMO was, I asked the PMO manager what the goals and measurable objectives of the PMO were, as there is no better litmus test of what the purpose of an organization is than the objectives for which an organization is held accountable. With this question the blank stare of the PMO manager transformed back into the energetic countenance that he first had at the start of our discussion. The PMO manager enthusiastically responded that the PMO had several key performance indicators (KPIs), 27 altogether, that were broken down into 3 KPIs for each of the 9 knowledge areas of the PMBOK.

At this point I mentioned to the PMO manager that KPIs are merely indicators of performance in key areas; they are not goals and objectives. It was also at this point that I realized that I needed to talk much slower. The PMO manager responded that the purpose of the PMO was to develop the standards for the management of projects and to measure and improve upon the behaviors and activities associated with managing projects. This included staffing, methodology development, tooling, training, and ongoing self-assessments. And though they do not have a written mandate for the PMO or measurable goals and objectives, if graded in the above criteria, the PMO would be an A+ organization.

After hearing this, I let a few moments pass before saying my next words, which were intended for not just the PMO manager but his boss, the CIO, as well. I sat up straight, placed my folded hands on the table, and said, "Gentlemen, what we have here is a failure to communicate." This produced a flustered look from the PMO manager and a chuckle from the CIO, who had yet to join the conversation.

I then proceeded to share my perspective on the kinds of projects and project management needs that exist throughout an organization as well as what an organization might want its PMO to do about those needs. I took out a piece of paper and started by drawing a simple square while asking the PMO manager to think about all the projects that exist throughout the organization as being inside. Next, I bisected the square into four quadrants. Shown on the x-axis or the horizontal dimension was the degree to which the projects of the organization were either the formal projects of the organization or the wide variety of business-as-usual projects, often called informal or accidental projects. Shown on the y-axis or the vertical dimension was the degree to which the projects of the organization were either managed in accordance with scientific plan driven management approaches or managed in accordance with the principles of complex adaptive systems, referred to as CAS. The state of this drawing at this point in the discussion is depicted in Figure 10.4.

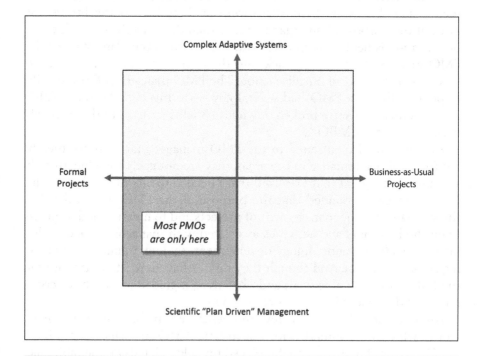

Figure 10.4   Organization-wide project management

I explained to the PMO manager and the CIO that this was my view of organization-wide project management: all the projects throughout the organization, both formal and informal, and the approaches for the management of these projects, both plan driven and adaptive. I also suggested that if one were to grade a PMO on its maturity acumen in terms of how well the PMO served the organization, one should look at each of these four quadrants and assess PMO effort and results, with effort being viewed as the means to the ends, such as best practices, and results being viewed as the ends to be achieved, such as the achievement of specific PMO goals and objectives.

As shown in Figure 10.5, I then offered the PMO manager and his CIO an assessment of their PMO. On a maturity scale of 1–5, I awarded the PMO manager a 5 for the scientific plan driven management *people, process,* and *tools* work that was accomplished for the formal projects of the organization. I did mention that this score of a 5 was a gift as it is inconceivable to me how one could go about developing a strategy for the means to the ends without first truly understanding and having a consensus for the ends to be achieved by way of a mandate, mission, vision, goals, and measurable

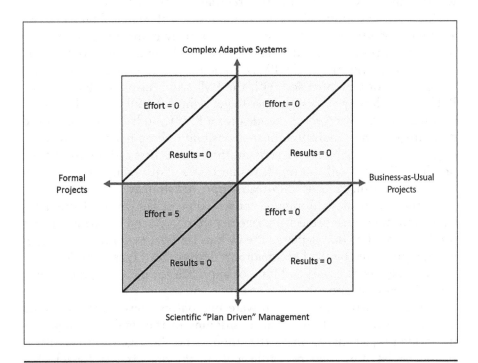

Figure 10.5 Organization-wide project management assessment

objectives. Since the PMO manager did not have any measurable goals or objectives, a score of 0 was awarded for that part of the assessment. And for the other three quadrants for which projects exist throughout the organization and for which the PMO manager had no notice or care, scores of 0 were given for both the means to the ends and ends to be achieved. With a resulting score of 5 points out of a possible 40, I then asked the PMO manager and CIO for what kind of test would a score of 12.5% be an A+ grade.

At this point in the discussion, the PMO manager's face had turned a bright red color and his demeanor had changed from overly confident to overly defensive. It was also at this point that the PMO manager's boss, the CIO, finally joined the conversation, and what he said only made the PMO manager more agitated. Though the PMO manager was well outside of his comfort zone, the CIO got it and knew exactly where this conversation about organization-wide project management was going. More to the point, the CIO had invested the time and money to attend the Gartner PPM and IT Governance Summit because despite all the hard work of the PMO to date, the prevailing sentiment of the leadership team and CIO was that the PMO was just not that relevant to the business.

Yes, there were noticeable gains in many areas of technical project management performance, but there were also many points of disconnection between the project-related business needs of the entire organization and the focus and priorities of the PMO. To no discredit of the PMO manager, these points of disconnection with the PMO and misplaced focus of the PMO are leadership responsibilities to get right. After all, it was the leadership team that conceived of the idea for a PMO, funded it, and approved its strategy. If they abdicated this responsibility, chose not to be involved, or just did a poor job of management, then that is first and foremost their problem. There is only so much blame that a PMO manager should receive for executing a leadership-team-approved strategy.

By the end of our 30-minute conversation, as shown in Figure 10.6, an organization-wide project management typology and its characteristics had been sketched that depicted the various landscapes of project management, represented by the four quadrants derived from type of project (formal vs. business as usual) and type of approach for managing the project (plan driven vs. adaptive).

As we were wrapping up our private, one-on-one consultation, I offered by way of a high-level recap and positioning of the totality of organization-wide project management that there is no shortage of project-management-related business needs throughout the organization for which a

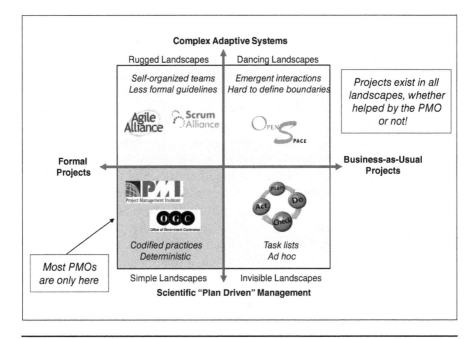

Figure 10.6   Organization-wide project management typology

PMO can serve, be of tremendous value, and be held accountable. And as with any other business unit in the organization, the PMO must have an unambiguous mandate, a clear mission, ideally an inspiring vision, and most certainly a set of prioritized goals and measurable objectives as set not by the PMO manager, but by the leadership team. Therefore, the quantified dollar value of the PMO is the leadership team's analysis and best guess assessment of the benefits of having fulfilled the mandate of the PMO, their PMO. I also suggested that for most PMOs just getting started, there is nothing wrong, when driven by the needs of the business, with having a focus that is initially limited to the formal projects of the organization and the plan driven approaches for the management of those formal projects. But as those foundational project-management-related business needs are met and as the PMO matures, there is a lot more it can do for the business.

This story reveals a perspective that is all too common in the formal project management and PMO community: a perspective that a PMO can reach a high level of some kind of knowledge-based standard for maturity, and when it does there is little else for it to do aside from managing the various formal projects that come its way. This myopic perspective about projects, approaches for the management of projects and project-related work, and narrow views on organization-wide project management maturity is that other villain that impacts the maturity acumen of PMOs.

It is worth noting that in the various Business Driven PMO workshops that I have conducted all over the world, there is an organization-wide project management exercise that we do at the end of the workshop. In this exercise, we list out all the various projects that exist in every nook and cranny of the organization as represented by lines of business, divisions, departments, and business units. These are the projects that are often referred to as informal or accidental, and these projects will never be found, nor necessarily should they be found, in the PPM tool of the PMO. Then we list out and put a dollar value on some of the typical project mishaps that can and often do happen in these projects. Without much difficulty and, more importantly, without anyone's disagreement, it can be shown that the difference between doing a poor job and a good job in the management of these projects is collectively a tremendous dollar amount. We then discuss the following questions:

- ◆ Does the value of doing a better job at managing these informal and accidental projects that exist throughout the organization merit consideration of some kind?
- ◆ Who by title should give consideration of some kind to improve how these informal and accidental projects are being managed?
- ◆ Who by title knows best the value of doing a good job instead of a poor job in managing a project?
- ◆ What percent of PMOs, whether strategic PMOs, enterprise PMOs, IT PMOs, or any other kind of PMOs, have done anything to improve the management of informal and accidental organization-wide projects?

As shown in Figure 10.7, in workshops conducted all over the world the answer to these questions are very similar and not a particularly positive reflection of the maturity acumen of the formal project management and PMO community.

With respect to informal and accidental organization-wide projects, how is it that the formal project management and PMO community can be so obtuse? Can you imagine any other discipline in which the expert in that discipline recognizes the need for the discipline and purports to be the expert in the discipline, but then relegates to functional management the job of figuring out how to do that discipline in their functional units? I can't.

Two memorable examples that I like to give that are contrary to this obtuse project management community mind-set are security and human

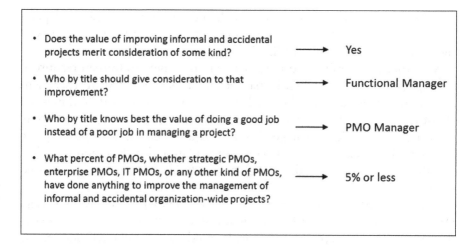

Figure 10.7   Organization-wide project management improvement

resources. Years ago, when I was an IBM trainee, my manager called me into his office and told me that I had violated IBM's security policy by leaving my desk unlocked after hours. I had failed the security audit. In my defense, I mentioned to my manager that as a trainee yet to be assigned to any real work, aside from the training program, my desk was empty with the exception of a few pencils, paper clips, and rubber bands and that perhaps the security inspector should actually look in the desk and not just check to see if it is locked. My manager replied that I should just get in the habit of locking my desk.

The offense was not major and I soon forgot all about it, at least until the following month when my manager called me into his office again. It turns out I failed another security audit as my desk was once again not locked, and it turns out that my manager was actually serious about locking my empty desk; I had thought at the time he was joking. Now my manager is very upset because I have single-handedly met his quota of security violations for the year. Any more violations and he could be in trouble, and if I got another violation, I could be terminated. I quickly learned IBM's security policy and complied with it, empty desk or not.

The point of the story is that the IBM security team by way of policies and measurements took a broad and comprehensive view of security and ensured that it was in place. Did the IBM security organization personally visit every field office and perform inspections? Of course not, but they had a level of responsibility and accountability for the overall security program, strategy, best practices, and measurements. If a security office can affect the day-to-day activities for the betterment of divisions, departments, and field business units throughout the organization, then why can't a project management office?

My other memorable and personal example involves human resources. Again, many years ago when I first became a manager at IBM, I was sent to new manager school, where I learned, among many other things, all about our policies for performance planning, counseling, and evaluation, known as PPC&E. As a manager, it was a requirement that we put in place for each of our employees a performance plan and a development plan, and that we conduct and document quarterly interim reviews of assessed performance.

In my seventh month of management, unbeknown to me, there was an HR audit in my branch office, and it was expected, per the audit process, that with 10 direct report employees I would have 40 PPC&E documents in my people management records: a performance plan, a development plan, and two interim reviews for each of my 10 direct reports. Needless to say, I failed that audit too. I mentioned to my branch manager, who was not at all happy about my PPC&E audit failure, that I had been quite busy, citing all kinds of big, competitive deals that I was working on with my team, none of which tempered his annoyance with me, as my audit failure was also his audit failure.

Again, the moral of the story is that the IBM human resources team, just like the IBM security team by way of its policies and measurements, took a broad and comprehensive view of human resources and ensured that effective people management was in place. Did the IBM human resources organization personally visit every field office and perform inspections? Of course not, but they did have responsibility and accountability for the overall human resources program, strategy, best practices, and measurements. Once again, if a human resources office can affect the day-to-day activities for the betterment of divisions, departments, and field business units throughout the organization, then why can't a project management office?

In addition to these analogies, I often like to provide an example of this myopia that the formal project management and PMO community seems to be afflicted with that is right under its own nose. Just by sheer happenstance, I was in Australia earlier this year to conduct a number of Business Driven PMO workshops. On the flight from Perth to Melbourne I was looking forward to catching up on my business reading and in particular I was looking forward to reading the current issue of *Project Manager*, the bimonthly magazine of the Australian Institute of Project Management, the AIPM.

Imagine my surprise when I spotted on page 7 of the December/January issue a full column ad for a new project management application targeted to some of those folks in the organization who have those informal and accidental projects that most PMOs don't even view as real projects. I could not wait for the next day's Business Driven PMO workshop in Melbourne to begin, as I was keen to use the example of this new project management application as one of many reasons why organization-wide project management should be of importance to PMO managers and project management professionals. At the right time in the workshop I held up the current issue of the AIPM professional magazine and asked the following questions.

Is anyone in the audience a member of the AIPM? As everyone in the audience was a member of the AIPM, this question brought a little laughter and a number of raised hands confirming membership.

I then asked if any of the members of AIPM had read the recent issue of *Project Manager*. Almost everyone raised their hands.

I followed this question by asking if anyone remembered the full column advertisement for the exciting new project management application that was announced on page 7 of the magazine. Not one hand was raised.

I then asked if anyone had ever heard of a little company called Salesforce .com. All hands were raised again.

I then explained for all those who either didn't care much about organization-wide project management or suffered from poor reading comprehension that in their very own professional magazine for project management, Salesforce.com announced a new project management application called do.com. I then asked if anyone knew who the typical users of Salesforce.com were. To no surprise, all in attendance understood that the users of Salesforce.com are typically sales professionals. I then asked if anyone in the audience knew what sales professionals called all of those sales things that they are working on. And again to no surprise, all in attendance understood that sales professionals call those things that they work on projects.

By now the audience is sensing that I am about to drop the hammer on them and I did. I asked them how is it that they can be so myopic that they can't see all the organization-wide projects, tools, and best practices and project-related needs that exist in their companies. And even when such things come to them in their very own professional magazines, they have no ability to notice and understand the ramifications that project management has throughout their organizations, not to mention do anything constructive about it.

If the formal project management and PMO community has consciously determined that it need not bother with project management things that are outside the tiny, little box of formal projects and plan driven approaches, then so be it. That projects exist organization-wide is hard to be oblivious to. That these organization-wide informal and accidental projects, tools, best practices, and outcomes are of significant importance is not debatable. What is debatable is how much longer the formal project management and PMO community, assuming there is no cure for its myopia, will be of significant importance.

Maturity acumen can be impacted in a number of ways, both good and bad. The bad news is that most PMOs are far less mature than they think. This can be said of the formal project management and PMO community at large as well. The good news is that project management has proven itself indispensable, and businesses that do a good job of both formal project management and organization-wide project management will out compete those that don't. Toward this aim, the potential for today's PMOs to be relevant throughout the organizations for which they exist to serve is virtually unlimited.

Section 3

PMO Future

Future (noun)—the infinite period of time that follows the present.

11

Perspectives on the PMO Domain

There are many perspectives on the PMO domain that range from what a PMO is to what the future of the PMO is and everything in between. Of course, the most prevalent perspective on the PMO domain comes from those who are right in the center of the formal project management and PMO community. Their perspectives in the form of research, tempered advice, and views on the state of the PMO are very important, though often limited in perspective and practical application.

There is no shortage of research, nor is there a shortage of opinions. Some of the perspectives, research, and opinions that I have enjoyed following and learning from over the years come from our project management standards organizations, namely the Project Management Institute and the U.K. Office of Government Commerce, leading research firms such as Gartner and Forrester Research, and leading project management vendors and consulting firms that are too numerous to list. From these organizations, there are more than a few *heroes* who have weighed in and contributed significantly to the PMO domain, such as Matt Light, Michael Hanford, Robert Handler, Donna Fitzgerald, Audrey Apfel, and Daniel Stang of Gartner; Margo Visitacion of Forrester Research; Kent Crawford of PM Solutions; and Terry Doerscher, Steve Romero, and Doc Dochtermann formerly of Planview, Computer Associates, and Microsoft, respectively. To these ladies and gentlemen, thank you so very much for all that you have contributed and all that you continue to do.

It would not be hard to write many, many pages that featured the various contributions of these heroes of mine. I have heard them all present, read most of their published works, and I have worked with some of them quite closely over the years. Though it would be beyond the scope and physical page limitations of this book to write about all these heroes, there is one that I would like to single out and call attention to. His name is Robert Handler and he is Vice President and Distinguished Analyst at Gartner.

For quite some time now, Robert Handler has advocated that most large organizations and many small ones have interdependent and adaptive social systems that are constantly in flux, and therefore the approach to managing projects must be managed differently, more adaptively, in order to succeed. Handler was the first leading authority on PMOs and project portfolio management (PPM) to not just cover the emerging field of study known as complex adaptive systems (CAS), but to actually embrace it and explain it in the context of its impact and importance to PMOs. In the 2010 Gartner PPM and IT Governance Summit, Handler gave a presentation on CAS to an audience of CIOs and PMO directors of the nation's leading and largest companies and explained how what most organizations do under the umbrella of PPM is becoming dangerous. He went on to explain how today's businesses do not operate in a simple, singular construct that is isolated from the forces of change, but rather a multidimensional, complex world, a CAS. His message: Attempting to use scientific plan driven management techniques that made sense a century ago when things were less complex is no longer a viable or competitive option. Views of PPM and the PMO must change and applying bloated technical project management techniques must stop. Strong words and he means them.

Handler has introduced CAS to the PMO domain and has urged PMOs and PPM performing organizations to introduce agile and adaptive techniques in the management of the formal projects of the PMO.

Naturally, in the context of Figure 11.1, I am referring to the embracement of CAS by the PMO in terms of the management of the PMO and PMO-related activities, as opposed to the agile community's embracement of CAS, whose Agile Manifesto, composed in 2001, well represents the principles of CAS. Hence, our agile brethren are years ahead of us in the knowledge and practical application of CAS within their domain.

I often get asked for an example of how an organization can become more adaptive and apply some of the principles of CAS. My favorite example is the one Harrison Owen, pioneer of CAS and inventor of Open Space Technology, often gives during the introduction of an Open Space Technology event. Open Space Technology is an approach for conducting highly effective meetings, typically with a large group of people, for the purpose of solving a problem, but beginning without any formal agenda beyond the overall purpose and call to action for attending the meeting.

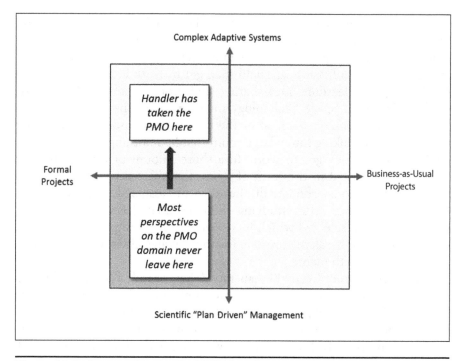

Figure 11.1 Perspectives on the PMO domain

In describing CAS, Harrison Owen often asks his audience if anyone can think of a complex system that can feed 10 million people, provide any cuisine that they want to eat, be open 24 hours a day, have on hand a two-week supply of food, and be economically viable for all parties, the buyer, the supplier, and the investor. After a few moments of silence, Harrison Owen says, "New York City." He makes the point that there was no master plan for the plan driven development for that which represents what you can find to eat in New York City; rather it was an emergent and adaptive evolution.

Once Harrison Owen has given the audience a primer on CAS, he then gives an example of how Open Space Technology works. He describes the time that IBM called him in to help with the 1984 Olympics. IBM was the lead corporate sponsor and was working with over 70 other corporate sponsors in what could only be described as complex program management. With seven months to go before the start of the Olympics, there were far too many open problems and unresolved issues to count. Plan driven program management had reached its limitations.

Harrison Owen suggested that IBM call an Open Space Technology meeting of all the corporate sponsors; he would facilitate it. Unlike a traditional meeting that has an agenda, audio/visual equipment, and comfortable theater-style seating for the participants, in an Open Space Technology meeting the participants sit in a circle, put up their own agenda in the form of a bulletin board, and then get to work in a marketplace of breakout spaces, learning, idea sharing, and problem solving. In the case of the IBM Open Space Technology meeting to get the 1984 Olympics mega-program back on track, after the corporate sponsors got over their initial shock of walking into a large room that had nothing in it but a large circle of chairs, they got to work. In a short amount of time, numerous issues were surfaced in the form of white flip chart papers taped to the walls, organized to consolidate duplications and assigned to specific meeting areas and times. After studying the consolidated issues on the wall, participants then selected which issues were of most importance to them and attended the breakout sessions for those issues along with other participants who did the same.

The process wasn't overly bureaucratic. There wasn't a prescribed methodology or a lot of rules. In fact, there was only one rule, called the Law of Two Feet. If you are not participating or learning, then use your two feet and go away and find a place where you can participate or learn. Over the course of the Open Space Technology meeting, committed participants met with one another, learned, shared ideas, and contributed to the development of an updated program plan and schedule of many important tasks and deliverables. The work that was done in that one day could never have been accomplished using traditional plan driven program management techniques. Not even the best program manager could possibly arrive at an equivalent work output in terms of the updated program plan and schedule.

Not long ago, I gave this example of CAS in the Business Driven PMO workshop in Canberra, Australia. After describing the example of the IBM program in support of the 1984 Olympics and relating that example to the PMOs of today, I noticed that one of the attendees, Adrian Lejins, had a broad grin on his face while at the same time all the other attendees were deep in thought and had serious-looking expressions on their faces. I asked Adrian what it was that he found so amusing. His answer was that everything that I had just described was exactly their PPM environment and what they do, but he didn't know there was a term for it.

Adrian went on to explain that as the portfolio manager for the Department of Human Services of the Government of Australia, they do quite a bit of formal, plan driven, project, program, and portfolio management. They are very good at it. Their portfolio is very well planned, at least initially. But then massive things happen, such as the flood of the Brisbane

River, the wildfires of Western Australia, and other acts of nature and unforeseeable changes. When these things occur, the Australia Department of Human Services does just what Harrison Owen has advocated for nearly five decades; they call a meeting of those committed and able and, in effect, they sit in a circle, put up a bulletin board, and get to work. The end result is not just an updated portfolio but the best possible response to the emergent and adaptive environment in which their programs are carried out and the citizens of Australia are served.

By way of comparison to the Australian government's Department of Human Services, just think how the responses by the various U.S. government departments to Hurricane Katrina in New Orleans might have been if they had only employed some of the principles of CAS. Remember some of the following mishaps:

- ◆ Hundreds of firefighters were held in Atlanta for days of training on community relations and sexual harassment before being sent on to the devastated area.
- ◆ Trailer trucks carrying thousands of bottles of water to Louisiana were halted for days because of incomplete forms.
- ◆ Hundreds of buses that could have been used to evacuate citizens sat idle in a parking lot.
- ◆ Thousands of mobile home trailers intended for those who lost their homes sat in a field for months.
- ◆ Resources in the form of emergency workers, buses, and planes offered from neighboring states could not be accepted because there was no system in place to authorize approval.

These kinds of mishaps, whether in the context of government organizations or businesses, are the kinds of mishaps that are inherent in the management of projects, programs, and portfolios. This does not mean that scientific plan driven management is no longer of importance; to the contrary, it is and will continue to be. But our plan driven management systems must be tempered with the appropriate adoption and use of CAS techniques. Otherwise, unless the project that we are managing is limited to a three-story parking garage with one S-curve, concrete, steel, wood, a bit of paint, and with the exception of weather and a few local building permits we know we can deliver on time, the practical application of project management and of PMOs will fail most of today's businesses.

In addition to CAS, another perspective on the PMO domain is the recognition that project management is ubiquitous. It is not just limited to the formal projects of the organization and it is certainly not limited to formally trained and certified project management professionals. There-fore, as shown in Figure 11.2, PMOs are not limited to just the traditional views of PMOs in terms of being a strategic PMO, enterprise PMO, or an IT PMO. PMOs can and do exist throughout the lines of business, divi-sions, and departments of enterprises of all shapes and sizes.

Though the formal project management and PMO community has some-what of a blind spot for and does not know how to contemplate the idea of projects and PMOs outside of its formal concept, it would not be hard to argue that the collective value to an organization of these ubiquitous, business-as-usual projects and their various PMOs is substantially greater than that of the portfolio of formal projects and the formal PMO.

When it comes to ubiquitous project management that exists through-out the enterprise and the wide variety of organizations that are created and often called a PMO, I must confess that I have a strong bias for their existence. Though I have been in the formal project management and PMO community for the last 15 years, the first 15 years of my project management and PMO experience were all out in the field business units. In these field business unit PMOs, whether a temporary program office or

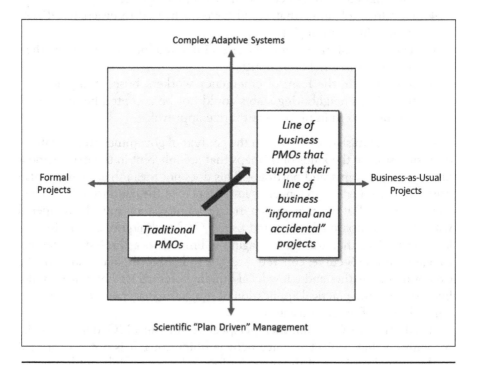

Figure 11.2   Perspectives on the PMO domain—line of business PMOs

a permanent office that manages projects, there was never any confusion over the purpose and value of the PMO. The PMO and projects of the PMO were always a means to an end and never an end unto themselves—a premise the formal project management and PMO community would be well served to remember.

I sometimes find myself at a loss as to why our project management industry associations do such a poor job of recognizing the totality of projects that exist in an organization, the kinds of people that manage those projects, and the variety of organizational types that act in a supportive or even directive manner. Are they unable to realize that an effort to make a sale is a project? An effort to develop marketing collateral is a project? An effort to conduct a customer satisfaction survey is a project? An effort to maintain plant equipment is a project? An effort to create a business partnership is a project? An effort to research a market is a project? An effort to acquire a company is a project? An effort to staff a new department is a project? I could go on and on.

Is it possible that the formal project management and PMO community thinks that all these projects should be contained within a single PPM system and all the various project participants be contained in some kind of shared resource pool? Surprisingly, I hear this view all the time. Is it possible that the formal project management and PMO community thinks that all these informal and accidental projects are not real projects and hence should be called something else so as to not confuse the real projects from the not-real projects? And heaven forbid, let's not call the people managing these projects project managers, as that should be a title reserved for trained and certified project managers who manage the real projects of the organization. Surprisingly, I hear that view too all the time.

To help make the point about the existence and importance of the ubiquitous projects of the organization, I would like to share the real-life example of a company that had a mishap with one of its ubiquitous projects. A publicly traded software company had a sale that was publicly forecasted for its second quarter. The sale, which the sales team and I too for that matter refer to as a project, was a $2M sale and it represented 10% of the company's $20M second-quarter forecast. The particular effort of this sales project spanned nine months, employed several resources, had a very definite and unique outcome, and was guided by a plan and schedule of tasks.

Regrettably, the sale slipped and did not close in the second quarter as forecasted. In project management speak, the schedule was missed. As a project mishap, the missed schedule meant that the second-quarter forecast of revenue for the company would also be missed. After the announcement of its financial results, as all publicly traded companies are required to do, the stock price of the company dropped from $83 per share to $42 per share. Hence, the market capitalization (value of the outstanding shares) fell from $3.1B to $1.6B representing a $1.5B loss.

Immediately after these results, someone was fired. Was it the salesman whose sales project did not come in on time? Was it the sales vice president who authorized the forecast of the sale for the second quarter? Was it the CFO of the company who is responsible for all aspects of financial management? Or was it the CEO of the company with whom the buck stopped?

Is there anybody missing from the list of potential candidates to be fired? The company had a PMO. Why wasn't the PMO manager a candidate for dismissal? After all, this was a project. Why would a project mishap that cost a company $1.5B not be grounds for firing the PMO manager? If not, how big would a project mishap have to be before the PMO manager becomes a candidate to be fired? Is it possible that this sales project is less important than those formal projects of the PMO like the server upgrade, the accounting system implementation, and the rollout of the current version of Microsoft Office? No doubt the formal project management and PMO community feels that way, but do the shareholders who saw their stock holdings cut in half feel this way? I suspect not.

No, the PMO manager was not fired; the CFO was fired, and by the end of the year the CEO had lost his job too. The PMO manager wasn't even a topic for discussion. For those who believe project management is a profession, then there is no poorer example of the profession than to have a company thrown into financial and management chaos over a project mishap, while at the same time no one within the profession had a care, concern, or role to play.

If this were only one isolated and unique example of a project outside of the formal projects of the PMO, then perhaps it could be dismissed. But it is not. The projects that exist outside the project mix of the formal PMO are too numerous to count. Individually, some of these projects are very important to the organization and collectively they are tremendously important. That the formal project management and PMO community is unwilling and unable to address in an effective way the project management and PMO needs that are inherent because of the ubiquitous projects that permeate all areas of today's businesses, is nothing short of stupefying.

This is a perspective on the PMO domain that is most in need of improvement within the formal project management and PMO community and one that offers tremendous opportunities for those willing and able to accept the challenge.

12

Perspectives on PMO Manager Career Paths

As a collective group, PMO managers are highly talented business professionals with a potpourri of valued skills that take years of experience to amass, such as strategic analysis, business management, people management, natural servant-leadership, situational leadership, problem solving, conflict resolution, and yes, project management too. But as talented as PMO managers are, most of us are not going to be promoted to replace our bosses.

Consider the following PMO manager positions: head of the strategic PMO reporting to the CEO, head of the enterprise PMO reporting to the COO, head of IT PMO reporting to the CIO, head of line of business PMO reporting to the VP of the line of business, head of a program office reporting to a functional department manager. In virtually all these examples, and many more, when the boss of the PMO manager is promoted or leaves and that position is open, rarely will it be filled by the direct report PMO manager. Not always of course, but by a very wide statistical margin it is unlikely that the career path of the PMO manager will be a vertical one. That doesn't mean that PMO managers cannot climb high up the ladder of organizational promotions and increased levels of responsibility, authority, and earnings. They can, but the path upward is much more likely to resemble a rock-climbing wall than a ladder.

Naturally, no two companies are alike in terms of how they manage people and especially how they manage the managers. One would think that once one has achieved the stripe of manager, regardless of the department, one would have reached a higher level of trusted importance to the organization and a higher level of job security; one would be half correct.

No doubt, a manager has earned a higher level of trusted importance and has been entrusted to manage not just people, but a small piece of the business. Rarely, however, does becoming a manager increase one's job security or put one on a career path for guaranteed promotions. In fact, in most organizations, there is far greater risk of losing a job as a manager than as an individual contributor. The management position of PMO manager is not immune to this premise; rather it is an example of it.

Within the formal project management and PMO community, I often hear a very limited, risk-averse, and defensive perspective on PMO manager career paths. Whether at conferences, within the collective blogosphere and online communities for project management, or in discussions with other PMO managers, the prevailing sentiment is one that suggests that once a project management professional (PMP) becomes a PMO manager, there is very little else to achieve professionally but defend one's PMO and one's job. This is highly regrettable though not inaccurate if one's perspective of the PMO manager career path is that it exists only within the traditional view of what PMOs are and where they exist in an organization, such as a strategic PMO, enterprise PMO, or PMO located somewhere within the IT department.

I have a different perspective on the career path of PMO managers, one that is based upon and that has emerged from three decades of PMO-related experiences. As shown in Figure 12.1, there are numerous career options for

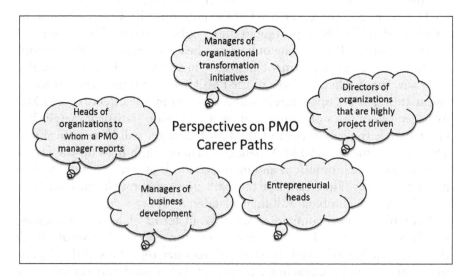

Figure 12.1   Perspectives on PMO manager career paths

PMO managers. Though not at all a complete set, five of these PMO career path areas I have witnessed over the years are (1) heads of organizations to whom a PMO manager reports, (2) managers of organizational transformation initiatives, (3) directors of organizations that are highly project driven, (4) managers of all kinds of business development functions, and (5) entrepreneurial heads of companies of all shapes and sizes.

Let's start with heads of organizations to whom a PMO manager reports. Increasingly, more and more companies, especially large companies, are recognizing the value of their PMO managers. It is not uncommon that a PMO manager of a large company such as an IT PMO manager is identified as a high-potential management candidate and placed in an executive development program. And after a few years of executive development, including an executive staff management position or two, the former PMO manager is a leading candidate if not slated to be the next head of IT. Hence, PMO managers in large companies most likely have this potential—the potential to work with immediate management and the leadership team to plan and realize a career.

It is interesting to note that years back, when large companies could afford their large corporate staffs, this two-step-style career advancement was the norm. Not only was it expected and part of the management development process, but promotion of a member of a department or organization to the head of it was highly discouraged and frowned upon, as it simply invited too many personnel issues and in many cases it advanced an unready manager to a management position likely to be beyond their immediate capabilities.

Manager of an organizational transformation initiative is another career area for PMO managers. Just about every organization faces and goes through transformations. In some organizations this is a once-in-a-blue-moon proposition, but for most organizations this is a regular occurrence. Who better than an experienced PMO manager to lead in the management of organizational change? In fact, more and more businesses are using the term change management office to describe this functional group. Though organizational transformation initiatives and such offices are typically viewed as residing high up in the organization and reporting to the C-level, they can also exist at lower levels in the organizational hierarchy such as a subsidiary, division, or line of business. A quick examination of just about any company's supply chain model would reveal many organizational entities going through transformation that would be well served by the leadership of an experienced PMO manager.

Directors of organizations that are highly project driven represent another career area for PMO managers. One particular organization type that

I have seen many PMO managers lead successfully is professional services. A professional services organization is inherently project driven. And in many cases, professional services organizations struggle greatly with their core delivery processes and management of revenue recognition. It is not uncommon that professional services managers lack the management of projects and management of project manager skills that experienced PMO managers possess. In other cases, professional services managers can be continually blindsided by the sales executive's commitments to customers in the form of promised scope, schedule, and budget beyond that of the agreed to statement of work. Whereas a professional services manager may not have the clout or acumen to prevent such happenings, an experienced PMO manager brings to the table process integrity and meaningful metrics to ensure the success of customer-facing projects and to prevent mischief and friendly fire.

Marketing is another area of the company that is highly project driven. Marketing projects in brand management, product management and development, lead generation, and competitive analysis represent just a few of the many kinds of projects that drive the marketing function. Increasingly, large companies are implementing marketing PMOs that report to the head of marketing and lead in the oversight and management of these projects. This represents two kinds of opportunities for experienced PMO managers: first, as the head of the marketing PMO, and second, as a staff or division manager within the marketing function in support of areas of the marketing strategy such as new market initiatives, international expansion, and the like.

Another area of course is business operations. More and more businesses in virtually every industry such as manufacturing companies, transportation firms, pharmaceutical firms, and others have offices, sometimes called a PMO but many times called something else, that manage the business-as-usual projects of the organization. These are the projects that are unique and self-contained to the organization and not found in the enterprise PMO portfolio. Both operational domain knowledge and management of projects and portfolios acumen are essential in these positions. Experienced PMO managers with a command of the operational domain are the first choice of these firms for these positions.

In the event that the experienced PMO manager welcomes objectives-based management and compensation, then directors and managers of business development represent another large group of positions and career paths for experienced PMO managers. Such positions could be either internally within the business development function of a large company or externally with any one of the too-many-to-count businesses and firms that provide project management products and services. Who better than an experienced PMO manager who actually implemented and used a product to be the trusted customer advocate in the business development organization that directly or indirectly makes the sale? Other business development positions within these firms that serve the project management industry include channel management, development of new business partners, thought leadership, and international development.

Rounding out our short list of career options for PMO managers are entrepreneurial heads of companies and organizations, from very successful one-person start-ups to emerging businesses of all shapes and sizes. Examples of this are plentiful, such as Lisa DiTullio, who after a career in project management, including the director of the Enterprise Project Management Office, went on to found Your Project Office, a boutique firm that provides virtual PMO services to organizations that do not require a full-time, dedicated PMO. Today, Lisa DiTullio is a well-known and leading thought leader in the PMO domain, acclaimed author, and international speaker.

Another example is Tom Mochal, who after two decades of experience in IT project and program management founded TenStep, a firm that specializes in consulting and training in business methodologies. In addition to authoring the TenStep products and building a global brand, Tom Mochal earned the 2005 Distinguished Contribution Award from the Project Management Institute (PMI®).

Also on this list is my dear friend Cornelius Fichtner, who after a career in project management, including being the president of the Orange County, California, PMI Chapter, left the comfort of his big company PMO to found OSP International, a firm that provides Internet-based products for PMP certification training. You may know of him as the provider of the Project Management PrepCast, a downloadable exam preparation video workshop that can be viewed on a computer or handheld device, as well as the provider of Project Management Podcast, a wonderful free resource and subscription aimed at keeping PMPs abreast of the leading project management and PMO tips, techniques, and industry trends.

Additionally, a former colleague of mine, who wishes to remain anonymous, founded a home-based business, incorporating all his project management wisdom and experience to get through the initial start-up work that had to be done with no staff. At present, this home-based micro-business is turning over more than a million dollars a year in revenue at a 35% profit margin. With no boss and no employees and earning more than double his big company salary, the decision to depart the corporate world in pursuit of an entrepreneur idea and passion has yet to be regretted.

One last example of career paths for experienced PMO managers seeking an entrepreneurial opportunity is in this fast-growing market segment of home-based micro-businesses. These businesses are managed by just one or two people and have revenues up to $1 million; any more than that would be considered a small business. Although micro-businesses have spartan budgets and avoid frivolous expenses, their supply chain models are typically highly inefficient. Additionally, the owner-operators of these businesses usually do not have a professional background and developed skill set in IT and project management. Just think of the opportunity for cost reduction and increased capacity through projects to improve the supply chain. Now imagine being compensated as a virtual PMO manager, not based upon hourly rates, but on a percent of the improvement, pay-for-performance basis.

As an experienced PMO manager seeking an entrepreneurial opportunity, would identifying and delivering a portfolio of projects that delivered a half-million-dollar benefit for which you were paid not by the hour but at 50% of the improvement be of interest? Similarly, as an owner-operator of a micro-business, would having a portfolio of projects to significantly improve the supply chain of the business, for which you have to pay the performing project resource nothing until the benefits have been realized, be of interest? Not only would the answer to both of those questions be yes, but in the last few years and perhaps driven by the recession, I have seen several experienced PMO managers enter the entrepreneurial world on such a basis.

As always, most people find professional success and personal satisfaction when they figure out, or stumble into, what makes them truly passionate. Whether in the context of a large worldwide company, a home-based micro-business, or any of the possibilities that exist between those two extremes, experienced PMO managers possess a great deal of the needed skills to achieve and sustain success. It would be a mistake to limit the practical application of project management and PMOs, whether virtual or real, to just the traditional view of the practicing community.

So, although there are those who suggest the career path of a PMO manager is limited and once a PMP becomes a PMO manager there is very little else to do but defend one's PMO and one's job, count me not in this group. Like a 50-year-old farmer, PMO managers have a skill set and vitality that have broad application. With perhaps equal doses of passion, hard work, and a little luck, the options and potential career paths for experienced PMO managers are limited only by one's imagination.

Part 2

Business Driven PMO
Success Stories

PMO Success Story #1: Strategic PMO at Greek Prime Minister's Office

When a Dream Comes True!

Panagiotis Agrapidis, OSS-Organizational Strategic Systems

Introduction to the Situation in Greece between 1996 and 2004

It was between 1996 and 2004 when Greece faced four major challenges with firm deadlines: (1) adopt the euro, realigning its economy according to European Union standards; (2) utilize in the best possible way the European structural funds in order to modernize its infrastructure (i.e., roads, railways, ports, airports); (3) organize the Greek Presidency of the Council of the European Union; and (4) organize the Olympic Games. The magnitude of each one of the above challenges could create serious organizational and financial problems even for a bigger nation with a well-organized bureaucracy. Very few people both internally and internationally believed that Greece would adopt the euro and fewer believed the Athens Olympic Games would be successful. So how did Greece succeed in all of the above and later on in the financial crisis?

In the beginning of 1996, Kostas Simitis became the Prime Minister of Greece. He was often referred to as "the man with the block notes" for his ability to write down in block notes all pending issues and then to continuously follow up on Ministers' actions. The country was coming out of a period of high inflation rates and increased debt. Progress in the big infrastructural projects was lacking and the public sector bureaucracy was considered inefficient by most of the Greek political parties, the European Union, the IMF, and the OECD.

Business Problems to Be Addressed by the PMO

Facing a critical financial situation and the four challenges mentioned earlier, the Prime Minister chose to become the *project manager of the country.* The reasons were many, but let's just say that the targets were extremely diverse! For example, to beat inflation and decrease the debt in order to adopt the euro, you have to spend less. On the other hand, to modernize the country's infrastructure and prepare for the Olympic Games, you have to spend a lot. Last but not least, to prepare for and perform the Greek presidency of the European Union, in a time period during which the war in Iraq started and ten new members signed in Athens their entrance into the European Union, is nothing short of a political and organizational nightmare!

In this context it became clear that the availability of timely and reliable information would be of paramount importance. At the same time, the number and complexity of public contracts were reaching new heights. Hence, it was necessary to apply a kind of integrated project, program, and portfolio management, although in 1996, portfolio management was like a visitor from Mars. In fact, as often happens, an organization facing a complex and critical situation is open to experimenting with new and not well-established practices. In this context, it became possible to propose the creation of a *strategic* PMO (SPMO) at the Council of Ministers level, supporting the Prime Minister's Office. The name we decided to give to this effort was *Strategic Project Management.*

Our Story

It's all about timing. Being in the right place at the right moment. But it also is important to be prepared to propose the best solution, in the appropriate way to the right people (or, if you like, stakeholders).

Previous experience plays a key role, especially when we have to demonstrate that we can meet the client's expectations, executing with success that which is requested. In the beginning of my professional career I had the opportunity to work on large engineering and construction projects such as the Second Bosporus Bridge and Kinaly Sakarya Highway in Istanbul, Turkey, and the Esna Dam on the Nile River in Egypt. During the early 1990s, I also gained valuable experience in project and program management methodologies and tools working as a consultant in the PMO of Snamprogetti SpA, an engineering company with headquarters in Milan and one of the first Italian companies that had chosen, at that time, to adopt a strong matrix organization structure.

Consequently, I had the opportunity to work not only on the project management of a $2.5 billion petrochemical complex, but also the development of PMO procedures and software systems. It was in that context when I started to think that the PMO must be positioned directly under top management and it must control directly all organization sectors and resources. Willing to apply this idea in real life, I returned to Greece to establish and operate an SPMO at the Greek engineering company Asprofos SA.

Since the success of the SPMO was achieved during the first year, at the end of 1996, on behalf of Asprofos, I became the project manager for the creation and operation of a *Strategic Project Management System* (SPMS) for the Greek Ministry of Public Works, with the aim to collect and elaborate data from 22 internal divisions and during 1997 to cooperate with the Ministry of Transport and Telecommunications. The SPMS, in this case, had been adapted and operated for each one of the ten public companies under its auspices (e.g., Greek Railways, Metro, Public Transportation, Olympic Airways, Hellas Telecom, and Hellenic Post) supporting in parallel the Minister's office.

As the situation was complex and the results from the application of the SPMS were encouraging, the Prime Minister decided to create the *Strategic Management of Public Projects Committee*, which was coordinated by his Technical Office and supported by participation of the Ministries of Internal Affairs, Treasury, and Public Works. I had been appointed as a member of the committee responsible for the technical support of this initiative. The committee's scope was to coordinate the efforts of all relevant organizations (ministries, prefectures, state companies, etc.) in order to optimize the efficiency and effectiveness of programming, planning, executing, and following up of the totality of public projects.

The Strategic Management of Public Projects Committee had started its work establishing methodology, reporting, forms, and processes. From the initial phase of the committee's work, it became clear that the government sector had specific and unique requirements for project and program management, mainly because we had to take into account the power and politics involved in the decision-making systems. The crucial point here is to maintain neutrality and continuously support all ministries in order to be considered a trustworthy adviser.

The ongoing experiences of the Ministries of Public Works and Transport and Telecommunications helped the committee to make important decisions in a short period of time:

◆ The type and number of reports necessary to produce comprehensive and useful information for our stakeholders had been defined.

- Due to (1) the huge number of projects, (2) the number and diversity of sources from which we had to collect the data, and (3) the limitations on time, cost, and quality, we decided that the minimum amount of data for each program/project/public contract had to be collected. Three types of simple, one-page data forms (construction contracts, engineering contracts, and procurement contracts) had been prepared, adopting the terminology used by public contract national laws.
- The decision was made to utilize one of the best project management proprietary software packages worldwide in order to shorten the implementation phase and cover both Council of Minister's as well as each organization's needs.
- The implementation of an SPMO had been agreed on, with the aim to provide support for the committee's work from the technical and operational point of view.

Having to implement the SPMO in a very short period of time, it was decided to expand the three-person team working for the SPMS by adding gradually and according to needs an additional 13 employees in a three-month period. We preferred people with engineering degrees and at least three years of experience in the construction industry. It was also decided to adapt the SPMS in order to cover additional requirements of the committee and to facilitate the work of SPMO team members who had no experience in the specific software.

Through continuous meetings and on-the-job training, we succeeded in integrating all team members. During this phase no specific groups had been formed and no leaders appointed. The reasons for the creation of the SPMO had been explained in depth and the personnel effectively motivated. Everyone understood very well that delays would not be accepted, nor would failures in data collection and elaboration or inconsistencies inside or between reports. Our failure would cause the failure of an unprecedented attempt!

The committee decided to proceed gradually, starting with the 13 prefectures of Greece. Working continuously in close cooperation with committee representatives, the SPMO proceeded to:

- Visit each prefecture.
- Involve top management of each prefecture in the project.
- Officially appoint a representative from each prefecture, assigning him the necessary authority.
- Explain in detail the data we were requiring, helping them choose the easiest way to fulfill their obligations.

◆ Involve all participants in the definition of their organization's needs regarding the system.

◆ Install the proprietary software and organize seminars in order to utilize its full potential.

Maximum effort was also given to customizing the proprietary software in a way that even people with no computer experience could be in a position to use it. Since ancient Greeks said that "the measure of everything is man," I am firmly convinced that the above customization was one of our key success factors.

After the first data collection, we had adopted a three-phase process: (1) the data entry in the central database, (2) a first check regarding missing data, and (3) a second check regarding inconsistent data. For each one of the previous checks a detailed report was produced and sent to the prefecture's representative in order to correct/complete project data and forward them again to the SPMO. It must also be mentioned here that in prefectures where it was not possible to install the proprietary software, we proceeded to collect the data according to availability.

The data were updated every three months. It was the optimal solution both for the client (quarterly reports) and for our SPMO in terms of human resource utilization, time, cost, and quality. Because of this, we had decided to visit each prefecture every three months. We wanted to present and discuss the reports we had prepared for each organization, before presenting the same reports to others, including the Prime Minister. We wanted to establish personal relationships based on cooperation and mutual trust and to keep the communication channels open. Our slogan was "we are working to satisfy each customer's needs."

Regarding the committee's needs, every three months the SPMO collected project data on time and of the desired quality. The requested reports were produced on time and with the desired accuracy. Furthermore, the SPMO, utilizing the experience gained by its cooperation with prefecture representatives, had produced additional series of reports that were welcomed by the committee.

The identified targets were achieved rapidly. In a six-month period the Prime Minister decided that the committee had to start collecting data from all the ministries and consequently from all state companies. The SPMO team repeated the same methodologies and procedures that had been applied for the prefectures. After a transition period, and in order to operate in an efficient way, the SPMO was divided into two groups, taking into account each team member's behavior and needs. One group was responsible for the prefectures and the other for the ministries. A leader was appointed for each group.

After 2000, and with the continuous efforts of the SPMO, we had gained the necessary credibility at the Council of Ministers, despite the disputes created inside and outside the government. The data collected were referred to approximately 54,000 projects, with a total budget of approximately €47 billion, coming from 7,500 various offices.

The SPMO team was gradually reduced until the final transfer of responsibilities to the Ministries of Public Works and Internal Affairs, which had no plans to create SPMOs. From what I personally know, this system is out of use. Perhaps this small example can help explain why Greece, which succeeded in meeting all of its targets during that period, is (seven years later) in such a difficult situation.

PMO Success

For the first time, the Greek public sector introduced project, program, and portfolio management methodologies and tools. The main results were the following:

- Data from the totality of projects had been managed in a homogeneous and efficient way.
- A common language and a common way of reporting had been established.
- Top-down, bottom-up communication had become more direct and precise.
- The personnel involved at all levels felt part of an integrated work process, which ultimately increases the system's transparency and efficiency.
- *Credible* and *timely reports* based on reliable data had been produced for the Prime Minister and the Council of Ministers as well as almost all public organizations.
- The expenditures of government projects could be measured and monitored continuously at an aggregate level.
- Evaluation of any organization, sector, category of projects, and geographic area was now possible, as was comparing them with other similar ones.
- Timely recording of deviations and the ability to discover the real causes had been achieved.
- Transparency and efficiency in planning and execution of public contracts had been increased.

- ◆ Disputes on data reliability had been eliminated, allowing the councils more time for discussions of broader strategic issues.
- ◆ At the Council of Ministers level, support for the development of the Council's forward agenda had been achieved.
- ◆ The Prime Minister's briefing on the handling of issues had been supported.
- ◆ The legislative work of the government had been supported both in the law definition phase as well as the application of the law.
- ◆ Credibility was gained at the Council of Ministers, despite the disputes created inside and outside the government.
- ◆ The SPMO became an indispensable tool for strategy implementation and strategy execution.

The success of the SPMO is extensively mentioned in three different chapters in the former Prime Minister's book *Politics for a Creative Greece* (2005).

Concluding Thoughts and Advice

Remarkable economic and technological changes are transforming the world around us at an incredible pace. This process can either create serious problems for any type of organization or organizations have to accept the challenges and take the necessary actions. Governments, as well as all other types of organizations, have to increase efficiency, transparency, and credibility. The economic crisis mandates the acceleration of the adoption of such initiatives.

We are indeed proceeding toward a computer society that is enabling us to focus on the details, while having at our disposal an enormous volume of information. At the same time, we must adopt a holistic approach for the definition, implementation, and follow-up of the strategy of our organization, whether the organization is called a company, enterprise, country, or nonprofit. However, this strategy must be continuously transformed, following a dialectical means of communication with the external and internal environment of each organization.

The experience gained in Greece, under extraordinary circumstances, can be repeated in any other country or organization ready to apply a top-down approach in the application of project, program, and portfolio management methodologies and tools in a simple and concise way, even if the organization has little or no experience in project management. Especially for the government sector, the Prime Minister, who is the key stakeholder, has to support the creation of an SPMO at the Council of Ministers level, since a PMO can succeed only if it has the authority and autonomy required to get the job done. Positioning is the most critical aspect of the SPMO because it establishes its degree of authority, acceptance, adoption, and autonomy and thus its *ownership* of the responsibility for establishing, distributing, and supporting project management best practices within the organization.

PMO Success Story #2: e-Government Program

Yesser PMO: A PMO That Works

Suhail AlAlmaee, Strategic Planning and Initiatives Director,
e-Government Program (Yesser)
Mounes Rashid Shadid, Project Management Specialist

Introduction to the e-Government Program (Yesser)

The Government of Saudi Arabia attaches a high level of significance to the concept of e-government as well as the transformative process leading to its ultimate realization. The government also has demonstrated confidence that e-government can produce huge benefits for the national economy. Accordingly, Supreme Royal Decree number 7/B/33181, dated 10/7/1424 (7/9/2003) included a directive to the Ministry of Communications and Information Technology (MCIT) to formulate a plan to provide government services and transactions electronically.

Transformation to an information society requires a comprehensive, concerted, and collaborative effort in order to realize set objectives. To realize this requirement, the MCIT established the e-Government Program in 2005 in close consultation with the Ministry of Finance and the Communication and Information Technology Commission.

This e-government program, begun in 2005, initiated the modernization and transformation of government administration while enhancing service delivery to public and commercial stakeholders. The e-government program *Yesser* further developed a National e-Government Strategy and (first) Action Plan that covered the period from 2006 to 2010. Consequently, leadership of the strategy and action plan was given to Yesser.

Business Problems to Be Addressed by the PMO

Yesser started the implementation of more than 22 concurrent projects utilizing different project managers. Despite pressures to deliver projects on time and within budget, quality should never be compromised. Culturally and historically, the escalation of governmental involvement on this scale has been treated as a source of complaint, distrust, and resistance: widespread governmental empowerment is not fully practiced by all. Also, we found challenges in tracking project documentation such as request for proposal (RFP), proposal, contract, communication, minutes of meetings, and deliverables.

To adapt to these challenges, changes in how we manage projects are necessary. The clear need for a PMO is quite obvious. A PMO will lead to standardized project management practices following a preestablished methodology, which in turn will optimize resource utilization. Furthermore, a PMO will aid in recognizing the potential for failure, thereby mitigating the risk of failure in future projects. Moreover, we believe that utilizing the PMO for more than merely a simple *project storage facility* will improve the chances of project success in the long run.

Such effort naturally requires a strong sense of commitment by higher management. In order to make this important project a reality, top management will be called upon to consistently demonstrate their serious attention and full support.

The Yesser PMO objectives are as follows:

◆ Deliver successful Yesser projects.
◆ Build project management professionalism among Yesser program staff.
◆ Keep Yesser program management and stakeholders well informed.
◆ Serve as Yesser program project support for Yesser project management practices.
◆ Create one repository for Yesser projects.

Our Story

Based on the needs and concerns expressed above, Yesser management made the decision to establish the PMO; I was selected to become both project leader and PMO manager. Unfortunately for us, the general understanding within Saudi Arabia of a PMO is as a mere tool and set of templates or even just as an auditing mechanism; the PMO has never been considered to be a mechanism for changing and challenging managerial efforts.

Therefore, to educate this audience we initiated the implementation of the Yesser PMO with a slogan and a theme. Since our program name in Arabic (Yesser) means *make easy*, we selected the logo design shown in Figure S2.1.

Project Management Office

Figure S2.1   Yesser logo design

This slogan and logo mean that the PMO will ease the very process of business conducted by Yesser. We also wanted to express the apparently contradictory idea that although the work of the PMO may appear complicated to ordinary understanding, in actual practice the opposite is true: a PMO simplifies the complex, making it *easy*. We adopted the following slogan to express the reality of the PMO and to clarify our purpose and function:

Success through Simplicity

We spent one month and a half marketing this slogan and theme in order to educate Yesser staff. Also, we made attempts to convince management to empower project managers to simply report the actual status of projects. They were to even report *bad news* or to include in their reports information potentially putting the manager involved on the project at risk. During this time we focused upon and sought a *quick win* to illustrate the added value of the PMO; we developed a one-page weekly status report utilizing a single dashboard that summarized the project status. To their credit, Yesser management demonstrated strong support in making the decision that *all* projects should be added to the PMO dashboard and empowered all project managers to honestly report the true status of their projects.

After six months of adapting weekly status reports and one dashboard, we took the further initiative to create our own project management methodology based on PMI standards, putting into play our slogan *Success through Simplicity*. Inspired by the success of our previous use of the Yesser slogan, we named this methodology the YesMethod©, as shown in Figure S2.2.

Following our theme of *Success through Simplicity*, our methodology (see Figure S2.3) consisted of only ten templates: seven of them should

Figure S2.2 YesMethod©

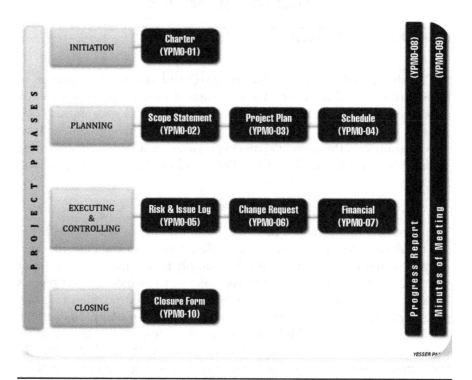

Figure S2.3 Yesser project methodology

be filled out consecutively depending on project phase, with one held in reserve; the two remaining templates should be used on a weekly basis. The ten templates were mandatory only as executed by the project vendor. However, in the in-house project executed by Yesser staff, only four of them became mandatory.

It cannot be stressed enough that the positive influence of top management is by far the most important factor in implementing a successful

PMO operation. In order to illustrate the necessity of this managerial effort and participation, we created the diagram shown in Figure S2.4.

In order to overcome the problem of tracking project documentation such as RFP, proposal, contract, communication, minutes of meetings, and deliverables, staff created a folder structure using the Microsoft SharePoint platform as a repository for PMO documents. This is shown in Figure S2.5.

Yesser PMO has worked well in its reporting function as a PMO by first making sure that project managers used the YesMethod© for two years until it became an integral part of Yesser culture. We then took the next step of automating part of the YesMethod© using Microsoft Share-Point: we focused on functions once done manually by the PMO; we've had great success in projects now being on the dashboard, weekly status updates, project changes, and project closure. With that accomplished, the PMO YesMethod© became the first tool in Yesser that contains a standardized process and a partially automated workflow. Additionally, at that time it was the only methodology that our vendors were required to use as a part of Yesser RFPs. Consequently, these successes have led top management to trust in the Yesser PMO and to then make the decision to move the PMO to the next level: as a managing and controlling

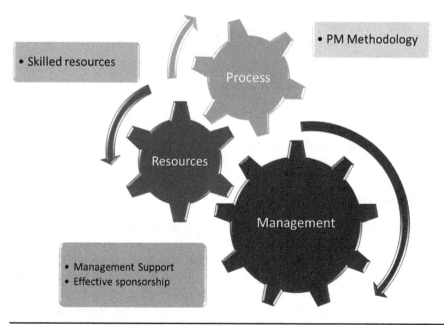

Figure S2.4   Diagram of managerial effort and participation

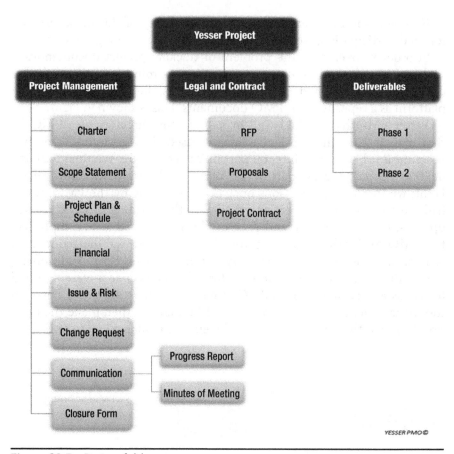

Figure S2.5   Project folder structure

PMO where we would begin to hire project managers and to manage portions of internal projects.

PMO Success

The Yesser PMO initiated first an effort through education to change management attitudes in order to convince different departments to release project management activities to Yesser PMO. This effort took six months of close work with different departments. Work was then limited to only new projects. The success achieved with these pilot projects proved to those involved the added value of management by professionals rather than having subject matter experts assume the additional burden of the project manager trying to bring projects to closure status. At that stage after six months, the PMO had 20 projects under our management (75% are direct Yesser projects and the remaining 25% are managed by subject matter experts/technical leaders working in other departments). Moreover, we have around 26 new projects in the pipeline for which we have been requested to act as PMO project managers. As a result of the above-implemented changes, the PMO has managed to reduce project delays by 32% and project change requests by 50%, a substantial business improvement.

The PMO's success has spread externally, especially where the Yes-Method© has become the first choice in project management methodology. This simple and effective program is being used increasingly by government agencies. Copies of the YesMethod© have been sent to 50 government agencies. Vendors have also been encouraged to better manage Yesser projects with greater success. Our PMO's reputation has spread to the marketplace as well, and we have received more than 50 requests to give presentations about the Yesser way of project management. Furthermore, the reach of the YesMethod© has become regional: two government agencies from two different Arabian Gulf countries have requested Yesser methodology in managing their projects.

Concluding Thoughts and Advice

Establishing a project management practice within an organization should be first considered as a change in management attitude, strategy, and level of commitment. With this in mind, we strongly advise that this effort should not start with immediately installing the methodology's templates and tools. Instead, we must always start with the human factor: spend time in marketing and education in terms of the added value of this method to everyone involved; also use slogans and themes that reflect the PMO's positive, inclusive intentions. Moreover, PMO implementation should be done gradually following a carefully developed rollout plan. Emphasize the flexibility needed to extend the time of implementation to receive the full buy-in benefits in each stage. Also, we suggest that you have a team with the right skills in place who will receive maximum authorized support. These suggestions will ensure the partnership between the PMO and the business units will always remain a matter of *success through simplicity made easy*.

PMO Success Story #3: Thomson Reuters Aranzadi

Adaptability, a Must Have Attribute of Any Successful PMO

Juan Arraiza, PMO Manager, Thomson Reuters Company

Introduction to Thomson Reuters Aranzadi

Imagine a family-owned Spanish editorial company, founded in 1929, a leader in providing legal content to legal practitioners in the Spanish market. That was Aranzadi back in 1999. That year, Aranzadi was acquired by The Thomson Corporation, a leading global company that provides professional information to the health, legal, financial, and education industries. In 2008, The Thomson Corporation and Reuters Group PLC combined to form Thomson Reuters. Since 1999, Aranzadi has had to adapt to enormous changes, some related to becoming a local branch of one of the divisions of a global corporation and others related to a very complex market situation, mainly due to the appearance of some very aggressive low-cost competitors.

Business Problems to Be Addressed by the PMO

Imagine a company, Aranzadi, that has never had a PMO (nor really knows what that is). Imagine a company in which nobody really knows about project management. Of course, the organization had projects that were named as such, *projects*, but there was a complete lack of professional project management knowledge, processes, or tools.

On many occasions there were not well-defined goals for projects. Managing projects was seen as something to be done by one team member on top of his/her role as a team member and on top of his/her functional day-to-day duties. There were no project cost tracking processes and tools (not even the awareness of needing them). I could probably continue adding

147

more examples to illustrate the context at the time, but hopefully by now the reader has gotten the point. And still, this was a company leading the market with modern, strong, and robust IT systems. Aranzadi was first to launch an online service of its legal information databases to the Spanish market back in 1998.

But the 21st century brought new challenges for which Aranzadi was not naturally prepared. One of the most important and difficult challenges was to make the cultural and organizational changes needed to be able to participate in and in many occasions lead international projects (as a consequence of being part of the Thomson Corporation), with English being the vehicular language and with different team members and expertise scattered in several countries and continents. That is a huge change if you think on a small Spanish company basis in which only a few people spoke English and almost none had any real experience in international projects. Many things were to change, and the challenge was to adapt to those changes in parallel to maintaining a leading position in the market.

Our Story

In 2004, Aranzadi's managing director decided to create a first PMO, reporting to the COO. I was one of the four members of that first PMO. Each of us was assigned a project, the goal of which was to study a segment of the market, identify wining value propositions, and finally to deliver products and services to meet our customers' needs.

We were trained by the corporation in a methodology focused on researching how our customers worked, not only when using our products and services, but in a holistic way. The underlying idea was that if you understand what your customers really do and therefore how important what you currently offer to them is, you will better assess helping them in two ways. On one hand, you will understand better how your current offer of products and services fits in their value chain. With this view you can evolve your current portfolio of products and services to serve your customers better. On the other hand, you will identify new ways of helping your customers with new products and services that may tackle the same or similar needs you currently meet or that may target new and different needs that your customers have in other areas of their value chain. That was probably the first time in Aranzadi history that a significant number of employees got real experience in applying some kind of project management methodology.

Also in 2004, the PMO, using PMI's *PMBOK® Guide* as a reference, defined and implemented a tailored project management methodology, depicting processes, activities, roles, and responsibilities, and creating a set of tools and templates to support them. Right after the methodology was ready, we prepared and provided training in project management to more than 100 people (approximately one-third of all employees), including ad hoc material and classes for different roles (upper management, project sponsors, project managers, and project team members).

In spite of all the effort, the good job the PMO did, and the general recognition from most of our colleagues, in the spring of 2005 upper management decided to dismantle the PMO. How could that be? What did we do wrong? In the last section of this chapter, I will share with you what I think was the cause.

In 2007, after a couple of years of hard work managing a very complex international IT project, I was assigned as the manager of a reactivated PMO. In this second stage, the office was set up as an organizational PMO reporting to the COO. Our goal was to provide project portfolio as well as project management services to the COO and to the departments reporting to him, which at the time were IT, editorial, and production. I started on my own, but within the following couple of years two colleagues joined me, one as a junior project manager and another one as a project assistant.

Between 2007 and 2010, we managed projects of different kinds, although in most cases related to new product development. Roughly speaking, we managed around four to six medium to large projects a year, most of which included content acquisition and preparation as well as IT work. All this was done in an international context with teams and platforms located in different countries such as Argentina, the United States, the United Kingdom, Spain, and India. The role of the project manager in this context was mainly to provide the overall picture, to guarantee good coordination among different groups, and to promptly identify, tackle, and resolve (or appropriately escalate) issues.

In this period of time more emphasis was placed on *people management* rather than *process management*. The project management methodology created in 2004 was adapted to be smaller, simpler, and more flexible. A minimum compliance to the processes and tools was mandated (mainly to comply with reporting requirements from the corporation), but then it was up to the project manager to decide whether or not to apply most of the recommended parts of the methodology.

With so many projects, we had experiences of all types. Some projects were a success in all aspects, including time, cost, scope, and quality, but also in benefits gathering, which was not the usual scenario, I have to confess, but we did have a few projects of this type. Most projects however failed to meet one or more of the aspects previously mentioned. They were late, the cost was higher than approved in their business cases, some features were de-scoped (or postponed to a later phase), or they did not end up bringing to the company the benefits that were expected.

Generally speaking, if the project delivered the product or service on time and with no significant cost, scope, or quality deviation, it was considered a success by the COO. Whether the product or service delivered afterward met or did not meet its business goal (in most cases to generate revenue) was another topic. Some projects were a disaster from a COO perspective because they suffered deviations beyond acceptable thresholds, but they still ended up delivering very successful products and services that brought to the company juicy profits. There were also other projects that met time, cost, scope, and quality expectations but were not well received by the market and did not meet their revenue goals.

The project portfolio was also managed within the departments reporting to the COO. The PMO also put in place operating mechanisms and tools to support decision making (see Figure S3.1). The two most fundamental mechanisms were a project portfolio dashboard and a weekly project portfolio tracking committee.

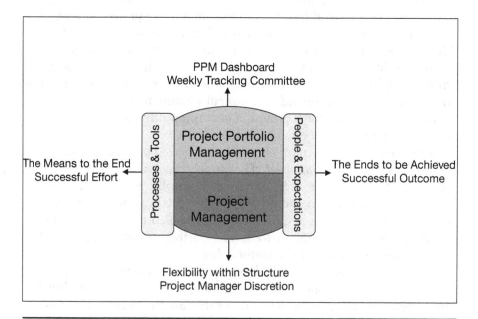

Figure S3.1 Business driven and adaptive PMO

PMO Success

In the spring of 2011, Aranzadi's COO was close to retirement and the company was defining a new organizational structure. As part of that reorganization process, the COO recommended that the PMO should evolve from an organizational PMO to an enterprise PMO, directly reporting to the managing director and managing projects end to end, from the ideation phase until benefits gathering. That proposal was taken into consideration, and now the Aranzadi PMO is transitioning from its previous responsibilities to the new ones.

Concluding Thoughts and Advice

In my view, the best way to assess the success (or failure) of a PMO is to consider the recognition that the organization demonstrates toward it. If the organization the PMO serves is satisfied by the value the PMO adds, then it will try to apply its best practices to other areas of the organization and it will promote and recognize its members.

If we consider the second PMO reactivated in 2007, we can fairly say it has been successful because it has not only added value to the organization but it also got its recognition. Aranzadi's COO recognized the work done by the PMO and recommended to the managing director that the PMO should evolve from an organizational to an enterprise PMO.

On the contrary, when the first PMO was created by the managing director, it was created to help him manage the project portfolio. However, instead of focusing on portfolio management, most of the effort was put into project management. Although the work done in project management was well perceived by most of the organization, it was not responding to the expectations of who had decided to create the PMO and it ended up vanishing.

Web Added Value™

PMO Success Story #4: British American Tobacco

Implementing Portfolio Management in a Global Organization

Marion Blake, PMO CoE Group Portfolio Management Office, BAT

Introduction to British American Tobacco

British American Tobacco (BAT) is the most international tobacco group in the world. We have a presence in 108 markets and employ more than 50,000 people. One of our key strengths is our broad geographic spread across both developed and developing markets, but this also presents great challenges. With a business that has grown both organically and through mergers and acquisitions, we have a history of federalism as well as an operational structure that encompasses four geographical regional business units and seven major central functions. We do not yet operate fully as a matrix organization and our current ways of working present many challenges for our global projects and programs. BAT is a very successful company, but like many global companies, we face increasing transformational change and the challenge this brings.

Business Problems to Be Addressed by the PMO

The Group Program Office (GPO) was established in 2005, primarily to provide methodologies, training, and consulting to global projects and programs. At the end of 2008, an internal audit report highlighted the shortcomings of the GPO with respect to the current needs of the business. At the beginning of 2009, the GPO was tasked with addressing the following business issues:

1. Providing visibility of global projects and programs
2. Defining and embedding controls and governance for these projects and programs

3. Enabling and facilitating resource allocation discussions and decisions across them
4. Ensuring the success of the key projects and programs

In early 2009, the CEO articulated his expectations for the PMO community:

> PMO *must support their respective leadership teams with facts on the table, by convening the conversations and ensuring that clear actions are agreed upon and followed up. They must help decision makers to allocate resources appropriately given the risks and rewards and enable the smooth execution of projects and programs that deliver business value.*

Our Story

The First Year

Our initial actions focused on gaining *visibility* over the size of the challenge. We needed to understand what projects and programs were in planning and execution, what resources they were consuming, how they were governed, and the level of success they were having. We tasked the global functions with completing a two-page summary for every project and program they were running to provide an initial sweep of information. This highlighted several challenges we would need to overcome: the inconsistency of data, differences in the way that costs and benefits were calculated, plus a lack of standardization of the way resources were estimated and allocated. Working with the global functions, we set about categorizing the projects and program list based on the following criteria:

◆ Budget allocated
◆ Benefits forecast
◆ Number of internal (and external) resources required to execute

Through this process we also identified key challenges we would have to address:

1. There were few, or no, standard processes to support the information we would require.
2. The information system in place was inadequate to support the processes we would implement.
3. We did not have a large pool of skilled PMO resources.
4. The organization's current ways of working did not lend themselves easily to standardization and centralization.

Having gained a better understanding of what would be required to address these challenges, we proposed an approach that would implement portfolio controls step by step, ensuring each was embedded and stable before progressing to the next level (see Figure S4.1).

Now that we understood what the business was spending on global projects and programs and what value they were expected to deliver, both of which were significant amounts, we next needed to define and implement controls to enable the efficient allocation of resources to maximize the return for the organization. The controls needed to ensure that any new projects and programs requiring resources would be prioritized against each other and existing projects and programs.

This of course is classic portfolio management, and we introduced a simple cross-functional gate approval process that integrated with the organization's annual planning cycle. Having done this, the next step in the plan was to introduce standardized reporting on project progress, risk management, and cross-functional dependencies as input to management decision-making forums. The focus on embedding the gate approval process across functions was also applied to the regional portfolios responsible for delivering global projects and programs. This process facilitated conversations between global projects and programs and the regional resources required to execute them. The subsequent discussions gave the regions

The Journey Plan

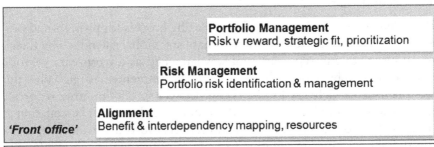

Portfolio Management
Risk v reward, strategic fit, prioritization

Risk Management
Portfolio risk identification & management

Alignment
'Front office' Benefit & interdependency mapping, resources

'Back office'

Gaining control
Baselines, exception reports, costs & benefits, consistency, Global & Regional engagement

Visibility & direction
What's in the portfolio, set ground rules & approval framework

No Big Bang – step-by-step approach, building on each level

Figure S4.1 A phased approach

more visibility of the projects and programs that would be coming their way for deployment, enabling the regions to schedule their resources and prepare better for deployment.

During the first company annual planning cycle, a cross-functional governance body was introduced to review and prioritize the portfolio of global projects and programs with the knowledge that there would be resource constraints applied that would require them to prepare recommendations as input to the management board. This first time around, the prioritization process was fairly broad and basic; brown paper and stickies were used to support the discussions, but for the first time a cross-functional and geographical team was having specific discussions about a group portfolio of projects and programs and the output was a prioritized recommendation input to the annual planning process.

We learned through this first planning cycle the importance of an agreed set of strategic outcomes at a more granular level than we had. This would have enabled the portfolios to complete a more comprehensive alignment and prioritization process. We planned to address this issue early in the new year.

By the end of the first year, we had met three of the four key expectations and were well on our way to achieving the fourth. We entered the second year with aspirations of identifying strategic outcomes to guide the portfolios, improving on our ability to prioritize and balance our portfolios and perhaps even experimenting with scenario planning.

The Second Year

Reporting: A standardized monthly reporting process for projects and programs was launched with a single template and global calendar. The Excel-based template and reporting tool was launched as a temporary solution until a more robust portfolio tool could be implemented globally (this was planned for delivery by the end of the year). The monthly reporting rhythm was adopted quickly and the report widely used. The collation at portfolio level of the monthly highlight reports evolved into an exceptions-based dashboard for presentation to senior management, enabling them to focus their attention and support where it was required.

During the implementation of the new reporting process, the inconsistency of data was highlighted, and it was agreed that the biggest challenge around this had been securing a single source of information that was consistent and of good quality. A commercial portfolio reporting tool was selected and implemented to address this challenge. The implementation itself would be a big challenge and, learning from previous attempts at implementing global tools, the approach focused on replacing initially only the existing templates and process before attempting to add better functionality. The reporting tool was a great leap forward in providing a single source of consistent portfolio information that eventually enabled us to introduce a standardized portfolio dashboard for the quarterly reporting cycle.

Risk Management: Building on the earlier successes, the team engaged with finance to align portfolio risk evaluation matrices with business matrices, ensuring portfolio risks that posed a threat to the business were identified, escalated, and managed within the group's risk management process. In support of this process regular cross-portfolio risk reviews were successfully introduced to identify and discuss group-level portfolio and business risks.

Strategic Outcomes: Early in the year a number of key strategic outcomes were agreed upon with the management board, enabling the portfolios, projects, and programs to ensure they were correctly aligned to deliver to expectations. This had a very positive effect on the portfolios, as they could validate their balancing and prioritization. It also made the annual planning cycle more sophisticated, yet also much smoother—we knew what to expect and we knew what was expected, so the resulting outcomes were more robust.

Governance Revisited: However, as expected in a global organization, things had moved on and it was felt that the levels of control and governance that were implemented in the previous year were no longer necessary; we had matured as an organization, and in order to simplify the perceived bureaucracy we were asked to review the controls to facilitate a more agile approach, which was deemed to have too many governing layers. The transition to the new governance took several months to complete; the same gate approval process remained the backbone of control but the operation of the process was pushed down a layer of management. There was no longer a need for central oversight. A key learning from this period was that slow was not good, the rhythm that had previously been embedded was disrupted, and many elements fell through the cracks.

But by the end of our second year we were confident that we had completed the first steps of our plan successfully, and as we entered year three we felt confident that we could now turn our focus on reviewing and improving what had been achieved. The global PMO community, which had gained experience and matured during this period, was positioned to focus on embedding the new standards to support the drive for consistent, relevant, and high-quality information as input to the evaluation, tracking, and reporting process.

PMO Success

Three years after starting the journey we can look back at some key successes:

- We have gained visibility of global projects and programs and improved the quality of information provided to decision-making forums.
- The project and program governance processes now facilitate cross-portfolio conversations across both global functions, which had previously operated in siloed isolation, and between functions and geographical regions.
- There is a high level of standardization and consistency of project and program information supported and enabled by the implementation of a global portfolio reporting tool, which drives the discipline of monthly reporting.
- The definition and approval of granular strategic objectives enable the alignment of portfolios to ensure they match delivery expectations.

Concluding Thoughts and Advice

None of our challenges were unique to BAT; we believe the step-by-step approach we undertook initially was a key to our successes and allowed us to understand how to manage and adapt to the changes within our organization as we implemented them. Setting realistic and achievable goals is very important to ensure that the basics are embedded before building on their successes. Understanding the pace at which change can be implemented is a key area; should we evolve at the pace of the fastest or the slowest? We learned that you can't always go at the pace of the slowest as it can impact the momentum that you build.

The Challenge of Standardization Versus Pragmatism

Some things must be standardized; otherwise the process cannot operate, but that does not mean that everything has to be or should be standardized. However, establishing a consistent data set, managed from a single source, as early as possible is imperative to ensure the PMO is not paralyzed by an avalanche of data and information. Our future plans must now turn to ensuring that we can measure the value of the PMO on our market share, revenues, and profits, with our primary focus on the processes and frameworks required to support business benefit management and realization. As before, we will tackle this one step at a time.

PMO Success Story #5:
An American Benefits
Administration Organization

A Tale of Two PMOs

Harlan Bridges, PMP, PMO Analyst, MESSA

Introduction

This association is a nonprofit membership association that administers health, financial, and retirement benefits to its membership. The association has been in existence for 50 years and regularly earns 98% satisfaction scores from its members. It employs 300 employees statewide and serves over 65,000 members. We place strong emphasis on member education, wellness, and preventive care. The call center is a Certified Center of Excellence and has attained Utilization Review Accreditation Commission accreditations in Disease Management and Case Management.

In order to stay competitive and to better serve the membership, new products are developed, information systems are developed or upgraded, and processes are created and improved annually. Often new regulations and laws affect the industry and create the need to make changes to the business in order to remain in compliance.

Business Problems to Be Addressed by the PMO

I joined a PMO that had been in existence for approximately three years. During this time the PMO failed to demonstrate business value. The PMO was not aligned with the business goals and objectives. The association had no clear understanding of the purpose of the PMO and the PMO was seen only as an overhead department that added no value. The other business departments sought to avoid interaction with the PMO as much as possible.

The project portfolio had more than 75 projects listed as under active development. In this portfolio, there were 12 number one projects and every project proposal submitted was approved. All these projects contributed to:

- An inefficient use of resources
- Cost and schedule overruns
- Low project quality
- Poor planning and execution
- Projects that failed to add value to the association

After three years, it was determined that changes in the PMO were needed or it should be discontinued. In redefining the PMO, our major goal was to ensure it met the needs of the business and added value by aligning the PMO objectives with those of the business. In essence, we tied our success to that of the business.

Our Story

The initial formation of the PMO was very inwardly focused and was implemented as a compliance organization. With no charter, and therefore no mission, vision, scope, or measurable objectives, this PMO struggled to demonstrate its value to the organization. No one knew why the PMO existed. The emphasis was on templates and ensuring that managers completed and submitted these templates correctly.

Functional managers were usually thrust into the role of project manager and expected to perform both their operational duties and those of the project manager. A lack of defined and documented processes made consistent project delivery very difficult, especially for these untrained project managers. After three years, it was time for a *big do-over*.

Our primary emphasis in our new PMO was to develop and maintain an outward focus. Using Nemawashi-style techniques and interviewing processes, we began the process of discovering the needs of the business. Our goal during this initial discovery period was to look for the problems and challenges the business faced. We sought to discover what the business expected from the PMO as well as how the business defined the value of the PMO. We identified our strengths, weaknesses, opportunities, and threats to success. As we performed this SWOT analysis, we focused on the business as well as the PMO.

During the first 100 days of the new PMO, we performed needs gathering and needs analysis only. From this period of intense analysis, we

Business Needs Assessment

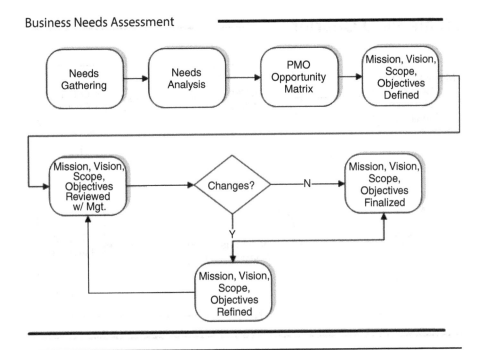

Figure S5.1   Business need assessment

identified the business needs and expectations. As shown in Figure S5.1, the results of this needs analysis were used to create an opportunity matrix that was further refined.

We created a mission statement, a vision, identified our scope, and defined the PMO objectives from the information gathered from our constituents. This led to the creation of the PMO charter as shown in Figure S5.2. Because this entire process was a partnership with them, the business was acutely aware of the value the PMO would bring to them. They had become owners through the process of creating the PMO charter and shared equal responsibility in the success of the PMO.

The PMO adopted a servant-leadership role, and though we were cognizant and focused on the needs of our constituents, we took the lead in creating solutions that would help the business reach its goals. We developed our services and functions with the goal of assisting the business to succeed and of adding value to the business. Our mantra became *if it doesn't add value, don't do it.*

Create PMO Charter

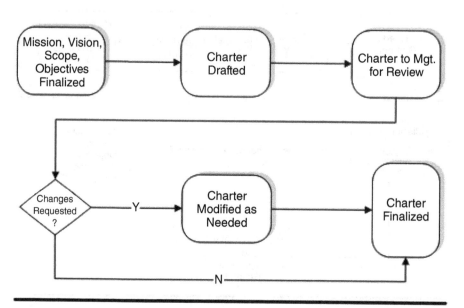

Figure S5.2   Create PMO charter

PMO Success

Project selection became the number one priority for the business. In order to address this need, we developed an annual Call for Projects process to assist in the selection of projects. The objective was to have no more active projects than we had resources and capability to support. All proposed projects were subjected to the Call for Projects process and only those approved were put in our project portfolio. Our project portfolio now consisted of only 24 projects of which only 10 are active. The number of active projects is determined by our resource capacity.

Resource allocation was recognized as a major challenge for the business, and the PMO created a process to make more efficient use of limited resources. By officially allocating resources and tracking that allocation, we were able to better identify what should be included in our project portfolio. This process increased the visibility and understanding around resource constraints. We were able to quickly provide *what if* scenarios when new proposals were brought to the executive steering committee.

We developed a project management process designed to be applied with the appropriate level of rigor, depending on the complexity and risk of the project. The consistent use of a project management process rather than focus on templates helped begin movement of the organization toward a culture of organizational project management.

Concluding Thoughts and Advice

It is imperative that the PMO be a value-add organization. This requires that the PMO understand the needs and expectations of its constituents. Focus should always be outward. Don't worry about performing a gap analysis. Don't be concerned with CMMI or OPM3® maturity levels. These are internally focused measurements, not measurements of value.

It is not difficult to measure the value of a PMO when the PMO and the business have worked together to develop the mission, vision, scope, and the objectives of the PMO. These then become the PMO charter, which is in turn owned by the key stakeholders. The success of the PMO is measured against the achievement of the objectives defined in the PMO charter.

Communication and continuous improvement are critical success factors for implementing and maintaining the PMO over the long term. Set up regular reviews of the PMO charter with the business to ensure that the mission, vision, scope, and objectives remain pertinent. Conditions or business needs may have changed, requiring the PMO to refocus and realign its efforts to ensure that it continues to provide value to the business. Stay focused on your constituents. Always add value, and the PMO will become a vital part of the business, no different than marketing, finance, or HR.

PMO Success Story #6: SIVECO Romania SA

Prevention before the Crisis

Jimmy Char, PMP, SKILLS Ltd.

Introduction to SIVECO Romania SA

Twenty-five years of work for Groupe Bull, the French-based international ITC company, not only helped to build my career through intensive international experience in managing all sizes of projects, but also shaped me as a business traveler who has the necessary motivation and ability to smoothly and regularly move from one project to another, from one team to another, from one country to another, and from one culture to another in the quest for and succeeding in challenging situations.

In September 2007, three years after the start of my last assignment for Groupe Bull, which happened to be in Bulgaria, I realized that it was about time for a change. The change that time was a bit different, not from location or country but, what many of us would like to reach at a certain point, a change that brought me on my own with a small but efficient consulting and training company in business and project management, which I am still running. SKILLS Ltd., the culmination of all my previous years of experience, was and still is based in Bulgaria and targets regional projects and clients from Bulgaria, Romania, Turkey, and Macedonia.

A month later I received a call from an old friend from a previous assignment in Romania, who proposed to me a new opportunity, the story I am sharing with you here. My friend was working for SIVECO, a Romanian-based company, with which I have had successful cooperation and effective partnerships during my previous assignments in different countries and with different accounts.

SIVECO Romania SA is the leading Romanian software house and one of the most successful software integrators from Central and Eastern Europe. The company develops and exports software products and high value-added consultancy projects to countries within the European community, the Middle East, North Africa, and the Commonwealth of Independent States area. Among SIVECO's customers are large companies and public agencies, to which the company provides efficient eLearning, EAS, Document Management, Business Intelligence, eHealth, eAgriculture, eCustoms, and eBusiness solutions, both on national and international levels. SIVECO was founded in 1992, and by 2007 it had 750 employees.

The discussion in that call revealed that in view of the growth that SIVECO Romania SA has registered the last few years, a new and different plan had to be prepared for the future. SIVECO was undertaking a restructuring plan in which several important entities and units would have to be launched in order to improve the efficiency of running its clients' projects. Restructuring also included the creation and development of the PMO. The PMO would be in charge of the improvement of the project managers' performance, how they are selecting, and winning, estimating, planning, conducting, controlling, and closing the projects. SIVECO's projects were already successful in scope delivery, but taking into account the rapid growth of the company as well as the international expansion, the creation of the PMO was at that time a strategic decision.

Given that SIVECO is a software house that deals mainly with complex projects and large international accounts, it was clear that the final result of this strategic decision was to do the groundwork for having, in the coming years, a well-functioning portfolio management office.

Business Problems to Be Addressed by the PMO

In November 2007, I began this new assignment by considering it a new project, having to address parallel needs and requirements and targeting many objectives with a set of deliverables, goals, and results, mainly:

- ◆ Optimizing the general costs of the projects
- ◆ Reducing the number of projects entering into crisis states; bleeding projects that are not meeting their schedules, budgets, and are costing the company a lot of money and resources
- ◆ Improving risk management
- ◆ Increasing profit margins
- ◆ Increasing cash reserves to cover the inability of clients to pay on time
- ◆ Increasing the productivity/expert ratio
- ◆ Optimizing the use of vertical resources in both vertical and horizontal projects

Our Story

The SIVECO management team was fully committed to having a PMO, and I was named to head it as a consultant on behalf of my company, SKILLS. I accepted the challenge knowing in advance that priorities may sometimes change and a PMO delivery value, as in many worldwide companies, might be difficult to achieve within the expected timelines. I accepted the proposal and moved to Romania. Reporting to the COO, I initiated the PMO unit, analyzing the needs and developing the solutions required. I had started the PMO and had the full support of the management team and was given power over a certain number of potentially available resources.

SIVECO Romania SA is a functional organization in which the business units form the different lines of business, headed by business unit managers that form SIVECO middle management (see Figure S6.1).

I started working on developing the PMO charter, a top priority task because the document to be fully accepted and supported by higher management. Small and big issues were discussed in that charter in a completely direct and transparent manner. From this document I wanted to clearly understand the *as is* (current state) of the projects as well as the procedures, processes, and the quality assurance system developed and applied internally. The objective was to find the weaknesses and define the points of improvement, all of which would secure the support for the PMO. The expected *to be* outcome was defined as much as possible in the charter, which once approved became the agreement between the management team and the PMO.

During the first month I had to meet with several business unit managers and project managers and deliver several presentations on my findings, thus gaining the support of the middle management team. In parallel, I started communicating the advantages of improving the current methodology for efficient project management performance and smooth transition of resources.

The *as is* can be simply summarized as somewhere between Levels 2 and 3 of the Organization Maturity Model levels. The *to be* can also be summarized as reaching Levels 4 and 5 in the next two stages of the Strategic PMO Plan. Each of these stages involved 18 months of hard work from all stakeholders connected with the company (see Figure S6.2).

The final objective of that stage of the PMO—initiation and development—was the shift of the current project management practices to com-

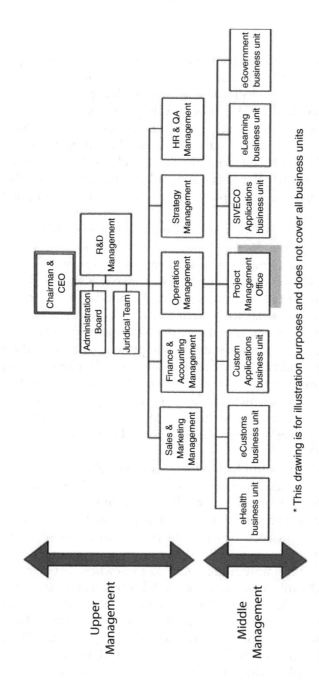

Figure S6.1 SIVECO organizational chart

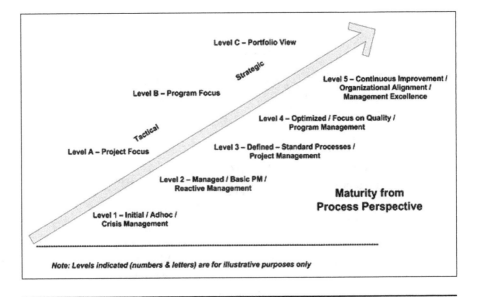

Figure S6.2   SIVECO maturity model levels

pliant standards and best practices as defined by *A Guide to the Project Management Body of Knowledge, third edition (PMBOK® Guide)*.

The gap analysis that I conducted shows that to achieve its objectives, the PMO must work on several axes and lines of activities that can be summarized (without going into details) as shown in Figure S6.3. All these axes of activities are the right start for any PMO wishing to achieve success. I developed the work plan and launched the implementation with several subprojects as shown in Figure S6.4.

Subproject 0: The creation of the PMO team. SIVECO management had authorized the nomination of five senior project managers to implement the different subprojects as defined per the Charter Project Plan.

Subproject 1: The development of a new methodology called SIVA-COP® (SIVECO Integrated Value-Added Code of Practice) that was introduced to a combined audience of management and user groups and later improved based on their comments and feedback. SIVACOP® covered not only the processes with their inputs, outputs, tools, and techniques but also the templates, work instructions, procedures and supporting platforms, software tools, and facilities, such as the project management software and project management information system (see Figure S6.5).

Figure S6.3   The PMO lines of activities defined in the charter

Subproject 2: The development and delivery of a comprehensive training plan for project management best practices in general and the new methodology SIVACOP® as follows:

◆ Project Management Fundamentals course delivered in six days during three consecutive weeks. This course covered the necessary explanations and knowledge transfer from the PMBOK third edition framework. The objectives of this course were (1) to prepare project managers for CAPM® and PMP® certification exams and (2) to prepare them for the following training sessions for the new SIVACOP® methodology.

◆ SIVACOP® implementation course delivered after the Project Management Fundamentals course in four additional days during two consecutive weeks. The objective was to train project managers on the use of the new methodology and to understand all templates, procedures, work instructions, tools, and facilities. The session was specially designed to prepare project managers to better follow the

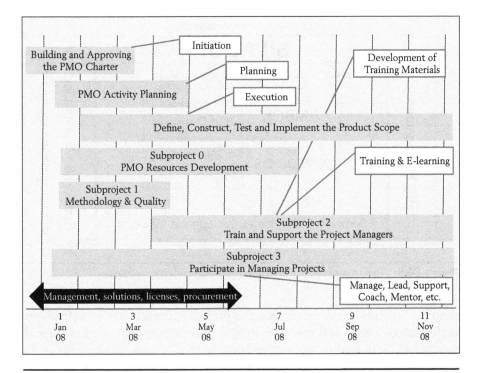

Figure S6.4   The PMO project plan summary

new methodology, thus improving the overall project performance of the organization.

The training involved 150 project managers and project team members. These training courses motivated project managers to pursue the PMI accreditation and certification and apply the international standards in their daily work.

After completing the new methodology and preparing project managers with the right training, the green light was given from the management team to start applying the new methodology on ongoing and future projects.

Subproject 3: The active participation of the PMO in ongoing and challenged projects. The role of the PMO in this subproject was to provide help to the project managers to better analyze the situation, to understand and resolve the issues raised, and to be able to find and take the right decisions to optimize their project management performance. The objective of

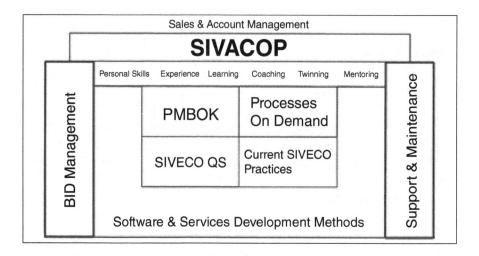

Figure S6.5   The new project management methodology concept

the PMO team was not to replace the project managers but to help them understand, choose, and take the right decisions in specific situations and to support them in their project endeavors.

Of the ongoing and recurring activities, the PMO was mainly involved in two major ones:

1. The aggregation of monthly project managers' reports to management for better visibility and justified management decisions.
2. The aggregation of the projects' workloads and availability of the company's resources for better sharing and optimization of all resources and especially the human resources, based on their priorities.

PMO Success

Running all the above subprojects in parallel with so many stakeholders involved was a true challenge and a risky initiative, but with the involvement and commitment of top management, the motivation of the project managers to achieve structured practices, and the support, patience, and dedication of the PMO team, the project managers found ways to do this in the most effective and efficient manner—effectiveness in identifying and working on the right problems and efficiency in fixing the problems in the best possible way. The success that was brought by the newly established PMO was considered enormous in its ability to move to structured practice.

Around the middle of 2008, signals started to come from various international financial and consulting institutions predicting a global recession and a financial crisis in the following years. A global financial crisis means fewer projects, less revenues, higher competition, and, generally speaking, difficult moments in all aspects of the business.

The global financial crisis had a heavy impact on all companies and businesses worldwide; however, SIVECO did very well, continuing to grow, and today it has 1,300 experts.

Concluding Thoughts and Advice

Management is always looking for fast results, and in the case of the SIVECO PMO, I shared such expectations and tried to deliver iterative solutions. However, for some longer deliverables, PMO success would need more time, patience, and durable efforts to truly deliver and prove its value and benefits to the organization.

PMO Success Story #7: An American Insurance Company

Luis Crespo, Senior Project Manager

Introduction to the Company

This company is a regional multiline property and casualty insurance carrier based in the western United States. It's a privately held company that is actually composed of three other companies that make up its three major lines of business.

It offers its insurance products exclusively through a network of independent agents and brokers; therefore, the ability to serve the needs of these agents quickly and in the right priority is of paramount importance.

Business Problems to Be Addressed by the PMO

When I joined the company there was no PMO in place. We had a growing number of project managers and an undetermined number of projects or efforts that were classified as projects. Although there was a Process Improvement Group in place, its main focus was to roll out ITIL® to the company.

From a 60,000-foot view, an outsider may have concluded a PMO was not needed. There was an abundance of templates, a lengthy and well-thought-out project management handbook, and a project management monthly team meeting.

However, that in itself was the challenge; none of these things were working toward the benefit of the project managers and more importantly the business. The PMO needed to identify what projects needed to be worked on, when they needed to be worked on, and how these projects would be tracked to ensure that these business investments were worthwhile. From my perspective, and frankly, after speaking to many of my colleagues from theirs as well, there was a lot of work going on but not everyone was sure if it was beneficial, and if it was, to whom.

Our Story

First and foremost, it's important to note that a PMO or something like it was not a novel idea at the company. As a matter of fact, just recently a well-respected project management consulting firm had been brought in to develop the templates and processes for the project managers at the time. That being said, I began attending the monthly project managers' meetings and I noticed a great deal of discord and noncompliance to the standards that had been developed.

The general feeling by most of the project managers was that the templates were mostly busywork, which they had no involvement in the development of, and the templates overall did not help but instead hindered the overall work they needed to do. In addition, if I was to ask anyone how many projects the organization currently had in process, there was no one answer. The first problem was there was no central system. There were at least three different systems or databases and just as many points of entry for the business to request work to get done. The second problem was that every request that came in would inevitably be classified as a project and an approved one at that. So, if the administrator from the third floor had a request for a new field for the intranet and the manager of the claims department needed a new system, these both would be entered into the system as projects. The third issue was who would work on these and when. The business was going through a major transformational effort, and after 20-plus years of not investing in IT, it was finally opening the floodgates. Unfortunately, the controls were not placed concurrently or in this case prior.

Enough of the problems (or in this case challenges that became opportunities to succeed); let's move on to how we solved them. Setting up the PMO required the authorization from the ultimate stakeholder in our department, which in our case was the CIO. He had given his blessing but we wanted to make sure this was more formal. So as with any project, we chartered the PMO and had it officially approved as an official body, complete with its roles and responsibilities along with the roles and responsibilities of senior management. This would ensure that this was not a one-way street, but that we would have buy-in from day one and we would be able to escalate issues when they arose. While we were getting the PMO chartered we wanted to make sure we took some baby steps as well, and we tackled one of the more prevalent issues that had permeated the company probably since day one. What is a project? More importantly, what was a project at the company at that point in time?

Without much fanfare but after some detailed analysis of prior completed projects, an e-mail was crafted and sent out to the organization that stated the parameters for a project for the organization. This was a key win for the newly not yet chartered PMO. It began to demonstrate our ability to first of all bring immediate value to the organization and second of all to do so with little bureaucracy.

The next step was to review and establish one central system in which all project management intake, scheduling, and time sheet recording would take place. Once again, we didn't try to reinvent the wheel, but realized that there were already tools in place we could either leverage or find a reason to replace. In our case we leveraged them until we technically could no longer and then replaced them with a more elegant solution. In both cases it was a matter of documenting a process, communicating to the user community, and weekly enforcement (in a good way) to ensure that everyone was applying the processes in place. By consolidating to one system and redefining what we called a project, we were able to narrow down our project list from over 200 to well under 50. Later we were able to whittle that number down even further once we introduced enterprise governance to the mix.

The next issue we tackled was the project management templates. Time is money, and in project terms an inordinate amount of time was being spent on updating long-winded status reports, extraneous and repetitive documents as part of the project kickoffs, etc., etc. This is not a knock against the consulting company that developed these documents. The level of rigor they introduced is well received in many companies and required in others. However, we were a company that was crawling and trying to walk, and someone had given us the playbook for a fox-trot. Once again, the first thing we did was review what worked. In this case, it wasn't much. Not that the material wasn't useful; as a matter of fact, we kept it as a reference, but the format and content were too much.

The next step was to decide to build or buy. Along the way we had an epiphany. This was more than just about templates. One of the major reasons this had previously failed was that templates were provided but there was no guide to go along with them. So when looking for a new set of templates, a key requirement was templates and processes. We were fortunate enough to find a product called Processes On Demand by BOT International, which provided both. They weren't the only ones but they were the right ones for us at the right time. We involved the project managers; we had them review the content we were going to push out in less than 90 days and had a project management methodology for them to follow. Immediately we saw adoption by the project management and end user community and were able to phase out the existing templates. This in turn allowed us to begin to perform compliance audits against each project to ensure the right tools and the right content were being provided for each project.

Once a good rhythm was established with regard to project methodology and process, we turned our attention to resource demand management. We knew for the most part which projects were being worked on, but there was still the issue of who was working on them and when. All the templates in the world were not going to solve this issue. One of the project managers from the project management office was dedicated full time to gathering, reviewing, and editing on a weekly basis all the data required to understand our demand management. It took about three months to get an initial baseline of the department's resources against the company's projects and from that point forward it was a matter of fine-tuning and getting additional data points. After 12 months, it was a fine-tuned process that allowed data mining and resource forecasting, which in turn allowed for an easier transition to project governance.

Project governance was the final piece of the PMO evolution at the organization, and it was a logical step given the fact that we had all the required pieces in place. We had a formal project methodology, a formal resource demand management process, and an established enterprise project management tool. Our executive management team needed a process by which to prioritize which enterprise efforts would be worked on by the business unit and by the enterprise. The PMO worked with each senior manager and devised a grading method by which to quantify and qualify each project request that came up for prioritization. In addition, the PMO worked on a formal demand management process, as shown in Figure S7.1, which tracked an idea from request, through prioritization, through project creation, and finally project archival. This allowed any end user in the organization to understand and appreciate how any of their ideas could end up becoming projects at the company.

PMO Success

The success of the PMO in my opinion could only be measured by the success of the projects that were overseen and by the acceptance of the audience, both direct and indirect. With regard to project success, the PMO was able to oversee the successful implementation of over 15 major projects during its tenure, along with dozens of smaller projects as well. The PMO also increased the likelihood of greater project success by conducting

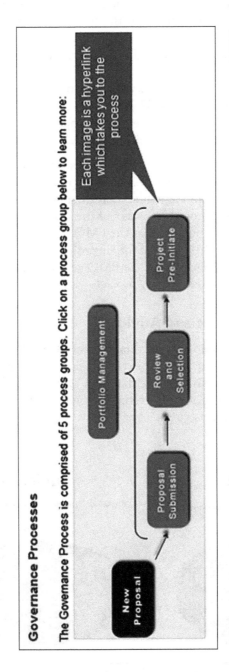

Figure S7.1 Governance process

bimonthly training on project management topics for well over a year and extended these training offerings into the lines of business. As part of its oversight, the PMO conducted at least 12 project reviews and project closeout meetings and was requested as ad hoc reviewer on other projects it did not directly oversee.

From an audience perspective, surveys were distributed to 40 users and 25 responded as shown in Figure S7.2.

As shown in Figure S7.3, we asked what impact the PMO services or tools had on the success of their projects:

- ◆ Forty percent responded that the PMO services and/or tools had a moderate impact on the success of their project.
- ◆ Twenty-eight percent responded that the PMO services and/or tools had a major impact on the success of their project.
- ◆ Twenty percent responded that the PMO services and/or tools had a minor impact on the success of their project.
- ◆ Four percent responded that the PMO services and/or tools had no impact on the success of their project

Concluding Thoughts and Advice

In retrospect, my advice to anyone thinking about starting, consulting for, participating in, or leading a PMO is to first and foremost plan with the end in mind. In plain English, realize that your efforts and/or contributions will not be measured by how many templates you created, dashboards you rolled out, or even projects you *rescued*.

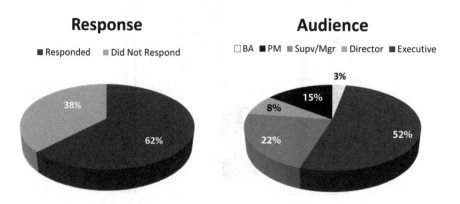

Figure S7.2   PMO survey response and audience

Impact of PMO Tools or Services on Project Success

☐ None   ■ Minor   ■ Moderate   ■ Major   ■ N/A

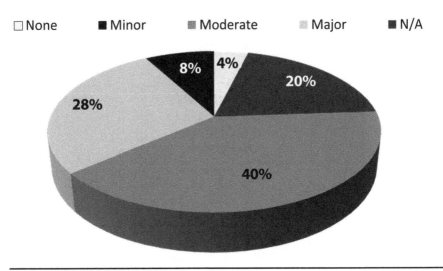

Figure S7.3   PMO survey of impact on project success

The true value of the PMO
will be measured by those who it serves.

In every situation that is different. There is no one book, one white paper, or one expert who can tell you how to do it or what to do. It will take research, but most of all it will take knowing your audience and knowing what business purpose and business value the PMO will bring to the organization. For those who have been asked to launch a PMO, I would ask you to challenge your management as to why they think one is needed. Although this may sound counterproductive to your mission, it will be your first step to figuring out whether or not you will actually be successful in the long run. As one closing thought, I remind all who take on this exciting and rewarding work to remember to be flexible and adaptable. No PMO ever stays the same as originally planned. The successful PMO manager will learn to adapt to the changing needs of the organization and even learn when a PMO has completed its mission.

PMO Success Story #8: International Facility Management Association

The Journey to a New Way of Working

Jennifer Drai, Director of Project Management Services, IFMA

Introduction to International Facility Management Association

The International Facility Management Association (IFMA) is a nonprofit professional association headquartered in Houston, Texas, dedicated to advancing professional facility managers worldwide. It has more than 22,500 members in 78 countries. The association's members, represented in 127 chapters and 16 industry councils worldwide, manage more than 37 billion square feet of property and annually purchase more than US$100 billion in products and services. Formed in 1980, IFMA certifies facility managers, conducts research, provides educational programs, and produces World Workplace, the world's largest facility management conference and exposition, and *Facility Management Journal*, its bimonthly publication, written specifically for facility professionals concerned with developing and maintaining productive workplaces.

Business Problems to Be Addressed by the PMO

IFMA headquarters has been established as a functional organization since its inception. This modus operandi served its purpose for the time being, especially as the association looked into positioning facility management as a recognized profession worldwide. With time, as is the case with many other functional organizations, IFMA realized that this method of operating made it difficult to adapt to constant business change as well as the ever-demanding needs of its global membership. A number of inherited and inefficient processes, a compartmentalized culture, and a poor flow of communication among staff made the senior leadership realize that a fundamental change in the way we operated needed to take place. Mike Moss, IFMA's COO, a Lean Six Sigma Green Belt who has a proven track record of experience in establishing and implementing effective business management processes aimed at reducing costs or increasing profits, took the lead on this initiative. He built the case for why IFMA's functions must transition into a project team-based approach if we were to pursue improved support for a diverse and global membership audience. However, because of its radical nature, it is well understood that this change can't happen from one year to the next. The migration toward a matrix organization structure, the establishment of a PMO, as well as the implementation of a carefully thought-through mobile workplace strategy on our upcoming office move would be some of the principal enablers of a project management culture.

Our Story

It was in summer 2011 after I returned from vacation that I was called for a meeting with the Vice President of Communications and the COO. As IFMA's Associate Director of Marketing at the time, I was in charge of creating, managing, and ensuring the implementation of marketing plans and strategies put in place for IFMA's various offerings. At the meeting, they both articulated a variety of current issues and situations that we were facing, which translated into the impending need for a project management culture. Having managed multiple projects as the head of the marketing department, I could not agree more—considering the number of frustrations I had often experienced. A big amount of marketing deliverables were constantly being affected by the lack of due diligence in planning and commitment to deadlines from other departments, who would put their own interests first.

There was no doubt that instilling a project management culture would help reduce the total amount of effort or *pain* experienced in project implementations. IFMA's common practice had been to execute projects right from the outset—without taking time to clearly define the need and requirements or develop a plan that addresses potential issues, as shown in Figure S8.1. As a result, the stress level experienced as projects evolved would grow exponentially. For obvious reasons, scope creep and/or rework would constantly be added to the projects as problems emerged. In contrast, if teams worked hard in defining requirements and developing a plan, problems would be anticipated and included in regular work—resulting in lower levels of stress as we approached delivery.

Adequate planning can reduce the level of stress

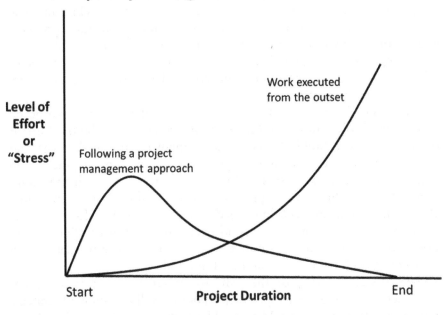

Figure S8.1   Level of effort over project duration

After agreeing on this reality and the imperative need to change for the good, the COO articulated that someone needed to guide this change and believed that, given my demonstrated work and professional qualities, I was the ideal person to do so. I felt quite honored and quickly envisioned how much more effective and able to react to business change IFMA would be if all staff were on the same accord and knew exactly what processes and methodology to follow as we implemented projects. I could not have been happier about this exciting and challenging opportunity that would contribute to taking IFMA to the next level. In addition, I was promoted to the director rank under the title of Director of Project Management Services.

The plan was for me to take on the new role once IFMA found my replacement in the marketing department and I helped aid a smooth transition. Ultimately, by being head of marketing for the past four years, I acquired extensive knowledge about each of IFMA's departments, products, and services. The transition period took about six months, including the time to find this person, but in the meantime, I took two project management courses. Interestingly enough, one of these was offered by IFMA—since it forms part of the four-course curriculum required for a facility manager to obtain our Facility Management Professional (FMP®) entry-level credential.

Although focused on the facility manager function, it does cover each of the core project management process groups and knowledge areas in detail. The second course was a weeklong project management fundamentals certificate program that focused on the discipline of project management. This course placed emphasis on the people side—including communication skills. As we all know, in life as in business, communication is key, and in project management there is no exception to this rule.

After taking these courses, the COO and I agreed it was time to proceed with the establishment of the PMO, as this would clearly be the formalized entity to help build a project management culture in the organization. Overall, we knew its main function would be to provide guidance in project management processes and methodologies, assist with the monitoring and controlling of the project portfolio—while at the same time offer the mentoring and coaching needed to effectively transform the way we approached the management and execution of projects. Before execution, we wanted to make sure that we were approaching this setup with the needs of both the business and staff in mind.

The first step in setting up the PMO was to create a strategy document intended to communicate its specific purpose, as well as outline its strategic guidelines so that any stakeholder could have clear expectations. The development of this document was two-phased; ensuring the executive team's buy-in was a priority. Composed of each department head, the executive team represents the entire organization. Although the long-term decision of transforming IFMA's culture into a project management one came from the top, the only way forward was to engage them and their teams in the process, taking their input into consideration from the beginning.

The delivery of the initial phase of the strategy document, aside from including an assessment of IFMA's current environment and needs, provided a lot of teaching. Although familiar with most terms, the majority of the executive team members had never considered managing their projects in any way than the one they already knew. With various examples, they quickly realized the benefits of running projects in a more efficient, consistent, and standardized manner. This led to PMO justification discussions as well as emphasis on the true nature of service of the PMO, which should be regarded as their medium to achieve their desired results more effectively.

Afterward, the executive team was presented with a first draft of strategic guidelines, including IFMA's PMO vision, mission, and guiding principles. It also came with a draft overview of the PMO's main roles and responsibilities, its critical success factors, as well as an exercise that required all directors to list their top three challenges. The results of the exercise led to the identification of the first priorities that IFMA's PMO should focus on, aside from its initial setup goals and responsibilities.

Following a number of meetings and continuous feedback with the executive team, IFMA's PMO strategic guidelines were agreed upon as shown in Figure S8.2.

In regard to the PMO's areas of initial focus, the different challenges that the directors listed they were facing were classified by themselves as high or low in terms of their organizational strategic value as well as the impact they could have on improving current processes. After analyzing the list, two-thirds was impacted by the current website status and considered high in regard to their value add—both to the organization and to the end customer. As a result, the successful delivery of the website redesign project was made one of the PMO priorities. Two other projects that ranked high due to their impact on value add and improvement of business processes were the office relocation project and the updating and documenting of our current customer service processes.

After the formalization of the PMO strategy document, I went about gathering and building basic tools to help the various project teams get started. I also purchased and installed an out-of-the-box project management toolkit. This PMO practices center, as we call it internally, consists of a collection of information housed on an intranet site. It is available

IFMA's PMO vision	IFMA's PMO mission
To empower and position the entire IFMA organization to effectively cater to the ever-demanding and changing needs of the facility management profession.	To act as a facilitating entity that is focused on integrating project management practices within IFMA's business units to enable them to establish and grow value over time.

IFMA's PMO Guiding Principles

The following guiding principles should enable IFMA's PMO to carry out its mission while being guided by its vision:

- Service: IFMA's PMO is dedicated to serve the needs of its customers (all IFMA stakeholders) and its success relies on the success of its customers.

- Effectiveness: IFMA's PMO processes and methodology shall enable effectiveness by being global, lean, nimble, transparent, flexible, supportive and based on recognized standards.

- Flexibility: IFMA's PMO will strive to find the right balance between flexibility and structure to guide and enable IFMA's project managers to achieve successful project results.

Figure S8.2   PMO strategic guidelines

to all staff in order for them to become familiar with standard project management methodologies and process steps—providing access to tools, templates, and reporting dashboards. Instead of reinventing the process for each new project effort, this PMO practices center provides an unbiased road map depending on the type and complexity of the project and allows teams to solely focus on executing the process. It also helps establish a common project management language among staff and acts as a PMO reporting tool for all project stakeholders. A following step is to evaluate the different project portfolio management tools available on the market and determine which one best suits IFMA's PMO.

PMO Success

Despite being in its most basic project management maturity level, IFMA's PMO has made a number of strides in advancing the organization toward a project management culture. Since its inception, I have been providing a series of presentations and training sessions that contributed to an increased level of project management knowledge and skills among staff. Many, especially the team members from the three main projects being run by the PMO, have become very familiar with the terminology, processes, and documentation required to ensure project accountability. I will continue to provide training sessions intended to explore the five basic process groups of any project, what they entail, as well as the different skill sets required to excel at each of them. As the priority projects identified in the strategy document unfold, the PMO will conduct another round of the executive team's challenge assessments to identify the next priorities to be undertaken. And last but not least, as the PMO reaches a new level of maturity, the information contained in the strategy document will evolve and the changes will be recorded as part of the change management process that the PMO will be guiding.

Concluding Thoughts and Advice

At times, one might think that a project management culture could stifle innovation; however, IFMA's PMO guiding principles of service, effectiveness, and flexibility look at achieving just the opposite. In an environment where everyone feels valued by the specific talents they bring to the table and empowered to make decisions based on their roles and areas of expertise, the opportunities for creativity to thrive are endless. When passion and commitment are constant, it becomes habit to regularly think about ways to delight members and customers. That's the type of culture we want to nourish at IFMA.

PMO Success Story #9: A Global 10 Company and the Consolidated PMO

Board of Director Level Project Management

Richard Eichen, Return on Efficiency, LLC

Introduction to the Company

This is a story about a large, Global 10 U.S.-headquartered company, consisting of over 4,000 legal entities grouped into five operating subsidiaries, each with its own country-specific financial structure, reflecting local reporting and regulations. Across all operating units, this company had over 50,000 employees, located throughout the United States and in 86 locations around the world.

As a leading member of the financial services industry, risk, compliance, and accuracy of reporting were all essential. This had to be balanced with the corporate culture of appearing to be a *local* company at each location, rather than the local outpost of a global firm. With such a high level of decentralization, it was mainly at the enterprise risk, cash management, and financial/statutory reporting levels where an enterprise view occurred.

Business Problems to Be Addressed by the PMO

The outside auditors identified a series of material weaknesses regarding the corporate consolidation and quarterly close process individually and collectively contributing to issuing financial statements late, to the point where additional delays could become an issue with the SEC. Both the number and severity of the weaknesses required a Board-supervised remediation program. Due to the highly independent operating cultures of each operating subsidiary, manifested in dissimilar accounting and consolidation software applications, finding a source of compromise within the Board's (and auditor's) time frame was politically charged and geographically difficult.

Typical of global companies with distributed responsibility, each subsidiary had its own enterprise PMO (EPMO), loosely adhering to a corporate standard. Due to a lack of common definitions for key project terms and gates/thresholds, it was impossible, for managerial purposes, to consolidate key project plans across these operating units into an enterprise view. In fact, a corporate-level EPMO did not exist, so even if they had tried to show the enterprise view, a central function, or capability, did not exist.

Our Story

There was no choice but to address and remediate the material weaknesses, providing constant input to the Board's Audit Committee as the highest global priority. It was decided that rather than take the considerable time and political capital to roll out a powerful standards-issuing EMPO, a lighter version would be introduced solely for the remediation initiative. If, based on success, this office would be formalized, that battle could be fought when everyone had more breathing room.

The Consolidated PMO (CPMO) was crafted as a reporting and conflict resolution focused entity, issuing normalized and standardized progress updates per identified material weakness. To stress its importance, the CPMO reported directly to the Board's Audit Committee. Each subsidiary EPMO was required to create a local project with the standard title of *Finance Transformation* focused on their role in each/any material weakness, the responsible person being the EPMO lead in each case. The organizational governance model is illustrated in Figure S9.1.

As is evident in the organizational governance model, conflict resolution was a key requirement of the CPMO, as previous experience in the rollout of global systems had been complicated by local differences in resourcing, expertise, timing, and will.

To ensure results and key definitions were comparable across all EPMOs involved in this initiative, certain key definitions were imposed, replacing any local definitions for consolidated reporting purposes. Each local EPMO would have to report according to these definitions; however, they could continue to run their individual initiative execution per their local standards. The goal was to minimize retraining and other local delays, in addition to consistency. Key standardized definitions included:

♦ High-risk project: On the critical path to material weakness remediation; precursor project to later activities/projects.

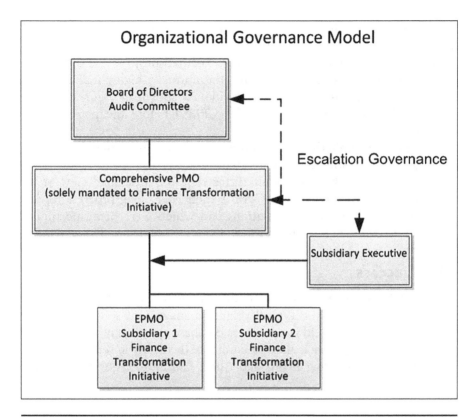

Figure S9.1 Organizational governance model

- ◆ Milestone: A gate where no further reworking is required as part of the handoff.
- ◆ Completed: The local executing party signals they have finished adding further time, resources, or activity to a project or subproject.
- ◆ Accepted: The recipient has attested to the accuracy, relevance, and completeness of the handed-off materials or results achieved. Only the CPMO could confer *accepted* status on a body of work.

High-risk projects had a mandatory pause built into the first deliverable stream so the team, the in-country/local EPMO as well as the CPMO could jointly access if the project was correctly staffed, resourced, and scheduled. Previously unidentified issues and roadblocks were also addressed at this time. These higher risk projects were labeled *P-Red* (for Priority-Red) and had increased visibility by the CPMO, often requiring weekly conference or video calls. Each P-Red project was assigned to a specific CPMO leader for continuity and visibility. Lower risk projects had a gate inserted at each project's midpoint for similar purposes.

The CPMO required that all locally executed projects use the following structure as a means to overcome the normally highly individualized nature of the various EMPOs worldwide. As shown in Figure S9.2, the template had to be approved by the CPMO before the project could commence.

Tracking was similarly highly focused on solely remediating the material weaknesses, as illustrated in Figure S9.3.

The Board and the Audit Committee required a detailed view of the overall status, provided by the CPMO, their goal being progress to date across over 100 parallel remediations and which were being postponed (and why), as shown in Figure S9.4.

PMO Success

The CPMO broke most of the traditional *rules* and best practices of a PMO or even an EPMO. Typical project management software was not used, with all details held in an Access database specifically developed for the CPMO. This approach allowed complete flexibility in reporting, brainstorming, and answering Board and Audit Committee questions. It also

---

Milestone
    Project Deliverables completely address ascribed role in larger initiative, completely achieve those objectives, and have been formally written into Project Mandate section of respective plan(s).

Objective
    Ensuring project outcomes address Corporate level initiatives by specifically linking to PwC or other identified needs. Written into Project Mandate so all understand the "why".

Measure
    Clear identification of specific initiatives, recommendations, weaknesses and how this project will address them.

Example
    Project XXX will achieve Project Charter and fulfill Business Case on mm/dd/yyyy by providing for faster closing of the books while providing walk-backs to the originating transactions.

Project	Phase	Milestone/measure

Figure S9.2 EPMO template

Local EPMO Project No. (sub ID-Weakness)	Project Name	Business Segment	Subsidiary Status							BoD Relevant Status	
			# Closed	Open - Severity Weight			Target Completion Date [2]	Self-Rated		BoD Dashboard Reference	Overall OPMO Rating
				High	Moderate	Low					
200-73030	Asset Management Follow-up Items	Asset Management	–	–	2	–	mm/dd/yyyy	Yellow		link	Yellow
221-73392	Legal/Reg/Compliance Follow-up Items	Legal	–	4	–	–	mm/dd/yyyy	Completed		link	Accepted

Figure S9.3   EPMO material weakness tracking

Line of Business	# BPRs	# Plans	Not Started	<----------- LOB Plans ----------->					<------- Steps ------->			<----- LOB Steps ----->		
				<---- In Process ---->				Com-	<--- % Complete --->			<--- Actual vs. Plan --->		
				Red	Yellow	Green	Total	pleted	LOB	IAD	IC	Plan	Actual	Variance
Corporate Compliance	126	54	49	1	1	1	3	2	0.9%	0.0%	0.9%	1.0%	0.9%	0.0%
Corporate Comptrollers	64						0							
Corporate Legal	10						0							
Enterprise Risk Managem	33						0							
Human Resources	9	3					0		0.7%	1.0%	0.1%	0.4%	0.7%	0.3%
Internal Audit Division	9	12	2				0	7	16.5%	0.0%	16.5%	16.7%	16.5%	-0.2%
Records Management	39						0							
Totals	290	69	51	1	1	1	3	9						

Figure S9.4   EPMO reporting

allowed the CPMO to be staffed by a set of senior business managers, reassigned from their operating responsibilities to this office.

Each remediation contained multiple components, from accounting policy to underlying system changes, but by having operational and functional managers running the CPMO, the focus was less on the *PMO process* and more on the results as they affected financial reporting.

Concluding Thoughts and Advice

Although initially each subsidiary had to self-diagnose its issues contributing to the remediations, it was quickly determined that a series of workshops would be required to understand, for the first time, the end-to-end financial period close process. Besides the expected outcomes in identifying roadblocks, systems issues, and process deficiencies, these workshops resulted in solutions spanning subsidiaries.

Execution became a complex matter. Given the overview mandate of the CPMO, executing on these recommendations had to be left to the individual subsidiaries, and a question arose regarding exactly who would execute any recommendations spanning more than a single subsidiary. After much debate at all leadership levels, it was decided not to build an internal consulting capability within the CPMO, as it would take too long and potentially complicate local cooperation.

If we had to do this again, we would require the CPMO to have a systems analyst, business analyst, and data architect capability as well as a permanent representative from the Corporate Controller's Office to ensure standardization across all remediations.

Early in the process we started to hear about who was going to fund these remediations, each subsidiary not wanting to increase its expenses. One battle where we went to the mat and won was having sufficient budget to fund all local initiatives. Had we not been allocated these funds, local subsidiaries would have had a valid reason to plan their local initiatives around future budget cycles, which was beyond our required timing.

At the end of this process, the CPMO was dismantled, as was the original intent. We felt this was highly beneficial since it highlighted the *crisis management* tone of the CPMO, giving it added internal (and necessary) political weight. As a side benefit, the subsidiaries did see the value of a corporate level EPMO, although they were reluctant to cede local autonomy in actual practice.

PMO Success Story #10: Dubai Roads & Transport Authority

From IT to All of It

Laila Faridoon, Director, Chairman's Office, Head of EPMO, Roads & Transport Authority

Introduction to Roads & Transport Authority

The Roads & Transport Authority (RTA) is a government organization responsible for the planning, design, construction, operation, and maintenance of the land and marine transportation networks in Dubai, United Arab Emirates. The organization was established in November 2005 as a specialized entity to concentrate on the challenge of planning and building a world-class transportation system for the city. RTA was established by amalgamating several departments and sections from three existing government organizations: Dubai Municipality (DM), Dubai Police, and Dubai Transport.

The government of Dubai is very progressive and the population of the city is forecasted to increase from 1.8 million in 2011 to around 3.3 million by 2020. Over the past few decades, Dubai has succeeded in developing its status as a major city, enhancing the well-being of its people and creating an environment that attracts business and individuals. RTA structure is based on the agency model, as shown in Figure S10.1; it has three sectors, six agencies, and one commercial agency. The authority is governed by a board of directors and each agency is managed by a CEO; the central headquarters of RTA is mainly responsible for planning, coordinating, and regulating activities, whereas the agencies are responsible for the implementation of the plans and all other operation activities.

Our Story

I joined RTA in May 2006 as the IT Performance Excellence Manager in the Information Technology Department (ITD). At that time, RTA was still

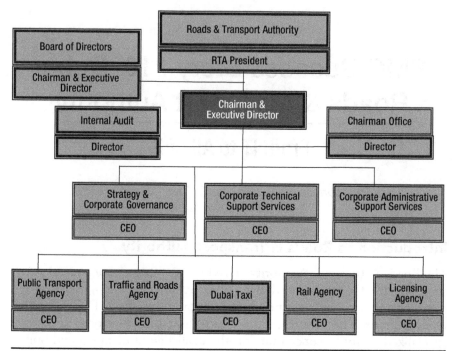

Figure S10.1   RTA organizational chart

using the IT infrastructure of DM. Even our e-mail addresses still carried the DM domain name. Major work was required to establish RTA's IT infrastructure and migrate all the legacy data and information. This actually translated into a large number of interrelated, overlapping projects that had to be completed in a short period of time. A total of 100 projects were running at the same time, varying from medium- to large-size projects. To ensure that these projects were managed effectively and efficiently, we established the ITD PMO. The ITD PMO developed policies, procedures, and templates for managing the IT projects. We also developed reporting systems and dashboards to track the status of all running projects. The ITD successfully completed 93 projects in the first five months and the remainder in the following five months, achieving all the established business objectives.

When I joined the Chairman's office in 2007, I realized that the project management issues on the RTA level are very similar to those in the ITD but only multiplied by a factor of at least 10! Some of the issues that I noticed were:

♦ Business projects are not linked to relevant strategic objectives
♦ No clear definition for portfolio of business projects
♦ Lack of projects integration or dependencies analysis across multiple agencies
♦ Projects are loosely coupled or being implemented as separate silos and duplication of work can be seen across the running projects
♦ Lack of formal coordination with stakeholders
♦ Nonexistence of enterprise program management standards; hence the organization is driven by its various vendors with different metrics, and therefore outputs and quality are not traced in the same accurate fashion
♦ Lack of consistent monitoring and control, risk assessment, and mitigation at corporate level
♦ Lack of rigorous assessments of business benefits realization
♦ Lack of consistent reporting methodologies and templates for project performance and progress

Based on my experience in the ITD, I knew that the solution was the establishment of a project or program management office on the enterprise level. So from that point on, I called the idea the *Enterprise Program Management Office* or EPMO.

The idea was welcomed by the Chairman; however, I was challenged by him to present it to all CEOs and get their buy-in, as this would help them in monitoring their projects. That wasn't an easy task considering the different business needs of each agency and management style of each CEO. To give an idea about the enormity of this task, I would like to mention that at that time there were over 170 projects running simultaneously in RTA. The total annual budget of these projects exceeded US$4.0 billion. These projects ranged from large multidisciplinary infrastructure projects such as the Dubai Metro to IT and business projects. Figure S10.2 shows the breakdown of the projects' budget into the different activities.

When I first introduced the idea to the CEOs in RTA, I was met with strong resistance and I could not convince them that the EPMO would provide a suitable solution to the existing project management issues. We continued using the existing reporting system with largely inconsistent templates and forms as they were coming from different agencies and departments and in some cases from contractors and vendors.

I did not give up as I felt that the Chairman was challenging me to test my abilities to identify and do what was important and not just what was popular. I enhanced my presentation by emphasizing the benefits of the EPMO for each individual agency and sector and tried again with each

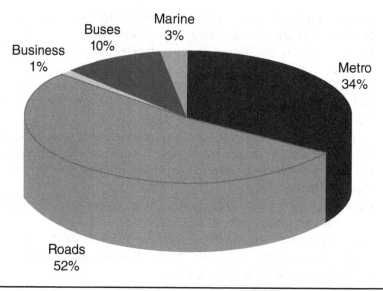

Figure S10.2   The breakdown of the projects' budget into the different activities

CEO. This time I was successful in persuading all of them of the impor-tance of the EPMO. Finally the EPMO was established as a section within the Chairman's office based on a decision of the RTA Board of Directors in 2007. The EPMO is primarily responsible to ensure selection, initiation, and execution of projects in line with RTA's strategic objectives and goals and provide a dashboard of projects' performance to top management. RTA also established satellite PMOs in the different agencies of the orga-nization that directly report to the relevant CEO. The different PMOs are reporting to the EPMO on a monthly basis according to the established reporting model.

The EPMO also developed project management policies to be used by all agencies and sectors across RTA. The policies had to be generic enough to suit the project management requirements of the varying projects im-plemented by the different agencies and sectors. It was left to each agency and sector to develop and implement their own project management methodologies in line with the overarching project management policy.

Several of the satellite PMOs were understaffed and in some cases they were not staffed at all. The EMPO faced delays in receiving the reports as well as resistance in implementing the policies. We held regular periodic meetings with the different personnel from the satellite PMOs to win them over and gain their trust. The main point that was emphasized was that the

EPMO was there to support rather than monitor and control them. The idea seemed to have worked because we ended up gaining the total trust of all satellite PMOs, resulting in the satisfaction of all major stakeholders. As can probably be understood, our major stakeholder was the Chairman. We developed reporting templates and dashboards to present the projects' progress and performance results on a monthly basis. Figure S10.3 shows one of the dashboards used in our monthly presentations.

PMO Success

To ensure long-term success and improvement, we developed a model for project management maturity in RTA. The model is based on the Project Management Maturity Model developed by Dr. Harold Kerzner as shown in Figure S10.4.

Moreover, we developed plans to raise the level of Project Management Maturity in RTA based on the model. Figure S10.5 shows the progress of maturity levels for the years 2008–2010.

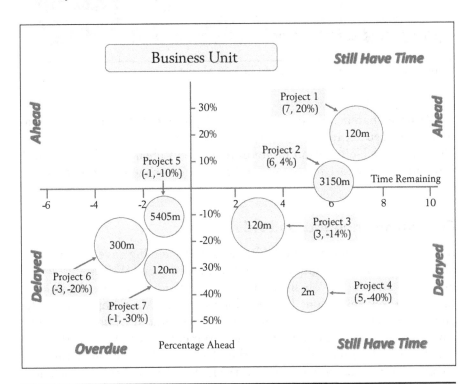

Figure S10.3 Sample of a dashboard used in monthly reporting to Chairman

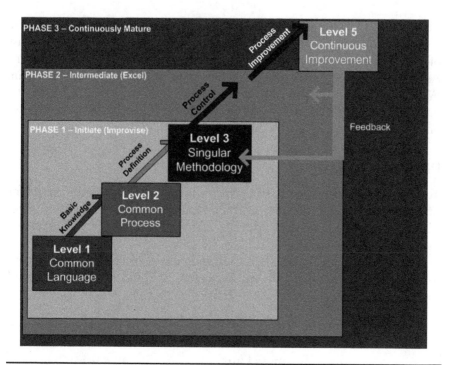

Figure S10.4   Project Management Maturity Model

We have shared our success story and presented it at many international conferences. In addition, many of the government organizations in Dubai and the United Arab Emirates requested to benchmark our EPMO. It became a showcase for project and program management offices in the region.

Concluding Thoughts and Advice

It was a challenge for me to establish an EPMO in a big government organization with all the complexity, political aspects, etc. With the practical implementation of the organizational project management model in RTA, there were several lessons learned along the way. Most importantly, the political aspects of the organization should be captured while building any governance model, especially in the government sector. Without the support I received from the Chairman, the EPMO would have failed; thus any PMO initiative must be sponsored at the highest levels of the organization. The implementation is better when phased in and should be very well

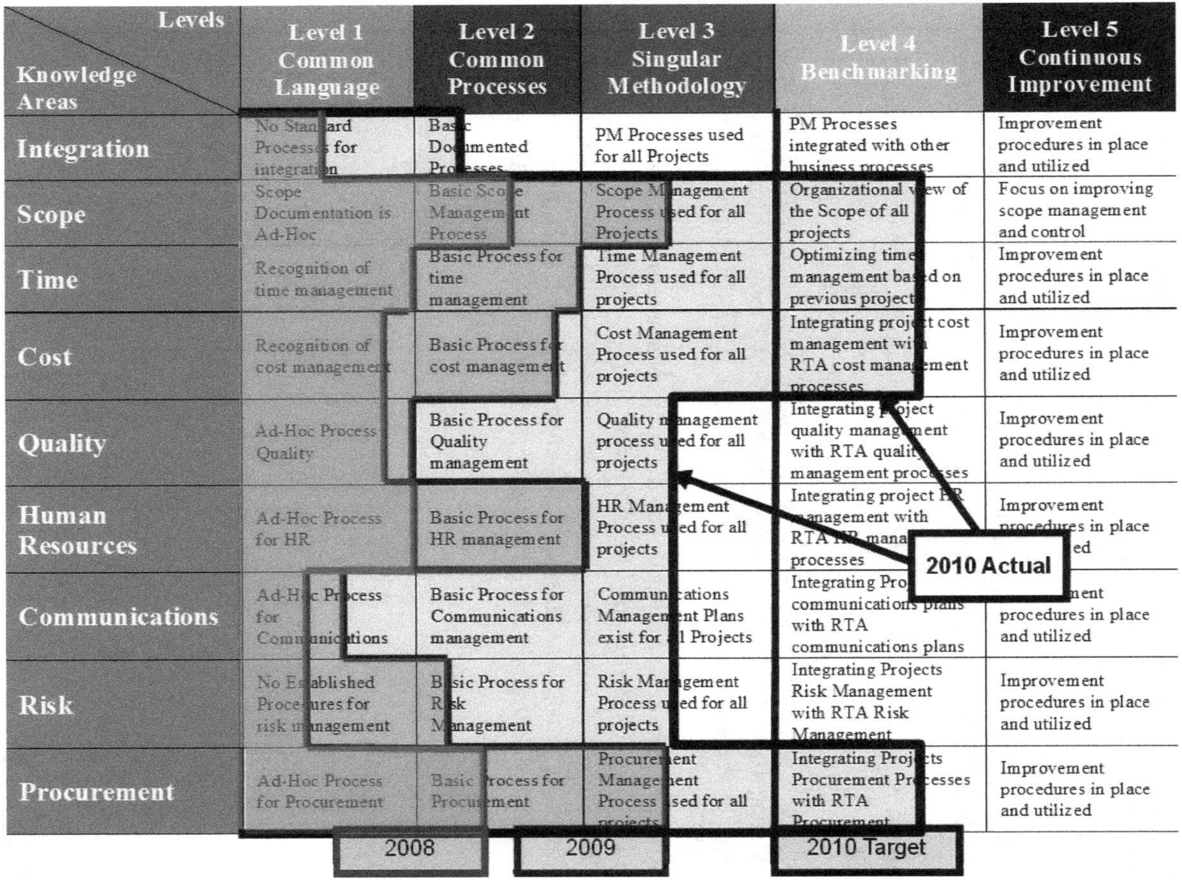

Levels / Knowledge Areas	Level 1 Common Language	Level 2 Common Processes	Level 3 Singular Methodology	Level 4 Benchmarking	Level 5 Continuous Improvement
Integration	No Standard Process for integration	Basic Documented Processes	PM Processes used for all Projects	PM Processes integrated with other business processes	Improvement procedures in place and utilized
Scope	Scope Documentation is Ad-Hoc	Basic Scope Management Process	Scope Management Process used for all Projects	Organizational view of the Scope of all projects	Focus on improving scope management and control
Time	Recognition of time management	Basic Process for time management	Time Management Process used for all projects	Optimizing time management based on previous projects	Improvement procedures in place and utilized
Cost	Recognition of cost management	Basic Process for cost management	Cost Management Process used for all projects	Integrating project cost management with RTA cost management processes	Improvement procedures in place and utilized
Quality	Ad-Hoc Process Quality	Basic Process for Quality management	Quality management process used for all projects	Integrating Project quality management with RTA quality management processes	Improvement procedures in place and utilized
Human Resources	Ad-Hoc Process for HR	Basic Process for HR management	HR Management Process used for all projects	Integrating project HR management with RTA HR management processes	Improvement procedures in place and utilized
Communications	Ad-Hoc Process for Communications	Basic Process for Communications management	Communications Management Plans exist for all Projects	Integrating Projects communications plans with RTA communications plans	Improvement procedures in place and utilized
Risk	No Established Procedures for risk management	Basic Process for Risk Management	Risk Management Process used for all projects	Integrating Projects Risk Management with RTA Risk Management	Improvement procedures in place and utilized
Procurement	Ad-Hoc Process for Procurement	Basic Process for Procurement	Procurement Management Process used for all projects	Integrating Projects Procurement Processes with RTA Procurement	Improvement procedures in place and utilized

2010 Actual

2010 Target

2009

2008

Figure S10.5   The progress of maturity levels for the years 2008–2010

planned with clear timelines, milestones, and targets. The initiative should be very well communicated, with frequent and clear messages of success to all stakeholders. Project management champions should be harvested in all organizational units to support the maturity efforts and to get the message across to other employees.

References

Faridoon, L. M. "Organizational Project Management Governance Model." 13th PMI-AGC International Conference, Bahrain, January 24–26, 2011.

Hamdy, K. A. "The Essential Role of Leadership in Managing Mega Projects: The Case of the Dubai Metro." In *Proceedings of the PMI North America Global Congress*, Washington, DC, October 9–12, 2010.

Hamdy, K. A. and L. M. Faridoon. "Establishing an Enterprise Program Management Office in a Large Government Organization." In *Proceedings of the 4th World Project Management Week*, Singapore, November 2007.

Hamdy, K. A. and L. M. Faridoon. "Program Management Office Maturity in a Large Government Organization." In *Proceedings of the 8th Australian Project Management Conference PMOZ8*, Melbourne, August 2008.

Kerzner, H. *Project Management: A Systems Approach to Planning, Scheduling, and Controlling.* 8th ed. New York: JohWiley & Sons, 2007, p. 891.

PMO Success Story #11: Baker Hughes Incorporated

The PMO Journey

Ricardo Ferrero, Region IT Director, and Kathie Mitchell, Process Improvement Manager, Region IT Baker Hughes Incorporated

Introduction to Baker Hughes Incorporated

The Baker Hughes story begins on April 4, 1895, when a 22-year-old man named Reuben Carlton (Carl) Baker arrived in Los Angeles with a brand new suit, confidence, a heart full of hope, and 95 cents in his pocket. Baker built a business that had revenues of US$92 million and employed 327 employees in 1941. By 1959, Baker Transworld was created and had 50 branches in 16 states of America. The company grew internationally and continued to grow through acquisitions, innovation, and business development. Baker Hughes Incorporated was formed in 1987 with the merger of Baker International and Hughes Tool Company—both founded over 100 years ago when R. C. Baker and Howard Hughes conceived groundbreaking inventions that revolutionized the fledging petroleum era. For more than a century, innovation has been part of our DNA.

In 2009, Baker Hughes Incorporated initiated its internal reorganization change initiative, called ONE Baker Hughes. It moved from a portfolio-managed product line organization with centralized leadership to a geomarket organization with 9 regional presidents and 19 geomarket managing directors servicing all the major markets. In 2010, Baker Hughes acquired BJ Services, bringing its employee count to approximately 58,000 and $19.8 billion in revenue, with facilities in 80 countries. Serving operations in more than 100 countries, Baker Hughes delivers solutions that help oil and gas operators make the most of their reservoirs. The company's history of technology innovation is a cornerstone of its success.

Business Problems to Be Addressed by the PMO

Prior to the internal reorganizational change initiative in 2009, the company structure consisted of six product lines under the parent company with multiple product lines and multiple IT departments, resulting in duplicated efforts across the globe. Moving to a ONE Baker Hughes organization also saw the move to a ONE Baker Hughes IT as well and the onboarding of a new IT CIO to support the change to a geographical focus with global IT support.

Changes resulted in challenges for the IT regions, such as the ability to find ways to support a very large number of end users with a limited team while, more importantly, delivering value to the business units to gain or maintain a competitive advantage. The introduction by the new IT CIO of the IT Big Rules set the framework for aligning IT supporting functions with each other and for the focus to be more on process improvement and program management.

To enable the IT organization to meet its objectives, launching a global portfolio management office and a PMO Center of Excellence initiative was a critical step toward consistency and efficiency. The completion of an internal IT PMO and project portfolio management (PPM) practice assessment across all IT functions was the first priority to identify areas for improvement. What were we doing right? Where could we improve? What was the plan to address the internal business problems? What were the quick wins? What was urgent? The outcome of the initial assessment provided the direction on what needed to be addressed and also identify the top priorities.

Although there were multiple PMOs within IT, each operated as a separate entity with different maturity levels, processes, tools, and templates. One of the first challenges was to work toward alignment consistency and common practice standardization. However, there were many immediate issues to take care of and it was important to build the house in the right order. Improvements in efficiency and effectiveness were accomplished by improving communication frameworks, standard processes, portfolio integrity, and building trust with our customers.

There were a number of workable business challenges to address. First, we needed to gain an understanding of the complex IT structure, learn how to manage projects and programs, and create a consolidated matrix region IT PMO virtual team to be the front end for both the customer and the remainder of the IT organization. We also needed to consider institutionalizing PPM tools (CA Clarity™ PPM) and their processes and structure; developing a stage gate process to better interface with the rest of the IT organization and teams; managing demand by implementing a work intake process; scoring models to build the relationship and level of communication; and building the required trust to support the business and the different IT teams, as shown in Figure S11.1.

Of course, important to our customers was the delivery of cadence; therefore, improved visibility was critical. Other important factors were to define the global IT PMO process, ensuring compliance with the IT Big Rules, and a global PMO team to agree on budget capacity impact throughout new project review processes. Additionally, there was a requirement to launch a new PMO Council with senior members from the other main IT functions and teams who would make the right decisions for both the portfolio and project management offices using the Center of Excellence as a model of reference. The PMO Council institutionalization and consensus on key decisions and direction presented a major challenge.

All these efforts should have been relatively simple to implement given that Baker Hughes is not adverse to change as an organization. Our century-long history bears testimony to this; however, the footprint from the former decentralized IT organization still existed.

Business had been impacted as a result of not having formal PMO and PPM organizations because information had not always been as reliable or

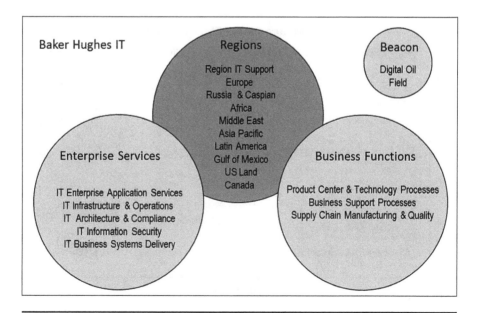

Figure S11.1   Baker Hughes IT

even available to communicate back to the key stakeholders, even while doing the project groundwork in a very effective manner and supporting our customers very efficiently. There was evidence of project delivery delays across the enterprise. No initiative had been taken to incorporate an advanced business driven PMO organization, which would result in focusing on transparency, control, consistency, portfolio integrity, lessons learned, reusability, resource management, forecasting, and cadence planning to manage capacity, delivery, and absorption.

In response to the IT CIO's request, we drafted a three-year plan on the basis of a maturity improvement model as shown in Figure S11.2, moving from reactive to proactive and toward business value creation.

The most important challenges were to define and implement common processes and methodologies to be able to reach a certain level of standardization and cost control. Was this to be the greatest opportunity for change and improvement or just the greatest challenge of all?

Our Story

From the very beginning, we were clear that any efforts should have a direct positive impact on the business value creation. "Do the right things for the long term" was our motto. Figure S11.3 shows the details of the

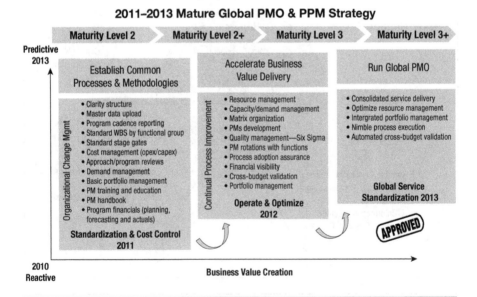

Figure S11.2   Three-year maturity improvement plan

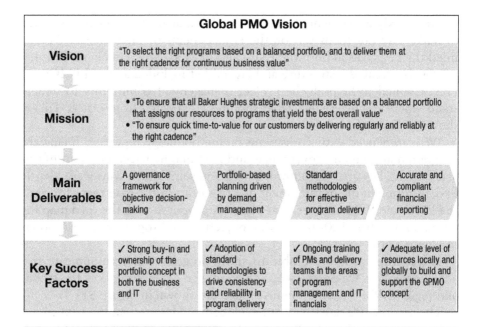

Figure S11.3   Global PMO vision

mission, vision, main deliverables, and key success factors that were developed to begin the process. The key point was to create and develop a clear road map that would provide the direction and improve the understanding about the enormity of this particular challenge.

Just as important as developing that road map was the monitoring and measurement of our performance along the way. We asked ourselves: How did we do? What went well? What went wrong? What lessons were learned? Typically, we asked all the questions about program management practices that should be applied to one's own vision and road map.

First and foremost, the key message was to ensure that we created value. The main key drivers included, first, to understand that there are no IT projects, only business projects. We work to support the business and it is important to listen to the business needs.

We recognized that we could not be driven by key performance indicators (KPIs), but instead must be driven by the value we created, and that KPIs should be used only as an indicator of whether or not we were on track. The objective was to move from just efficiency to effectiveness as well, while focusing on the few major issues that would indicate progress and to then communicate outcomes.

We quickly implemented a business value management process in order to make sure our focus was on the key elements of the business. We defined the key goals in both the PMO and PPM as shown in Figure S11.4.

We also created a structure and layers that included a global PMO and PPM Council to help all the project management community to understand where they were and what should be expected from others. This is shown in Figure S11.5.

We commenced with assessments on methodology, reporting, financials, program management, governance, and portfolio management. Out of the assessments, key areas for improvement and some quick wins were identified, resulting in the development of a first draft of the road maps for both the PMO and PPM. A three-year plan was proposed with the road map focusing on the first 100-day specific objectives and top priorities as shown in Figure S11.6.

It was important to be able to show progress and communicate the achievements as we progressed. The combined achievements of the global and regional PMO during the first phase are shown in Figure S11.7.

The second 100-day goal was developed and focused on the next phase of the key deliverables. It was critical to identify the top five things to work on. As shown in Figure S11.8, these were then developed into micro-strategies with each initiative translating into IT and business benefits, which became the business driven story.

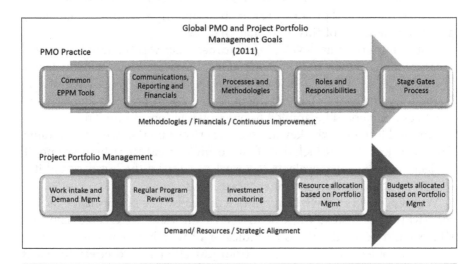

Figure S11.4   PMO and PPM goals

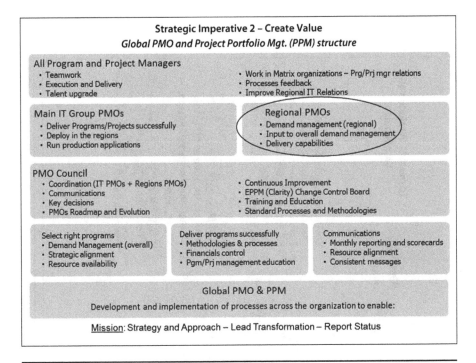

Figure S11.5   Strategic imperative

Clarity was the PPM system of choice; therefore great strides were made by each functional group to ensure programs and projects were structured in the same way to ensure consistency across the enterprise. Goals were defined for the Clarity team to ensure the PPM tool would be totally in sync with our tactical plan. A great deal of effort was devoted to defining and producing project cadence dashboards to provide clear visibility of program and project status for the business. Demand management and portfolio investment planning was another key area for development, as well as the implementation of a project manager development plan to provide additional training and development for project managers. Things were progressing, although somewhat slowly; we had a clear road map, a three-year maturity plan, senior-level support to drive the initiatives, and details were aligned, but we still hadn't reached our goal. It was important to stop and identify the problem areas.

The purpose of the project was to bring people and departments together, break down the silos, and work toward standardization and consistency. Moving forward, we needed to understand that when launching anything

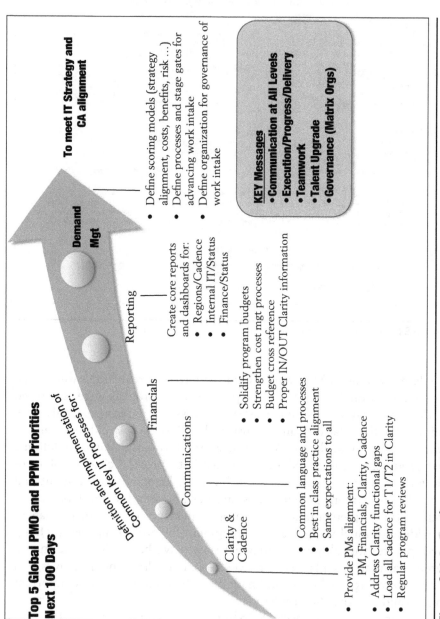

**Top 5 Global PMO and PPM Priorities
Next 100 Days**

Definition and Implementation of
Common Key IT Processes

To meet IT Strategy and
CA alignment

Demand Mgt
- Define scoring models (strategy alignment, costs, benefits, risk ...)
- Define processes and stage gates for advancing work intake
- Define organization for governance of work intake

Reporting
Create core reports and dashboards for:
- Regions/Cadence
- Internal IT/Status
- Finance/Status

Financials
- Solidify program budgets
- Strengthen cost mgt processes
- Budget cross reference
- Proper IN/OUT Clarity information

Communications
- Common language and processes
- Best in class practice alignment
- Same expectations to all

Clarity & Cadence
- Provide PMs alignment:
  PM, Financials, Clarity, Cadence
- Address Clarity functional gaps
- Load all cadence for T1/T2 in Clarity
- Regular program reviews

KEY Messages
- **Communication at All Levels**
- **Execution/Progress/Delivery**
- **Teamwork**
- **Talent Upgrade**
- **Governance (Matrix Orgs)**

Figure S11.6   Top five priorities

Q1 Achievements (detail)

Global PMO	Region PMO

• Activate PMO Council
  -Regular meetings
  -Common goals – global PMO cadence
  -Actions/minutes/agreements
  -PMO Council working/decisions/processes
• PMO/PPM assessments
• Longer term plan in place:
  -Vision/Mission/Strategy
  -Deliverables per quarter
• Top 5 priorities defined/agreed/some met
• Global PMO communications
• Clarity team quick wins
  -Regular weekly meetings, improvements
  -Regional cadence reports and dashboards
• PM alignment phase 1 completed
• Clarity structure around Prg/M.Prjs./Prj agreed/communicated
• T1s/T2s in Clarity – cadence info available and ready to report
• Key PMs and management liaison and feedback
	• Regional PMOs team set up
	• Regional PMO Council set up
	• Regular meetings
	• Team charter
	• Common goals: teamwork
	• Knowledge and best practice sharing
	• Regional cadence dashboards
	• Regional presidents reports
	• Regional monthly scorecards
	• Clarity education to regional ITs
	• Top 7 Regional Priorities defined
	• Regional processes definition
	• Clarity training usage delivered
	• Clarity capabilities training scheduled
	• Regional representation in PMO Council
	• Participation of regions on PDLC and gates process
	• First stages of demand mgmt definition
	• Consultancy – PMO and demand management

Figure S11.7   Global and regional PMO achievements

new, it takes time to implement change, especially when the legacy of the multi-silo culture from the past is factored in. This was a three-year project and, again, a further change for the organization and for the employees. We were setting up a global IT PMO foundation for the entire IT organization of nearly 1,000 people within a company that employs 58,000 people, but with a very small team to define and execute the deliverables.

With the complex matrix organization structure in place, there was no urgency for many to focus on these key deliverables because they had their own departmental goals and objectives to achieve; so, how could we continue to move forward to achieve these objectives and deliver the value to the business that had been agreed on?

The decision was made to move the global PMO team and the PMO Council into a larger Operational Excellence Center of Excellence with smaller teams to implement the changes required. This meant a further transition from a large nine-member PMO Council to a three-member council, with the key PMO subject matter experts becoming part of a larger Enterprise PMO Council charged with focusing on completing the key road map deliverables for year 1 that were missing. Additionally, the message was understood and there was further commitment at a higher

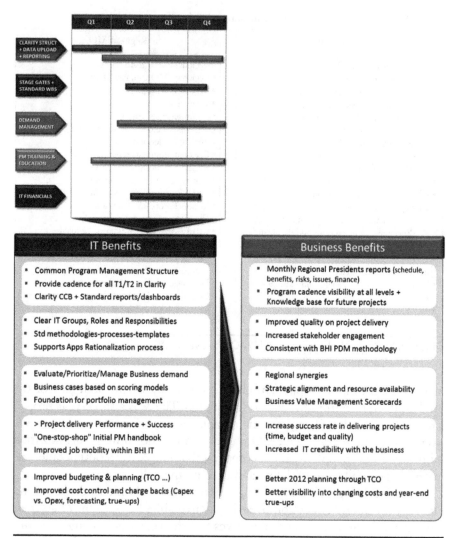

Figure S11.8   Business benefits

level in the organization to unify the IT PMO efforts in combination with other enterprise PMO efforts in order to enhance the significance and to make the business units successful as a whole.

PMO Success

There were a number of significant achievements resulting from the efforts of a small team. A virtual Region IT PMO team had been created worldwide with team members from the United States, Canada, Latin America, the Middle East, Asia, and Europe, all working together to achieve the same goals. The foundation had been clearly defined through the three-year plan and road maps, PMO goals were in place, and there was evidence of the benefits to both IT and the business (as referenced in Figure S11.8).

Great progress had been made at the Region IT level to define a process for demand management and prioritization, taking the business needs into account. A successful pilot of a business value management concept had been completed, and we now had business dashboards to show the move from *cost* to *investment*. All this took months of preparation, weekly communications through virtual team calls and meetings to continually focus on the initial objectives. To be able to achieve and be successful with just one initiative was indeed a milestone, and we are extremely proud of what was achieved in a short time, given the many challenges faced along the way.

Concluding Thoughts and Advice

With any project, there will always be hurdles. There will always be varied opinions and some form of resistance to change, but the important thing is that no matter how hard it may seem, never give up. If you have your road map and your plans communicated correctly, the appropriate thing to do is whatever the right thing is for the long term. Focus on the long-term vision that you have set up and continue to work in that direction every day. Overall, as you go through these major projects, as with any project, it is important to show progress and to communicate.

Overall, we believe that our biggest success is that we have left a footprint and the idea that the PMOs need to be business driven, focusing on creating value and on collaboration. The introduction of demand management and business value management was a great basic solid foundation to ensure that we worked on business projects and not on IT projects. History, if not written, is forgotten, so just as Reuben Carlton (Carl) Baker's journey started, we close this chapter in the same spirit—confident and with hearts full of hope, knowing that the journey and the story will continue because of the foundation we laid for others to follow.

PMO Success Story #12: Tryg

Establishing Business Governance

Ole F. Holleufer, Head of PMO, Tryg

Introduction to Tryg

Tryg is the second largest general insurer in the Nordic region, present in Denmark, Norway, Sweden, and Finland. It is listed on Nasdaq OMX Copenhagen. Tryg wants to be perceived as the leading peace-of-mind provider in the Nordic region, dedicated to providing peace of mind to our more than 2.7 million private customers and more than 140,000 businesses on a daily basis.

Tryg was formed through a merger between two of the largest Danish insurance companies in 1995, acquired the third largest general insurance company in Norway in 1999, and has established branches in both Finland and Sweden. From 1999 to 2002, Tryg was part of Nordea Banking Group, but became a pure nonlife insurance company in 2002. The company was listed on the stock exchange in 2005.

Business Problems to Be Addressed by the PMO

When Tryg was listed on the stock exchange in 2005 and the division from the Nordea Banking Group was final, the company was destined to follow a common path. The aim was to gather the different parts of the company as one entity to benefit fully from the investments made in Norway and Finland (Swedish branch established in 2006) and create a common Nordic insurance company to realize the synergies. One of the means to realize this potential was to establish joint cross-country staffs, including the IT department, and lay the tracks to develop common Nordic insurance processes driven by the business directors.

Our Story

The Tryg PMO was established in early 2005 as an IT PMO, as an element in fulfilling the IT strategy. The primary goal was to make it possible

217

to monitor a unified development resource pool and to track the performance and alignment of projects with the company strategy and goals in order to better optimize the use of the development pool by 10–15%.

Our starting point was to make sure that common project management and reporting processes were established and implemented. In doing so, we worked closely together with our methods department. In this way new project management standards were formed and implemented. We also developed a new portfolio management process. The new reporting tools reflected the mind-set of the business: projections for cost, benefit, and delivery dates as the foundations of the portfolio decisions and reporting focusing on deviations from these.

Aligning different mind-sets to the new standards was quite a challenge, but it definitely made sense, especially to governance bodies and project managers, when transparency was established and interdependencies between the projects were clarified.

The second phase of our journey was to establish business-owned process development and along with this business-owned prioritization bodies. The idea was to make the business directors responsible for the process development, making the head of the claims department head of process development for the claims process and so on for sales, underwriting, IT, and staff processes. At the same time, these process owners would form the Prioritization Forum, headed by the COO. The Process Owners Forum would be in charge of prioritization of the pool of development projects and as well the key coordinator of the business process developments.

We did not really succeed in this part for the new development projects. Monitoring and reporting the project portfolio went quite well, but the business development process did not. At the same time, the process owners felt that a lot of time was wasted on meetings without real impact, and they felt that a number of parallel prioritization and government processes were taking place. They had a point! In fact, almost all our development resources were occupied by executive management in the master plan and very few resources were deployed to support the work with process development.

Following a number of organizational changes, we changed the focus of the PMO as shown in Figure S12.1. We increased our focus on how to present the information to our prioritization boards in a simple and to-the-point manner and increased the support to the project managers, ensuring that their financial reporting was fully accurate, as well as closely monitored the development resource pool by the PMO. At the same time, more resources were dedicated to support the preparation of new projects, and

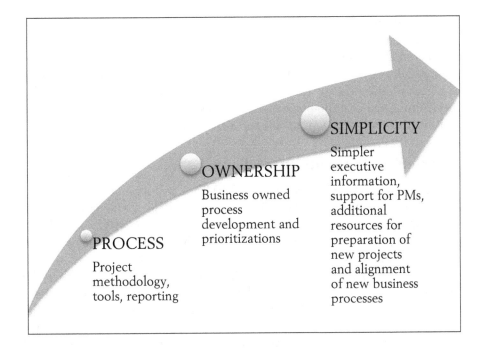

Figure S12.1 Evolution of PMO focus

the alignment of the business processes was supported in a better manner as well. At the same time, a new concept of specific benefit commitments for lines of business was introduced, demanding a precise benefit impact on future years' budgets for new proposed projects.

PMO Success

The success of our PMO was due to the fact that we have tried to understand the position of the decision makers. We tried to make our presentations as clear and simple as possible and tried to obtain the full portfolio overview including strategy, financial statements, budget impact, and the resource pool.

At the same time, we increased our close coperation with the project managers and made an effort to support them in the best way possible. We have taken over the resource allocation process in close dialogue with the line managers, making all resource requests part of the reporting process. Further, all new project initiatives are prepared more thoroughly and quality assured, including the impact on scarce resources and interdependencies with ongoing projects.

This makes the basis for decisions quite consistent by taking all major factors into account and at the same time demonstrating possible consequences of the prioritization choices. The governance structure has also been simplified and the business executives are now a genuine part of the prioritization process; we try to keep a close dialogue with them as well.

Concluding Thoughts and Advice

I believe that the basis of a successful PMO is to be perceived as a valuable tool for decisions makers. This means that the PMO is dependent on creating report and prioritization foundations characterized by high-quality output. It is likewise paramount that the foundations are perceived as meaningful tools to the business. The output must be very easy to comprehend, highlighting the prioritization dilemmas in a clear way. If the decision makers feel confident in both the reports and overall portfolio views regarding strategy alignment—long- and short-term goals, financial figures, budget alignment, and resource or competence dependencies, they will feel confident in the foundations of the basis of their decisions and appreciate the PMO.

Therefore, the prime concern of a PMO should be to ensure that business needs are understood. From here, the whole chain of portfolio and project management must be established and—very important—trust and cooperation between project managers and middle management must be established. Close ties to the financial department and lines of business are likewise crucial to success.

Finally, it is vital that the PMO has the full attention and support of management. Thus, a number of parallel procedures can be avoided and the information from the PMO will not be challenged in order to promote alternative agendas.

This is quite a job to accomplish—good luck!

PMO Success Story #13:
A Nigerian Telecoms Company

PMO Benefits

Henry Kazalma-Mantey, Head of Projects & PMO, Suburban Group

Introduction to the Company

This PMO success story is about a large telecommunications company in Nigeria. It was founded over 10 years ago and it caters to the retail, enterprise, and wholesale markets. The company's range of products includes IP backbone services, enterprise solutions, and colocation services. The customers of this company span across Nigeria and other parts of Africa and Europe.

Business Problems to Be Addressed by the PMO

Let me begin with a little history. The company didn't have a PMO before I joined, and there was little or no control over the projects being executed. This caused various problems: inadequate project scoping and budgeting, no proper internal and external reporting structure, and no department or unit looking at the overall company strategic objectives and linking them to projects that would help accomplish the objectives. Also, some projects were being executed without all the stakeholders within the company being aware the projects had actually commenced. All these factors led to duplication and poor execution of projects by various departments, amounting to huge wastages of company resources running into hundreds of millions of naira (i.e., Nigerian currency).

The company realized that if this was to go on for another year, it would be out of business. My first task upon joining the company was to do an audit of all the projects executed to date. I gathered as much information as I could find on all the projects and broke them down into different categories: value, relevance, and cost.

I looked at 15 projects that were executed and focused on the top 10 in order of relevance and the total project cost. The projects analyzed are anonymously depicted in Figure S13.1.

Number	Project Name	Project Cost (Naira)	Successful?
1	Project Alpha	>15,000,000.00	No
2	Project Bravo	>32,000,000.00	No
3	Project Charlie	>230,000,000.00	No
4	Project Delta	>450,000,000.00	Yes
5	Project Echo	>80,000,000.00	No
6	Project Foxtrot	>60,000,000.00	No
7	Project Golf	>4,000,000.00	Yes
8	Project Hotel	>120,000,000.00	Yes
9	Project India	>45,000,000.00	Yes
10	Project Juliet	>110,000,000.00	Yes

Figure S13.1   Project analysis

We can see that out of 10 projects that were executed, 50% were successful. When you consider the huge resources expended to deliver these projects and the loss of projected revenue from the projects that failed, a success rate of 50% was totally unacceptable. I will not go into details of what happened after a report on the findings was published, but suffice it to say that the need to quickly set up a unit that would help put an end to such wastage was even more glaring.

Our Story

Some of the questions you get asked a lot when setting up a PMO in an organization are: What is a PMO? What is its function? How is it going to help our company achieve its objectives? If I had a naira for every person who asked me these questions, I'd be a very wealthy man! Even though at the highest level in the organization I was told that the staff would cooperate, it was a totally different story when the actual work started. I met some form of resistance from every corner. Many of the staff just did not understand why things had to change.

Being new to the company, I had to rely on others to get the information I needed. My first instinct was to hire new staff for the PMO, but after I had a chat with all the project managers and officers in the organization, I realized that I could use most of them but they would have to buy into the new way projects would be delivered. Some of them easily saw the benefits and came on board, especially when I presented the data showing the delivery of projects over the years. The rest of the staff was not that easy to win over. I remember when I had a meeting with members of staff from various departments and I informed them that they would need to start sending daily, weekly, and quarterly project reports on a regular basis. The staff grudgingly agreed but it never happened. It became a daily battle getting staff to do their reports, send out e-mails to stakeholders, and calling for and attending meetings when due. Many people just felt that they were being given additional tasks and responsibilities that would have little or no effect, so why not go back to the *old system* that worked just fine for them? They didn't realize that the *old system* was going to run the company bankrupt.

PMO Success

What factors would you use to determine if a PMO was a success? In my opinion, a PMO is successful if it can adequately show that the company's strategic objectives are being met, projects are delivered on time, costs are reduced to a minimum, and the quality of the deliverables is of the highest standards. It is also important to note whether the stakeholders, especially the financiers and the clients, are happy. This will lead to more business for the company and, hopefully, more profits.

The first hurdle we had to overcome was getting the staff to accept the new measures we had to put in place to make the company move forward and to position it to take its rightful place as one of the best and most innovative telecom companies in Nigeria. We were about to embark on a very expensive expansion program that would involve the delivery of a lot of projects and the launch of various cutting-edge products. If executed properly, it would definitely propel the company to be one of the top three players in the telecom sector in the next two years. We couldn't afford any slipups. I believe one of the most important measures we took was to get the buy-in of most of the staff, especially those who worked on projects. It became clear that many people just didn't believe in what they were doing and were not inclined to do their best. People needed to understand the reason why the company had made the decisions to move in a particular direction and the benefits that would come to the company and to them.

By the time we had embarked on countless sensitization sessions with various units, things began to fall into place quite quickly. In fact, we had many people in the company pleading to be part of the PMO. What a turnaround! Members of staff now believed that they each had an important role to play, so they went about their tasks with a new vigor. Each project manager and officer received extensive training to prepare them for the tasks ahead. All this made tracking and monitoring of each project a whole lot easier. Projects were initiated properly, tasks were completed, status reports prepared and sent on time, deadlines were met, and deliverables were delivered when due. There were many project-related risks we encountered along the way, but we were able to mitigate these risks in a timely fashion as they were identified in time and appropriate measures were taken.

By the end of that year, we had successfully delivered some of the biggest projects the company had ever embarked on. The company went on to become the largest provider of IP services in Nigeria, with customers in the wholesale, enterprise, and retail markets.

Concluding Thoughts and Advice

About five to seven years ago in Nigeria, the term PMO was very rare. It was a concept that was quite new, only common in engineering-related industries. Today that has changed. The organizations that have PMOs cut across different sectors. I think the trickiest part of selling the concept of a PMO to any organization lies in how well you can demonstrate the value it brings to the organization. Can a PMO really help drive the business goals? Can it really help the business grow?

The Nigerian government in recent years has embarked on several projects that have clearly not met their objectives, and the citizens have demanded better accountability. Many have said that what the Nigerian government needs to do is establish PMOs in all the ministries and agencies that would oversee the execution of all key capital projects. This would surely help to ensure that the deliverables are met on time with the highest quality and also keep the cost to the barest minimum. Will this be done? Only time will tell. I, for one, will definitely push for it.

PMO Success Story #14: Tyco Flow Control

A Tale of the 3 Ps

Wai Mun Koo, Global PMO Manager, Tyco Flow Control

Introduction to Tyco Flow Control

Tyco Flow Control (TFC) is a major business segment of Tyco International and a leading global supplier of flow management, water and environmental systems, and thermal control solutions through three main lines of business: Valves and Controls, Water and Environmental Systems, and Thermal Controls. The range of products that it carries includes valves, actuators, controls, pipes, fittings, emissions and water quality monitors, and heat tracing and de-icing systems.

TFC is a world leader in the industry, with over 15,000 employees in 100 offices, located in 24 countries worldwide, and approximated annual revenue of $4 billion. It has a strong global presence supplying critical products and services to vital industries including oil and gas, mining, chemicals, marine, power, waterworks, and commercial and residential building. To solve challenges in the most critical environments, TFC partners with customers to keep their operations running safely, minimize downtime, and enhance life cycle performance. Through its portfolio of trusted brands that includes Crosby, Raychem, Erhard, and more, TFC is committed to bring essential infrastructure to local communities around the globe to ensure a more sustainable future.

Business Problems to Be Addressed by the PMO

In order to serve and align better with its customers, a strategic decision was made in 2010 to have a corporate-wide reorganization of the business from a regionally operated to a vertically managed structure. Functional departments and operational teams started to break and reform internally. Due to its wide range of products and services, TFC depends a lot on its IT infrastructure and systems to provide the necessary support for its business operation.

As more and more IT projects were being initiated to support the business under the new organization structure, it was apparent that the distributed style of managing the projects locally was inefficient. Differences in local practices and standards had become the new problems, with project managers managing projects in their own ad hoc ways. There was no visibility into the number of projects running concurrently and the amount of money invested in them. Projects were delayed and put on hold with no proper reason given. The figures in the monthly project reports were nowhere near the reality.

All these issues had become a challenge for the CIO, who was trying to align the IT group with the business back then. Frustration grew as more and more people were confused by the misleading figures, resulting in more conflicts and project delays. Monthly reporting had turned into a daunting task, if not a nightmare, for many project managers. A change was desperately anticipated. We needed a consistent approach to manage all the projects globally and share the information centrally to address the concerns with respect to efficiency, effectiveness, and timeliness of information.

Our Story

In order to address the problems faced by TFC's IT group, a Global Program Management Office (GPMO) was established. The first task for the newly formed GPMO team was to define its objectives and set the team's direction. Several discussions were conducted with the CIO and other key stakeholders to understand the critical problems at hand and their top priorities in order to derive the objectives for the GPMO. The discussions produced a list of objectives that can be broadly grouped into four main categories:

1. **Visibility:** Provide a 360-degree view of project information to the business.
2. **Standards:** Define a methodology and standard processes for project management.
3. **Governance:** Develop a framework to monitor project execution and ensure compliance with the methodology and processes defined.
4. **Alignment:** Establish a way to measure performance and make appropriate changes to realign the business whenever necessary.

In short, these objectives can be roughly summed up in the GPMO's mission statement:

> *The Program Management Office (PMO) will coordinate on all projects globally and take the lead as the project management center of excellence, set standards and the best practices for managing projects in terms of Process, Portfolio and Performance for the Tyco Flow Control IT Group.*

I was fortunate to be anointed with the sacred task of building the GPMO team and preparing them for the upcoming challenges. As every journey starts with a travel plan, the first thing that I worked on was creating a two-year road map for the GPMO team. The finalized road map includes strategically placed milestones to mark the deadlines for the key objectives to be achieved, as shown in Figure S14.1.

The 3 Ps Concept

After laying down the road map and getting it approved by the CIO and key stakeholders, the focus was shifted to moving the team members around to get the required work done. A 3 Ps concept was proposed to restructure the GPMO team internally into three groups, each with a specific set of roles and responsibilities. The main idea was to have each group focus on different key areas, while at the same time collaborate among themselves to develop action plans in order to drive the required changes to meet the objectives defined in the road map. The 3 Ps represent the Process, Portfolio, and Performance groups, and they form the building blocks for the GPMO, as shown in Figure S14.2.

With the new 3 Ps structure in place, the team members no longer just focused on managing the day-to-day project activities. They were assigned new roles and responsibilities for the 3 Ps groups as described below:

◆ **Portfolio group:** The portfolio group is responsible for managing the training on the project portfolio management tool and driving its adoption globally. They also manage the portfolio and projects pipeline, while at the same time facilitating project prioritization and execution to meet management demands. As part of their duty, they have to collaborate with program managers, project managers, and business leaders to schedule projects and allocate resources efficiently.

◆ **Process group:** The process group is responsible for leading the development and pushing the adoption of the project management

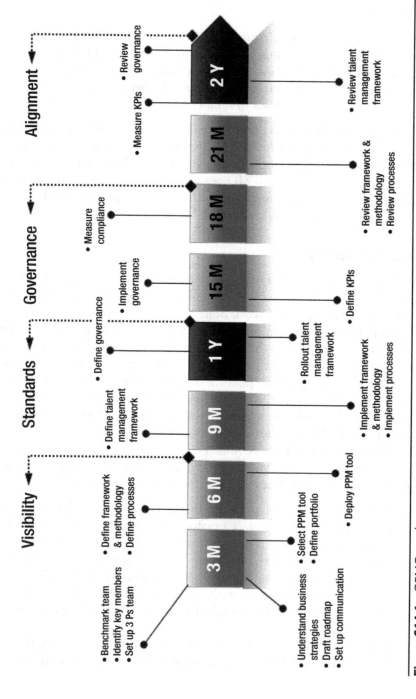

Figure S14.1 GPMO road map

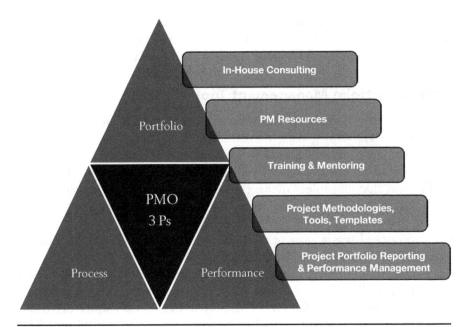

Figure S14.2   GPMO 3 Ps building blocks

methodology and standards across the business. They develop tools and templates to be used by all project managers and business analysts in project execution. The group also provides training on project management methodology and conducts regular audits to ensure there is a high level of compliance in the project executions.

◆ **Performance group:** The performance group is responsible for developing and maintaining the project manager competency and development program whereby they measure and benchmark the competency of project managers and put together training plans and development programs based on individual needs. They also help to define project management key performance indicators and lead initiatives to improve performance and project management capability in the team.

As with most change management endeavors, it was not as smooth as expected initially. People were skeptical about the 3 Ps concept and most were too ingrained in the mind-set that *project managers just manage projects*. It took quite a while to convince people and forge the mind-set through persuasion and countless pep talks, but once we crossed the hurdle, things started to fall in place. Enthusiasm grew, new ideas started to pour in, and the morale of the team was at an unprecedented peak. That was the period when many great ideas and initiatives were being developed, some of which will be highlighted in the following paragraphs.

Project Portfolio Management Tool

Project visibility was always a painful topic for the CIO in the past. He used to struggle with getting the number of running projects and their status. No one could tell him how many projects there were and the total amount of money the company had invested in them. The root cause for this was that all project managers were managing projects using Excel spreadsheets that were usually stored in their local machines. There was no way to do project reporting efficiently. The first thing that the portfolio group proposed was a project portfolio management (PPM) solution to enable project managers to manage projects consistently using a more efficient tool that stores the project information centrally, and at the same time provides flexibility and ease of project reporting. After evaluating some of the big names like HP PPM, Serena PPM, and Daptiv PPM, the portfolio group eventually settled on building an in-house PPM tool. The rationale behind this decision was to start with a simple custom-made tool after determining the maturity of the team was not at a level that can cope with a more complex solution. After a month of conceptualization and identification of key functions, and another two months for the development work to complete, the first version of the PPM tool was successfully launched with much anticipation.

PATH Program

During one of the discussions with the key stakeholders, it was noted that the competency and maturity of the IT team needed improvement. Unfortunately, the project management skill set and knowledge the team had back then were generally well below expectation. Many project managers were actually converted from a business functional role after involvement in several projects. The competency issue turned out to be a key reason for those projects that were poorly executed. In view of this, the PATH program, the brainchild of the performance group, was conceived. It consists of a framework that dictates a method to profile, benchmark, and monitor the competency of a project manager. This will be translated into development programs with a series of training matched against the project manager's competency level and the skill set that are required for a specific job scope. The development programs will be managed by the performance group, with the progression of the project managers closely monitored.

GPMO Toolkit

In the past, we kept getting questions like: "What is my next step?" "What are the deliverables at the end of this stage?" "Should this be a change request or a budget?" from the project managers. Obviously, this was due to the lack of a common methodology and standard processes. The process group took on the responsibility, worked collaboratively with the key stakeholders, and delivered the *GPMO Toolkit* to address this. The toolkit includes a *GPMO Methodology Guide* that details every aspect of how a project should be executed in compliance with the standards defined by the GPMO. This guide serves both as a tool and as a reference for all project managers. The toolkit also includes a detailed process map that describes the processes for the IT team from idea initiation, project selection, project execution, and product monitoring to product improvement. This process map helps people to understand what needs to be done by when and by whom. The process group also created a set of standard project documents, tools, and templates in the toolkit that can be utilized by project managers to reduce their effort in the day-to-day project execution.

PMO Success

Two years had passed since the GPMO team embarked on the journey that transformed the way it performs strategic planning, portfolio management, and project management. As of early 2012, the PPM tool that we launched a year ago recorded a total of 38 successfully completed projects, 108 active projects, and another 69 requested projects in the pipeline across the entire organization. All projects are now accounted for in the PPM tool and project reporting is merely a few clicks away.

In the beginning of the transformation, we only had one certified PMP on the team. With the help of the PATH program, we now proudly host a stronger cohort of five certified PMPs, three PRINCE2® practitioners, and three certified in ITIL v3 Foundation. These figures imply at least 80% of the team members in the GPMO had gone through some form of professional training in either project management or IT service delivery. People are now more well versed in project management terminology and able to understand and apply the tools and models appropriately in their projects. In addition, having the methodology properly defined and the processes streamlined helped in reducing ambiguities and ensuring consistency in the way the projects are being managed. Greater efficiency was achieved, resulting in a higher project completion rate. Feedback from the business also shows that project managers are now more consistent in their work, with fewer missing steps and a higher quality of project deliverables.

Overall, the capability and maturity of the team have shown significant improvements over the past two years, with more projects completed on time and within budget. This is reinforced by the fact that project managers are now more productive and able to take up multiple concurrent projects due to better training, more efficient tools, and streamlined processes. The satisfaction level of the stakeholders has gone up as well since they are now receiving accurate and timely updates on the projects periodically, which provide them with better visibility. The business has also shown tremendous confidence in the GPMO as we have started to see an increasing number of non-IT projects being managed and executed by the team. In other words, although the GPMO team has yet to achieve every objective stated in the road map, they have at least proven their value to the business and have shown that they are on the right track to success.

Concluding Thoughts and Advice

When setting up a PMO, it is crucial to align its objectives with the business expectations, as the value of the PMO depends very much on this. Talk to the people in the business and hear what they want. Do not take any working model off the shelf and try to implement it for your PMO. This will not work, as each PMO is unique. A success story for others might not fit your bill. Having said that, avoid relying too much on the people in the business to tell you what they want the PMO to be. Exercise your judgment cautiously and validate each requirement you have gathered. Do not forget that you are the expert in this domain. If possible, manage setting up the PMO like a project. First, gather the requirements from the business and understand where you are and where you want to be. Next, identify the gap and come up with a road map and project plan to close it. Form a team and assign specific tasks to people to work on. Track it and monitor the progress periodically. If necessary, adjust the road map to suit the pace of your team and realign with the business objectives accordingly.

Every long journey begins with a small step. See you at the finish line!

PMO Success Story #15: Ericsson Korea Project Office

The Story behind the Success

Yechie Labay, Director of Program and Project Management, Ericsson Korea

Introduction to Ericsson Korea

For the past 13 years I have been working for Ericsson, a leading global information and communications technology company providing technology and services in the telecoms and IT industry. I was asked to move from Japan to Korea in September 2009 to start looking into an engagement we had in Korea with one of the telecoms operators.

Korea is one of the most advanced countries in the world, and the Korean people are hard workers, educated, and very proud of their culture and achievements. They are considered to be very quick and early adapters of new technologies, and today 95% of the Korean people, at least in Seoul, have a smartphone. They are also advanced users of the Internet and the mobile Internet.

Business Problems to Be Addressed by the PMO

The Korea market in general, and the telecoms in particular, were a well-regulated and well-protected market. Over the years, they had only local companies, or joint ventures (JVs), and the majority of the competence and delivery was within the local part of the JV. They were working almost in a partnership in such a very customer-centric way that sometimes the companies needed to make compromises to adapt to market requirements. This had resulted in highly customized products for the operators; however, this over customization caused late deliveries, although the market leaders didn't think so.

Our customer was very surprised when they found out that the speed of their mobile Internet network was far behind that of other global operators.

233

For instance, when I started the engagement with them back in 2009, their network speed was 7.6 Mbps in Seoul, whereas the rest of the world was already at 14.4 Mbps and in different stages of 21 Mbps deployments. My former customer in Japan already was at 21 Mbps in their network and they were testing 42 Mbps.

Our Story

After previous successful engagements, I was asked to set up the PMO for the Ericsson Korea office in Seoul. This is how I began my journey in Korea and it continues today.

In the last three years that I have been coming to Korea I have established a PMO, a services sales department, and a customer engagement team for managed services. The story behind the PMO establishment is one of the most interesting and challenging assignments I have ever had in my 13-year career at Ericsson.

When I started looking into the PMO setup, I began with the regular activities of gap analysis and planning the setup with the needed activities, and indeed we had lots to do.

I had two main focus areas to work with: (1) the PMO-related activities, processes, procedures, recruitment and head hunting, governance, etc. and (2) the setup of the project organization that will deliver and fulfill the upcoming contract.

The latter part was the more complicated one, since at Ericsson Korea we didn't have the needed head counts and competence to deliver the contract. The line/functional organization was rather small and without the competence needed due to the lack of investments in Korea for many years from Ericsson headquarters.

So I had to set up a project organization that was mainly based on expatriates and contractors from abroad, and that was a challenge by itself—how to find so many people in such a short time. Thus, I began searching for the top management layer of the project. The idea was to bring in a handful of five to seven people who would build up the rest of the organization. Otherwise, it would be too difficult to manage the whole operation and set up the needed PMO.

While all this was happening, an unexpected event took place, which escalated the whole operation and setup to a new level I never expected. Ericsson headquarters decided to buy part of a local Korean company and set up a JV in Korea. This company was supposed to be the legal entity, as it is now. The reason for the escalation to a new level was that in the newly established company, LG-Ericsson, Ericsson had well-established PMO processes and governance whereas LG had none.

My challenges began when I realized that I had to start by giving presentations to the new JV management about project management and that the level of these presentations needed to start with the basics:

- What is a project and what is a line/functional organization?
- What is the definition of project manager, sponsor, stakeholder, etc.?

I had to start with the very basics of PMO and project management with the JV management. This is something that never happened to me before at Ericsson.

My first step was to set up a new steering committee with the new management covering both the PMO setup and the project setup. This was a wise move because I soon realized that what I was thinking of as a PMO setup and project setup would not work for the new company and I would need to find new solutions for the given situation.

The understanding from the new JV management regarding setting up a PMO was that for the project organization I would set it up, whereas in Ericsson, we have one PMO for the company (the local office) that takes care of traditional PMO activities.

To clarify this part, before the JV, LG never worked in a project organization. Every time they needed to deliver a new product or technology, they set up a line/functional organization to deliver the project. So the people couldn't accept the concept that they would have to work for a project manager and report to him for project-related matters. The line managers couldn't accept the new situation as well, since they felt they had lost control over their employees on the team. The solution was to move all of them under me in the PMO and they would report to me as their line manager.

My new PMO had to have two sections: the service delivery organization (SDO) and the line/functional organization PMO.

Service Delivery Organization

The SDO was focusing on setting up the project organization that would be delivering the new, soon to come contract and ensuring that the right people and competencies were in place. We set up a 250-person organization that covered all the project execution and project delivery functions such as:

- Supply chain management
- Procurement management
- Contract management
- Financial management and control
- Process management

The SDO had to define and redefine some of the existing company processes and policies to ensure that the customer gets what they contracted for with no impact on *internal* issues and politics. This was not easy for anyone, since we needed to change some processes that had been in place for many years, and people didn't want to change them.

The SDO managed 450 additional people as subcontractors, and we had to create a new set of processes for that as well.

The total budget the SDO dealt with was more than US$100 million, and the prime goal of the SDO was to—no matter what—just make it happen. This meant that it doesn't matter if we are a new JV, we have cultural or language issues, processes and people we need to deal with—just make it happen with the needed quality and the given budget. One of the most critical skills that I utilized for the SDO was communication; I had to communicate clearly and rapidly.

Line/Functional Organization PMO

The other section, as mentioned earlier, was to set up the line/functional PMO that eventually will develop the project management practices in the new JV, train new project managers, and support the new contracts and projects. The total head count of the PMO was 35 people, made up of, among others, the following:

- Program managers
- Project managers
- Project controllers
- Contract management
- Project administrators

This is the classical PMO department that is concerned with process and governance, planning for the future for competence development, and looking into portfolio management.

PMO Success

Today the PMO is responsible for more than 15 projects with over US$250 million budgets. It provides training and development for project managers and is considered an innovation center when it comes to the projects it delivers and the solutions it finds for the challenging requirements from its customers.

As of July 2011, the SDO became the division that holds all the needed expertise for contract delivery in Korea, and the PMO is part of it, along with other competence centers. The projects are running as more classical project organizations. The SDO and PMO are the resource and expertise providers for the projects.

Concluding Thoughts and Advice

In terms of concluding thoughts and advice to share, I would offer the following three points to consider when setting up and managing a PMO. First, determine the focus of your PMO. No two PMOs will have the exact same focus, so this has to first be determined based upon the business conditions of the company. Second, ensure that your PMO organization will work for your company and not just be a typical PMO structure. Many PMOs fail because they are set up to be one of the many theoretical PMO models that are often described and presented within the project management industry. And third, establish and use the PMO steering committee to help keep the PMO focused on fulfilling the strategic needs of the business. Many PMOs fail because they do not truly consider and align themselves to the needs of the business.

PMO Success Story #16: RACE Consulting LP

Is the PMO a Vehicle for Creating Business Value during Times of Crisis? The PMO Story of a Greek SME Firm in the AEC Industry

Vanessa Matsas, PMO Head, PMP, PRINCE2® Practitioner, IPMA-D

Introduction to RACE Consulting LP

RACE is an independent small-medium enterprise (SME) specializing in planning, designing, and performing project management for transportation projects. By delivering services throughout a project's life cycle, the firm undertakes partnership roles in design and build, early contractor involvement, and BOT/DBFO/PPP projects. Although the Athens-based firm was established in 2007, RACE's experience dates back to 1994. Today, it is one of Greece's leading transportation engineering and design consultancies and is a preferred partner for many contractors, government agencies, and local authorities. The consultancy services offered by RACE are comprised of transportation planning, traffic volume analysis, highway and hydraulic designs, road safety audits, rail designs, topographical surveys, and cadastral maps.

RACE's culture is characterized by dedication to fulfilling each stakeholder's needs within the context of the firm's technical expertise, social responsibility, and professional ethics. RACE's fundamental principles are the quality, safety, and environmental aspects of each project that are ensured by its specialized and experienced personnel. RACE's workforce is its most valuable asset. For this reason, a large investment is made every year for employee development with emphasis on training and technical excellence, as well as on soft skills. The highly trained engineering team has extensive experience in complex, multidisciplinary projects involving clients from different cultures. Additionally, an in-house team of certified project management professionals (PMPs) has integrated processes of project management (PM) within the company to be applied to both internal and external projects. This integration of technical and PM competences facilitates approaching every project holistically.

Business Problems to Be Addressed by the PMO

Today's aggressively competitive business environment has stimulated companies to become more efficient, competitive, and flexible. Greece's declining public finances since 2008 have negatively affected the number of transportation projects initiated. This is mainly due to scarcity of funding resources combined with investors' unwillingness to enter the Greek market. RACE's management team realized the need to undertake the necessary reforms in order to rationalize the company's structure, differentiate its services, and improve its competitiveness in order to expand further and compete on an international level. Consequently, the management team created the firm's 2011–2014 strategic plan, which involves:

♦ Entrance into new markets by providing PM services for the transportation industry
♦ Differentiation of the firm's existing services and augmentation of the product's life cycle by means of incorporating Building Information Modeling (BIM) methodology and asset management functionality
♦ The firm's transformation to a value-creation driven organization

The PMO was recognized by the strategic plan developed as one of the main drivers for implementing and achieving the strategic objectives. The PMO will accomplish this by addressing the following business problems:

1. Project governance: By defining and implementing a new governance framework that meets the challenges of projects with different risk profiles.
2. Project selection: By following the throughput model,[1] the PMO connects the market demand with the internal capabilities, resulting in value creation.
3. Project prioritization: By prioritizing projects in order to face both human and capital resource constraints.
4. Stabilize project success: By defining and establishing a value-driven delivery approach to ensure that the majority of projects initiated will meet all their requirements.

These issues were to be tackled over time, since the development of the PMO was to be done gradually, in six phases (each with a planned six-month duration).

Our Story

Our PMO story began back in 2009, when Christos Rados, the company's CEO, gave me the lead of a small task force with the assignment *"... to determine ways that would improve our operations' efficiency, increase our market share and finally increase the company's bottom-line results."* The story unfolds by confronting this assignment through the implementation of a PMO in six-month phases, shown in Figure S16.1. Throughout the phases, the CEO would gradually increase my authority and responsibilities, therefore having the PMO's role evolve over time.

Phase 1: Restructuring the Organization

In order to understand our firm's current standing and therefore establish where we ultimately wanted to go, I benchmarked our firm against other organizations in our local industry. Then, together with the senior executives, we began analyzing the existing business model and brainstormed ideas regarding increasing operational efficiency and enhancing the firm's services. During this period of analysis, we also addressed two of the firm's existing weaknesses: the lack of structured communication channels and our ineffective organizational structure. Even though we are actually a project driven organization, our organizational structure was functional. We concluded to progressively change our organizational structure from a functional to strong matrix.

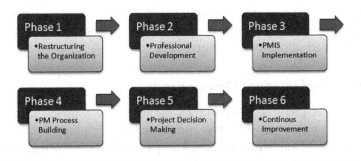

Figure S16.1   The six-month phases for RACE's PMO implementation

Although a seemingly easy task, obstacles arose with respect to the functionality of the changes. Apart from the need to incorporate the PMO into the new organizational chart, modifications needed to be made to the existing departments. The firm originally operated using a multidisciplinary approach; each functional silo would carry out its operations and projects independently. Before product delivery, the departments would collaborate with each other in order to integrate all the designs (highway, hydraulics, etc.) to generate the end product. This approach was driving our operation costs high. It should be mentioned that even before the implementation of the PMO, each project had a team leader and there were processes in place that would assist them with running their projects. We needed to increase functionality and efficiency by implementing appropriate communication channels, providing a structured and standardized approach for managing projects, and by changing the way we operated, from multidisciplinary to interdisciplinary. In this new environment, project teams would be formed at the beginning of each project with resources from all the necessary departments. Although functional departments still exist within the organization for planning, reporting, and accounting purposes, the model is now dynamic in the sense that the colocation of project teams is encouraged in order to facilitate collaboration, better communication, and decision making.

It was during this phase that we realized that PMO implementation is really all about change management, in that we were really restructuring our organization as a whole. My position as the PMO head facilitated this transition via continuous communication. This was essential in order to minimize the anticipated surfacing of concerns regarding changes to the former structure and to clarify the role and responsibilities that the PMO department would have. As Elias Georgoulakos, one of our lead civil engineers stated at the time, "I feel that all these changes are in the right direction; though, I am concerned that we may shoot ourselves in the foot by increasing bureaucracy in the attempt to improve efficiency." A vital aspect for the effective integration of the PMO with the new structure was top management support. To this end, a direct reporting line to the CEO was established as shown in Figure S16.2.

Phase 2: Professional Development

After the first phase, the second six-month phase was initiated. Professional development in PM was promoted to employees through the coordination of two eight-week workshops at 12PM consulting, an Athens-based project, program, and portfolio management consulting company.

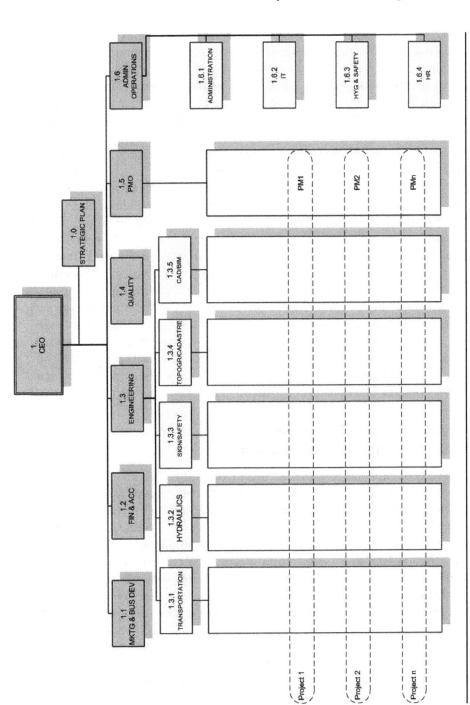

Figure S16.2   RACE's new organizational structure

Alongside the workshops, we collaborated with Theofanis Giotis, the CEO of 12PM consulting and president of PMI's Greece chapter, with the aim of familiarizing our technical personnel with PM terminology and helping them recognize the need for the PMO within our firm. This stimulated the employees' interest in PM; today more than half of RACE's technical personnel are PMP certified. A few are also PRINCE2® Practitioner and IPMA Level D certified.

In this phase, my key responsibilities included creating PM templates and processes, ensuring that they were appropriately used, and assisting project managers with document control, namely managing, organizing, and archiving project-related documents. In parallel, Windows SharePoint Services (WSS) was implemented in order to serve as a single web-based repository for accessing project documents. Additionally, I ensured that projects were not initiated without sponsor approval and fund authorization. By further developing and mentoring project managers and encouraging them to use PM processes, I helped them get accustomed to the new environment and to apply their knowledge from the PM training they had received. At this point in time, the only documents that the project managers were required to have were the project charter, work breakdown structure (WBS), project schedule, and lessons learned. This was done because (1) the firm preferred to be flexible and (2) so that the project managers would not be bombarded with a heavy *bureaucratic* policy.

Phase 3: Project Management Information System (PMIS) Implementation

After the organization became accustomed to using PM processes, the third phase was initiated; this is where the PMO actually came into play. Here, I was to evaluate, implement, integrate, and test our PMIS, which is comprised of WSS, MS Office suite (including Project Professional for scheduling and Visio for WBSs), MS Project Server, Replicon's Web TimeSheet (WTS), and Replicon's Integration Manager. WTS is used by our project teams to record time against projects and the Integration Manager is used to update project schedule information and time sheet information between WTS and the Project Server. This integration allows for real-time project progress and costing updates, facilitating decision making, efficiency, and reporting. It was here that the need for a PM-oriented solution surfaced that would systematically help me with the PMO's asset management of processes and templates as well as with dashboards. After evaluating the available solutions in the market, BOT International's *Processes on Demand*[2] was acquired to facilitate our needs. Additionally, we received invaluable consulting services regarding setting up our PMO and PMO best practices from Mark Price Perry, the founder of BOT International.

Once both the PMIS and the PMO site (using Processes on Demand) were deployed, I presented them to the organization (see Figure S16.3). In order to increase involvement and buy-in, I requested that everyone make suggestions and comments regarding these new systems. The end result was accessible and organized information that everyone found easy to use, along with a methodological approach to managing projects.

Phase 4: PM Process Building

In this phase, my responsibilities included the introduction and implementation of various PM methodologies such as risk management, critical chain project management (CCPM), and PRINCE2. CCPM improved team collaboration and assisted quality measurements using the project dollar days index. The PRINCE2 methodology assisted me with establishing a new, more effective project governance framework. Gradually, we improved product quality by monitoring key performance indicators (KPIs) that the engineering departments created. Furthermore, we coordinated several internal workshops for our technical personnel regarding quality and how our firm defined value; value was to be aligned with the objectives of both the buyer (our clients) and seller (our firm).

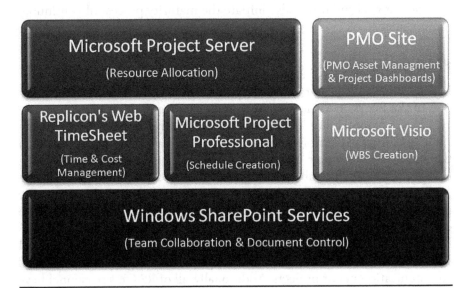

Figure S16.3 RACE's PMIS

Phase 5: Project Decision Making

Once the PMO was organized, the new project governance framework was established, and the ideas of PM and value creation had matured within the firm, it was time to initiate the fifth phase: advancing the PMO's role to a strategic one. After increasing my authority level, my team and I would ensure that all projects selected would be aligned with the firm's strategic objectives. Other responsibilities included project prioritization, return on investment tracking, and creating additional value for the firm and its clients. A project selection process was determined, along with the identification of selection criteria, development of project scoring, and incorporation of quantitative economic models such as net present value. Once everyone in the organization was familiarized with these and their uses, they understood the reasoning behind projects' initiation.

Today, we are still in the fifth phase and in the process of introducing a new, project-oriented performance appraisal management system within our firm. This will assist with enhancing the competencies, skills, and performance of our teams. Additionally, it will improve the selection and allocation of the appropriate resources to each project, thus increasing the probability of the projects' success. Our forthcoming goal is to initiate the sixth phase, which will involve a maturity assessment against an industry standard, such as OPM3® or P3M3®, and obtaining certification. This process will involve identifying our strengths and weaknesses in order to achieve our goal and it will also initiate the maturity process of continuous improvement.

PMO Success

In our case, the key ingredients required for the successful implementation of the firm's strategic plan were and are integrity, simplicity, transparency, and accountability. The same principles were adopted for the firm's value-creating PMO implementation. The acceptance and sound fusion of the PMO with all other departments were physically possible by taking into consideration the above, by gradually introducing the PMO to the organization in five six-month phases, and by carrying out the previously mentioned approaches. One of the PMO's first objectives was to be able to communicate effectively, using PM terminology, with the whole organization. Through the active participation of all technical personnel in the PM workshops, we established a common language and thus have improved communication in our projects. Additionally, all of RACE's personnel have gained the basic knowledge of how to manage projects. Furthermore, by establishing standardized PM processes, there is consistency between all projects and project-related documents. Since project managers are required to prepare project plans with their team members, they have become more efficient in the sense that they are committed to the plan they put together.

After accomplishing the fundamentals, we confronted the challenge of resource constraints that we faced as an SME. Firstly, this was achieved through successfully prioritizing our projects. Secondly, having a structured PMIS facilitated proper allocation of human resources, thus increasing efficiency within our organization. Thirdly, the readily available information for project teams and management has provided the organization with a crystal clear picture of the status of all projects. Before this, since the nature of our business creates a considerable amount of downtime, it was difficult to pinpoint when and how much idle time our personnel had. Today, as a result of this available information, we feel more comfortable with the fact that employees will have some idle time and we now work toward utilizing it to our benefit. Every project team now works toward a predetermined goal and strives for the optimal outcome. Just as important is the fact that we have met our goal of project success stability (see Figure S16.4).

Before the PMO was created, many projects were initiated for the achievement of benefits such as profit generation and expanding clientele. Management found that although we were meeting the short-term goals, long-term goals and the alignment of projects to the strategic objectives

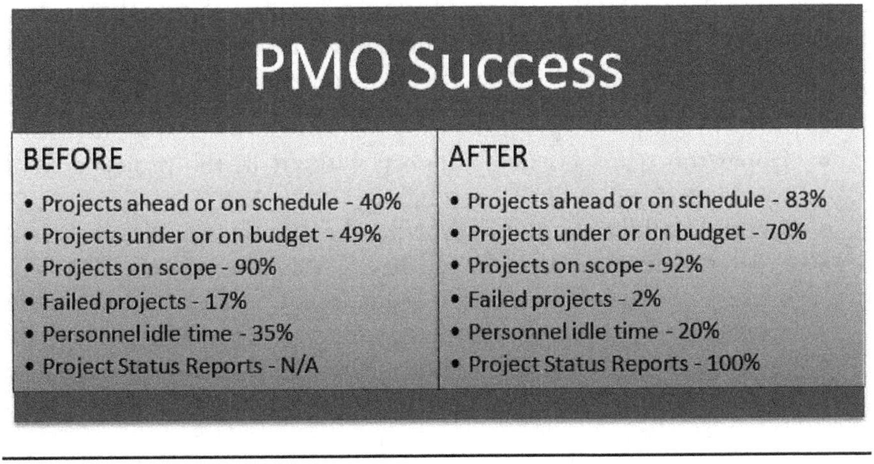

PMO Success

BEFORE	AFTER
• Projects ahead or on schedule - 40%	• Projects ahead or on schedule - 83%
• Projects under or on budget - 49%	• Projects under or on budget - 70%
• Projects on scope - 90%	• Projects on scope - 92%
• Failed projects - 17%	• Failed projects - 2%
• Personnel idle time - 35%	• Personnel idle time - 20%
• Project Status Reports - N/A	• Project Status Reports - 100%

Figure S16.4   RACE's PMO Success

were not being achieved. The PMO created and implemented a new project selection process that incorporated the use of quantitative economic models such as net present value as well as tracking KPIs like return on investment and product dollar days. The resulting accomplishment is that today projects are selected based on the value (utility) that they create and the realization of not only short-term goals but long-term strategic objectives.

Concluding Thoughts and Advice

Greece's 2009 fiscal crisis has developed into a full-blown economic/social crisis, which affects all industries. The country's AEC industry suffers greatly; on the one hand, the tight fiscal policy has drastically reduced the government's funds for infrastructure investments; on the other hand, public-private partnership initiatives have been suspended due to the country's financial risk. In our firm, the immediate effect of the above situation was the steep increase of initiated projects. It seems like a paradox, but it's not; our firm strives to maintain its market share and bottom line results via internal projects, a strategy that focuses on long-term value creation. During 2010 and 2011, the number of internal projects increased by 400%. The value-creating PMO had the most determinant role for the successful implementation of all these projects by selecting, prioritizing, directing, and managing all the competing constraints.

So, what are the lessons learned? From experience, planning and communication make for the most important aspects when putting into effect changes or initiating projects. It is critical that the key stakeholders involved work together in order to develop a detailed plan, including how this change will be communicated throughout the organization. The following were imperative for the effective implementation of the PMO within our firm:

- ◆ Upper/top management's support; without it, the project's result would be either deficient or a failure.
- ◆ Get stakeholder buy-in by involving them in the planning process.
- ◆ Progressively introduce the change within the organization. This strategy allows for continuous evaluation of performance and easier acceptance by those affected.
- ◆ Short- and long-term goal setting aligned to the strategic objectives of the organization. Through the achievement of the short-term

goals, apart from the feeling of success, an assessment can be made in order to determine new needs and/or risks.

♦ The development of success criteria (KPIs) so as to monitor and control the performance of the PMO and to communicate its achievements to the organization. Additionally, KPIs aid in benchmarking for quality improvement and enhancement of procedures, services, etc.

♦ Well-defined and communicated authority, roles, and responsibilities of the PMO and its personnel.

So, what is the answer to our initial question? Is the PMO a vehicle for creating business value during times of crisis? Our records and results reveal that, in our firm, the PMO is truly a vehicle for creating business value.

References

1. Kendall, Gerald I., and Steven C. Rollins. *Advanced Project Portfolio Management and the PMO: Multiplying ROI at Warp Speed*. Boca Raton, FL: J. Ross Publishing, 2003.
2. Processes on Demand, BOT International Corporation. www.botinternational.com.

PMO Success Story #17: A South African Financial Services Company

PMO Value Demonstrated and Quantified

Colin Anthony McCall-Peat, Group PMO Manager, Gijima

Introduction to the Company

This company is a large financial services company in South Africa providing long-term insurance, health care, and investment products. Its website describes the business as follows: "We're a progressive African wealth management group, and for more than 50 years, we've been delivering innovative long-term solutions that empower our clients to take control of their finances and of their lives. And we do it by offering the best and broadest possible range of products and services to help them build and protect long-term wealth—including life and health insurance, investments, asset management and property development."

Due to the competitive nature of the business, a short time to market with new products is imperative to maintain market share and remain at the forefront of customer needs. This necessitates an agile approach to product development and project delivery.

Business Problems to Be Addressed by the PMO

When I joined the company, although a PMO had been established, it was not fulfilling any significant business purpose nor contributing to business goals and objectives in a tangible or measurable way. My mandate was to improve the efficiency of delivery of projects and to reduce costs.

Upon further analysis I identified the major business problems that needed to be addressed as the unreliable delivery of projects and the poor quality of the deliverables. These problems related directly to my given

251

mandate of improving efficiency and reducing costs, as these were merely the symptoms of the real underlying problems.

Our Story

One of the major challenges of a PMO is to justify its existence by providing evidence of the business benefits provided to the organization. Many of the functions of a PMO are difficult to quantify, such as the provision and enforcement of a standard project management methodology, providing project governance mechanisms, project and portfolio reporting, project manager training and coaching, provision and support of project management tools, etc. As part of my strategy I wanted to demonstrate tangible and measureable improvements for the business as a result of the initiatives implemented in response to the business problems.

Fortunately, the company had embarked on a project benchmarking initiative the year before I joined, but this initiative had been poorly understood and implemented. It had therefore not delivered any meaningful value to the company at this stage. When I analyzed the benchmarking service I was pleased to discover that this would provide me with the means to demonstrate and quantify the business benefits that I was planning to achieve over time. Benchmarking is the process of comparing the performance of an organization's business activities, typically a specific subset, against the performance of other organizations.

The benchmarking service was provided by an external specialist company called Quantimetrics, who use an extensive database of past projects from many different companies against which to compare the company projects. This enables a comparison against many different metrics, such as cost, delivery speed, productivity, quality, conformance to budget, conformance to schedule, and staffing index. The database of projects grows constantly as more projects are added with each benchmark submission. The project comparison is based on like-for-like projects taking into account the project characteristics such as size, duration, and technology.

The benchmark results for the year prior to my joining showed the major existing problem areas regarding project delivery to be poor quality and poor conformance to budget and schedule (unreliable delivery). Although cost of delivery was not highlighted as a problem area by the benchmark, due to the competitive nature of the business this was an area that I targeted for improvement as well.

My first goal was to rein in the poor quality issue. The measurement of quality in the benchmark was to quantify the number of errors encountered during the first month of operation of the new system or process. The results of the first benchmark indicated that the quality was 13 times worse than the benchmark. This means that for every 1 error that the average project encountered after implementation, we were encountering 13 errors. Quality is often impacted adversely due to compressed project deadlines, resulting in poor quality assurance and control measures during the project life cycle. It could also be due to an attempt to reduce project costs by reducing the project duration and therefore limiting the quality aspects of the project. This is often a shortsighted strategy, as the cost of poor quality far outweighs the cost saving achieved through the compressed project duration. Resolving the errors after implementation comes at a premium cost compared with preventing or identifying and resolving the errors early in the project life cycle.

To improve the problem of poor quality, I implemented two major resolution initiatives. The first was to improve the testing process. This was predominantly a quality control initiative as it sought to identify the errors before implementation but not to prevent them from happening in the first place. The second initiative was a quality assurance initiative, whereby more effort was devoted to the early stages of the project life cycle to ensure that the design and development activities were peer reviewed and more thorough than previously done. Coupled with this was more focus on the up-front scope definition to prevent the extent of scope change during the project life cycle.

The problems of poor conformance to budget and schedule related mainly to the scope control issue, where the scope was not finalized until late in the project, resulting in rework. This problem was addressed through stricter scope definition and sign-off during the planning stage, as well as more rigorous project schedule baselining and monitoring. Formal change control was enforced, requiring the cost and effort impact to be approved by the project steering committee before being incorporated into the project.

The requirement to focus more on the accurate scheduling and schedule management necessitated some training and coaching of the project managers and project administrators. For this purpose, a practical training course was compiled and delivered. This course was based on the company methodology, thus enabling the attendees to utilize the skills immediately on their projects upon returning to the workplace. Coaching was also provided by the PMO to assist project managers with their schedules and with problems regarding the usage of the scheduling tool.

PMO Success

Figure S17.1 shows the benchmarking of the quality aspect of projects prior to my joining (year 0) and for the five subsequent years.

As you can see from the graph, the quality was extremely poor at the start of the benchmark and improved dramatically after the measures were taken during my first year of employment to address the root causes of this. The quality did deteriorate slightly during the subsequent years, but this was due mainly to a strategic focus on fast delivery of products to market in order to gain competitive advantage. However, the quality measure remained very close to the benchmark, unlike the starting point, where it was unacceptably poor compared to the benchmark.

The cost of delivery is measured as cost per function point in the benchmark. Figure S17.2 shows the cost benchmark over time.

The costs in the first benchmark were $215 per function point. These were reduced over the five-year time frame to $100 per function point. The costs are a function of the other aspects of the project, such as the duration and quality, but maintaining the costs at a fraction of the benchmark costs was a gratifying result for the organization.

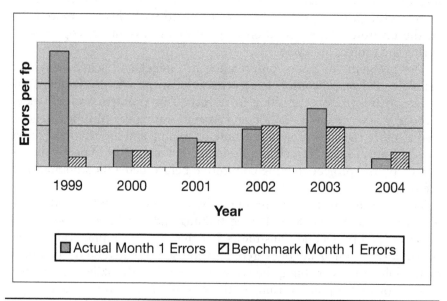

Figure S17.1 Quality: month 1 errors

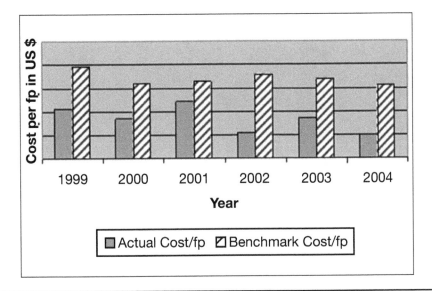

Figure S17.2   Cost per function point

Concluding Thoughts and Advice

The establishment of a PMO must always be considered with the desired business goals in mind. A PMO establishment should never be viewed as a *one-size-fits-all* situation. Knowing the business goals for the PMO, one can then specify the measures that will be used to quantify the degree of achievement of these goals over time. If this is not done, then the risk is that the contribution and value of the PMO will be questioned by management and may result in the demise of the PMO. By agreeing with the mandate and the measurement process and criteria up front, the focus and goals of the PMO are clear and the benefit added can be better quantified and evaluated. There will then be no doubt as to the value add of the PMO from a business perspective, and it will take its rightful place with the other major business functions as a major contributor to business success.

PMO Success Story #18: ABS Nautical Systems

PMO Start-up: "Changing Culture"

Christopher McCourt, PMO Manager, ABS Nautical Systems

Introduction to ABS Nautical Systems

With over 25 years of delivering fleet management software to the marine industry, the company started as Nautical Technologies Corporation, with its flagship product known as SafeNet. In 1990, the American Bureau of Shipping purchased a majority share of the company, which became known as ABS Nautical Systems, LLC (ABS-NS). In the early 2000s, ABS-NS embarked on a new software platform for its products and customers. The new platform was named NS5 and it contains several modules that assist marine owners and ship managers to manage their respective fleets. The core modules are Maintenance Management and Supply Chain Management.

Throughout those years, ABS-NS ran a relatively lean staff of about 45 people worldwide to cover sales, product development, consulting, and product support. It was an environment where people joined and learned on the job. Our projects were generally managed in an informal manner; however, as the organization grew we needed a process that was similar for all implementations. We also needed to enable team members to step into or out of projects without disrupting the process. Late in the first quarter of 2011, we had a senior management change at ABS-NS. Demetri Stroubakis joined the team as a SVP of Operations. As Demetri was reviewing the current operation, he was struck that we did not have a more formal process to manage our implementation projects. At that time, I was working in the product development area of the organization managing internal development projects. Shortly after his arrival at ABS-NS, I met with Demetri and we discussed the need for a more formal process to manage software implementation and other related projects. That begins our journey (which is still in progress) to cultivate a culture of project management that would be a differentiator between ABS-NS and its competition. Together, I worked with Demetri and Darren Unger, Director of Global Consulting, to create the PMO within ABS-NS.

Business Problems to Be Addressed by the PMO

In April and May 2011, I started to research the development of a PMO and began reviewing project management maturity models, using this as an input to discussions with Demetri and Darren regarding the PMO formation. Figure S18.1 displays common characteristics of PMO maturity. We needed a common model and an agreement about where we were from both a strategic and a tactical perspective.

Strategically, it was clear that we were moving from an informal to a formal project management process, but from a tactical perspective, we needed to have at least a common language and process to move forward. The decision was clear that we needed to form a PMO. The question was where and how to start. We reviewed some lessons learned from current and past projects and there were some major themes that initially emerged: (1) expectations management, (2) schedule performance, and (3) internal coordination within ABS-NS.

With many projects, it became evident that a gap existed between what our expectations were for the project and what the client believed they

PMO Maturity Model			
Stage	Type	Scope	Characteristics
5	Center of Excellence	Strategic Alignment	Manages continuous improvement and cross-department collaboration to achieve strategic business objectives
4	Advanced PMO	Business Maturity	Applies an integrated and comprehensive project management capability to achieve business objectives
3	Standard PMO	Process Support	Establishes capabilities and infrastructure to support and govern a cohesive project environment
2	Basic PMO	Process Control	Provides a standard and repeatable project management methodology for use across all projects
1	Project Office	Project Oversight	Achieves project deliverables and objectives for cost, schedule, and resource utilization

Figure S18.1 PMO maturity model

would receive. With our implementations, the main problem areas were project scope (what was to be delivered) and schedule (when would it be delivered). In general, our project kickoff meetings went well from a technical perspective (technical details of the software modules); however, less emphasis was placed on formal project planning and documentation. From that perspective, it is quite easy to see that any implementation would most likely suffer from schedule issues resulting from a kickoff meeting that really did not align ABS-NS and the client.

Another aspect of schedule performance was that any project plan that was created was sort of written in stone. We did not treat the project plan as if it were a living document. The major issue that ABS-NS faced during its implementation engagements was internal coordination within the departments of the organization. Our departments communicate well on a regular basis, but there is a distinct difference between everyday business communication and structured communication that is required to successfully manage a software implementation project.

There are three major parts to internal coordination on any implementation project that can have a direct impact on project success: (1) transition from sales to operations, (2) product enhancements, and (3) project communications and status visibility. Our story begins as we worked to take on our challenges and to change the culture of the organization through the development of tools and processes that can be readily used by 80% of the organization.

Our Story

We quickly realized that we needed to create a lightweight, workable process and complement the process with specific tools that were familiar to the organization. During my investigation of options, I came across a book entitled *Business Driven PMO Setup* (Perry 2009), and when I started reading the book, I quickly realized that Processes on Demand (POD) was highlighted as an example of a PMO methodology. I also reviewed a similar methodology from a competitor. With ABS-NS, we had some interesting discussions regarding PMO tools, and ultimately we decided to go with POD.

Most of our discussions centered around the need for the product, who would work on the implementation, and would anyone even use it. We quickly implemented POD and within days we were up and running.

We also arranged formal project management training for staff from all areas of the organization including executives from sales and operations.

The training gave all participants the common language and understanding of project management principles, which enabled a quick adoption of the PMO website that we implemented. So now, we had tools and processes in place to apply to current and future projects.

We customized the PMO process to include some basic but very effective tools to initiate and manage projects. Those tools included the project charter, work breakdown structure, stakeholder analysis, communications plan, and a risk matrix (register). As shown in Figure S18.2, one of the customizations that we made to the project charter was to add a flexibility matrix to the scope section of the document.

The flexibility matrix aligns the clients' expectations with ABS-NS's project management process. When any issue arises on the project, a quick review of the flexibility matrix will enable the project manager to develop strategies to address issues while keeping the client's confidence in the process and the project.

PMO Success

After several months of a formal PMO in place, we achieved many of our initial goals when implementing the PMO. We had a project that was in progress for about six months with a major client in the Americas region, and the client was very concerned about the overall progress of the project. After a meeting with the client, we refocused our efforts and reviewed scope, costs, and progress and found some challenges with the execution of the project. These challenges stemmed from issues with project management, the work to be done (scope), and management of expectations.

ABS-NS responded by sending in two senior product consultants to assess the work to be done. The consultants worked directly with me and I

Project Constraint	Least Flexible	Some Flexibility	Most Flexible
Scope	X		
Schedule		X	
Cost			X

Figure S18.2   Flexibility matrix

worked with senior operations management to address resource issues and any other obstacles that were present. We went in with the premise that we must show some progress and then address future work with a new project plan. Communication was a big issue as well. We set up weekly conference calls with the client. In addition, communication with the consulting team on-site was on a daily basis.

Within three weeks, the project started to stabilize and we started to regain the client's confidence on the project. After two months of being back on track and carefully managing expectations, the client complimented our work and was impressed that we were driving the project.

This project also included a third-party software integrator that was working on a core system for the same client. In addition to that turnaround, we successfully recovered three other projects and commenced three others with a more formal approach. Every project is bound to have issues; now we can manage the issues and expectations much more effectively.

Other measures of overall success are formal project review meetings every month held with key members of the management team within ABS-NS. We worked with another division of our parent company to develop a project charter for a multiyear project for a leading petroleum company. The charter we developed is currently supporting the governance of this project. Overall, we have buy-in from our management team, key executives within the parent organization, and key clients. We at ABS-NS are very excited to continue this journey of improving our PMO, processes, and tools.

Concluding Thoughts and Advice

Although there is much more to accomplish, we hope that this example of the creation of a PMO will serve as a reminder to those contemplating this journey, and also to those who are on the journey, that starting with the basics and building from there can give the team the momentum to be successful. At ABS-NS we use the following strategy to improve our processes and tools:

1. Revisit and revalidate goals, both strategic and tactical.
2. Support the team; this is a vital component to success.
3. Create opportunities for learning and improvement.

My main goal as a PMO manager is to support all the members of project teams. We use Lunch and Learn webinars as a way to give team members opportunities to continue to learn about project management. We also have quarterly PMO meetings to review our progress against our overall goals. One example of this is the introduction of formal requirements analysis and business analysis within the organization. We see this as a vital and complementary component to our overall project success.

References

Perry, Mark Price. *Business Driven PMO Setup: Practical Insights, Techniques and Case Examples for Ensuring Success.* Fort Lauderdale, FL: J. Ross Publishing, 2009.

PMO Success Story #19: ON Semiconductor

PMO Success: Adapting to Change

Frank R. Myers, Ph.D., Senior Director Program Management, ON Semiconductor

Introduction to ON Semiconductor

ON Semiconductor (Nasdaq: ONNN) is a premier supplier of high-performance silicon solutions for energy-efficient electronics. The company's broad portfolio of power and signal management, logic, and discrete and custom devices helps customers efficiently solve their design challenges in automotive, communications, computing, consumer, industrial, LED lighting, medical, military/aerospace, and power applications. ON Semiconductor operates a world-class, value-added supply chain and a network of manufacturing facilities, sales offices, and design centers in key markets throughout North America, Europe, and the Asia Pacific regions. Global corporate headquarters is in Phoenix, Arizona. Revenue totaled $3.442 billion in 2011.

Over the period 2003–2011, ON Semiconductor has grown from being #48 in the semiconductor industry with annual revenues of $1.1 billion to being ranked #18 with revenues of over $3.4 billion. A significant portion of this growth has been driven by nine acquisitions since 2006. Some of the larger acquisitions include AMI Semiconductor in 2008 and most recently SANYO Semiconductor in 2011. Company growth through acquisition brings some unique challenges across all functions in the company, with the need to continuously integrate people, business processes, systems, and operations.

Business Problems to Be Addressed by the PMO

ON Semiconductor has three primary PMOs. A traditional IT PMO is focused on system and process continuous improvement along with IT integration of acquired businesses. A second PMO is focused on new product development within the business units and has processes that are well defined based on common phase gate approaches for product development. A third PMO was created under the COO of the company in 2009 to improve execution of the company's top R&D and cost savings programs. This PMO was created by recruiting an outside leader with significant experience managing large-scale R&D and post-M&A integration programs. In addition, the team was staffed with senior technical program managers, most with over 20 years of experience in the industry.

A very simple but efficient PMO architecture was established by the PMO as shown in Figure S19.1. Project selection was done at the discretion of the COO and his staff based on the magnitude of potential cost savings or long-term benefit to the company from key R&D programs. The team was regularly focused on the top ten *needle-moving* programs with cost savings and new revenue potentials in the tens to hundreds of millions of dollars. Implementation of the COO PMO proved to be very successful as execution of programs improved markedly (based on schedule and scope delivery performance). In addition, many of the PMO assets such as the custom project management methodology, reporting methods, and templates began to be adopted by the other PMOs and smaller

PMO Architecture

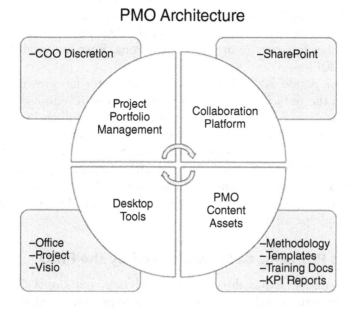

Figure S19.1   PMO architecture for operations (COO) PMO

program teams in the company. The establishment of this PMO clearly had addressed a business need by driving solid execution of large critical programs for ON Semiconductor.

Although the establishment of the COO PMO was a much needed addition to ON Semiconductor and showed great success, several factors drove the need to adapt many aspects of the PMO to meet the needs of the business. Large acquisitions and natural disasters required marked and sometimes urgent changes to the PMO. In the section below, I will describe how each of these situations drove adaptation in the PMO to meet the needs of the business.

Our Stories and PMO Successes

SANYO Manufacturing Consolidation

In January 2011, ON Semiconductor acquired SANYO Semiconductor (2011 revenue $1.1 billion), headquartered in Japan. With this acquisition came major challenges with respect to integration, including cultural, language, and regional barriers. In addition, in order to improve the profitability of the new semiconductor division, a massive manufacturing restructuring program was needed to reduce cost. The restructuring program involved consolidation and movement of internal manufacturing operations that were primarily in Japan to lower cost geographies, subcontractors, and foundries to generate annual savings of hundreds of millions of dollars.

The cost reduction program involved movement of thousands of product lines, hundreds of different manufacturing process flows, hundreds of pieces of manufacturing equipment, and ultimately the closure of multiple large manufacturing facilities. ON Semiconductor had never planned and executed a program of this size and this represented a major challenge from a PMO perspective. Execution of the program required the COO PMO to quickly adapt and address three key issues.

First, while on the surface, scoping and managing the portfolio of programs for a consolidation may appear to be a onetime event, it is not. The portfolio management is continuous throughout the life of the consolidation as business conditions change and risks and issues arise. To address this challenge, a small strategy team was formed led by a senior manufacturing technologist with significant experience in manufacturing consolidations and in the region. This leader also had multilanguage capabilities to allow for efficient communication between the teams. The strategy team consisting of operations leaders in both ON Semiconductor and SANYO successfully defined and managed the portfolio of projects necessary to meet the cost savings objectives.

The second issue to be addressed by the PMO was to rapidly put in place competent program managers. ON Semiconductor had a manufacturing facility in Japan prior to the acquisition of SANYO with people familiar with the internal program management methodology. Five senior engineering managers from the ON Semiconductor facility along with three managers from SANYO, all with multilanguage capabilities, were assembled to create the program management team. The advantage of this approach was that it provided the program with experienced leaders to drive the programs; good communication between Japan, the United States, and European teams; and an early injection of the ON Semiconductor culture, business processes, and network into SANYO.

The third and final challenge for this program was to rapidly deploy a PMO architecture, as shown in Figure S19.2, across the new teams to enable a consistent method of planning, executing, and reporting on the progress of the programs.

The collaboration platform, desktop tools, and content assets were utilized with little modification (some information was translated into

PMO Architecture

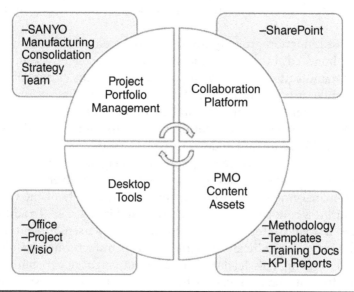

Figure S19.2   PMO architecture for SANYO consolidation

Japanese). The project management methodology, templates, and reporting methods were new to SANYO and were introduced through multiple training sessions, through the internal ON Semiconductor Japan program managers and through individual coaching and mentoring by members of the PMO from the United States. Reporting of the program progress was integrated into existing business processes including weekly reviews with the PMO and Consolidation Strategy Team, monthly updates to company executives, and quarterly updates to the Board of Directors.

Recruitment and relocation of the program managers, deployment of the content assets, training of the program teams, and detailed project planning were executed over a period of three months. The Project Strategy Team created 12 different programs to execute the consolidation. Execution of the consolidations began immediately after the formal acquisition of SANYO Semiconductor by ON Semiconductor in January 2011. The program teams were able to execute the programs and ultimately beat the project timing for cost savings by three months, thus creating huge savings for the company. The PMO successfully adapted to the changing needs of the business by creating a new organization in Japan, by rapidly deploying a team to manage the project portfolio, and overlaying the existing content assets to be successful.

Thailand Flood Recovery

On October 11, 2011, ON Semiconductor announced that its SANYO Semiconductor division's operations, located in the Rojana Industrial Park in Ayutthaya, Thailand, had been suspended as a result of recent flooding in the region. The severity of the flood damage to ON Semiconductor's production facilities in Thailand, and the prolonged inability of these sites to operate, caused major disruptions within the company's global supply chain. The operations located in the Rojana Industrial Park produced approximately 10–12% of ON Semiconductor's total worldwide output, creating a significant revenue shortfall for the company, and had the potential for significant negative impact to many customers. By late November, it had been determined that it was not financially viable to restart operations in Thailand and a decision was made to cease all production at the sites. The bulk of the operations had to be transferred to other ON Semiconductor facilities with available production equipment capacity and excess floor space, along with external subcontractors.

At the time the Thailand floods occurred, the COO PMO was extremely busy with the SANYO manufacturing consolidation and other programs.

The PMO had grown from a team of 7 program managers and the PMO leader with a portfolio of roughly 20 programs to a global team of over 20 program managers running over 45 programs. Although the team first considered adding additional program managers and overlaying the PMO assets and portfolio management approach, it was quickly recognized that due to the urgency of the situation and specific needs related to project selection and execution, a different approach was needed.

The Thailand flood had significant impact on ON Semiconductor's customers and revenue. Speed of execution was of utmost importance in the recovery efforts. To plan and execute the recovery, a temporary PMO was put in place. As shown in Figure S19.3, the COO PMO provided the PMO architecture and guidance on program structure and planning.

A senior leader in the region was selected to lead the recovery effort and a small team was assembled with engineering, procurement, and manufacturing expertise to rapidly define the programs necessary to recover the production capability. Five programs were defined to recover manufacturing capability in internal sites in Malaysia, Japan, the Philippines, and China. Two additional programs were defined to divert some portion of the manufacturing to subcontractors.

PMO Architecture

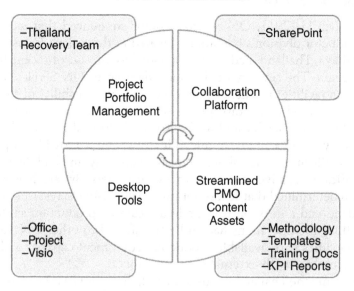

Figure S19.3   PMO architecture for temporary PMO

Due to the compressed timescale of recovery, there was significant overlap in the timescales of the project definition from the project portfolio management team and the program planning and execution by the project teams. Within the content assets, the project management methodology was streamlined and simplified by the COO PMO leaders to maintain only critical elements needed for execution. Special emphasis was placed on dynamic scope control due to the rapid and dynamic definition of the programs. More than half of the program managers deployed were not familiar with the project management methodology and short cycle training sessions were held. Several of the program managers were loaned from the COO PMO team temporarily to run programs and to facilitate training and program planning. Program key performance indicators were reported every two weeks to the COO PMO and senior members in operations. The status of the program was reported by the COO PMO to the executive staff of the company on a monthly basis and to the board of directors on a quarterly basis.

There was significant apprehension on the part of the customers and the senior leaders of ON Semiconductor with respect to the time it would take to recover production capabilities. Much of the replacement equipment needed had significant lead times (two to four months), with installation and qualification durations ranging from one to three months in many cases. In addition, some of the piece parts and raw materials needed were also impacted by the flooding in Thailand. However, through some very innovative efforts by the temporary PMO and project teams, manufacturing capabilities were reestablished much quicker than anticipated. ON Semiconductor made the decision to not restart operations in Thailand in late November of 2011. By mid-December, many of the product lines had restarted. By February 2012, the team had recovered 67% of the capability and over 95% by the end of April 2012. The success of this recovery was due to the efforts of a very nimble and focused team. The COO PMO addressed an urgent business need by providing a simplified PMO architecture and resources for project planning, execution, and communication.

Concluding Thoughts and Advice

I have given two examples of a PMO adapting to business needs. In the case of the SANYO consolidation programs, the PMO addressed the needs of the business by rapidly expanding into Japan with a team for portfolio management and bringing in multilingual program managers to drive execution. The majority of the existing PMO architecture was overlaid on this large program to successfully drive large cost savings. In the case of the re-covery from the floods in Thailand, the PMO responded by providing the necessary PMO architecture, a portion of the program managers, training, project planning, and communication to the company executives. In both cases the PMO responded by utilizing their expertise and resources to best meet the needs of the business. By constantly adapting the changing needs of the business, the PMO demonstrated significant value to the company.

PMO Success Story #20: Fujitsu Sweden

Building an Enterprise PMO

John O'Neill, Manager, Enterprise PMO, Fujitsu Sweden

Introduction to Fujitsu Sweden

Fujitsu Sweden is part of the global Fujitsu Company, which has 170,000 employees supporting customers in over 100 countries and net sales of US$55 billion. In Sweden, we are an end-to-end provider in the field of information and communication technology, serving companies and organizations. We help customers adapt their IT and operations to new needs and demands, helping reduce costs and increase efficiency. Fujitsu is a leader in Lean IT in Sweden, working, for example, at the forefront of service desk provision. The list of renowned global companies choosing to work with Fujitsu is long. In Sweden, our customers include Volvo Car Corporation, Husqvarna, Electrolux, and Scania.

We are also a supplier to the Swedish state and Swedish municipalities and county councils throughout the country, providing them with expert consultants as well as products and IT services, all via a general agreement with Sweden's Legal, Financial, and Administrative Services Agency. Moreover, via our regional offices we are an important local IT partner for companies all over Sweden.

Business Problems to Be Addressed by the PMO

At the beginning of 2011, each of the major outsourcing accounts had its own PMO or at least a PMO manager. These PMOs managed internal projects and the reporting of external customer-driven projects. There was a program and project management (P&PM) function, but at that time it only provided PRINCE2® (hereafter referred to as PRINCE2) templates and project management training from an external provider. Some of the problems facing the management team and each account were:

◆ Despite the fact that PRINCE2 was the approved project steering model, there was inconsistent application of PRINCE2 and varying levels of project management maturity.
◆ Each account PMO was fixing its own problems in the areas of reporting, budget preparation, cost tracking, and risk management.
◆ There was no proper information sharing and discussion about project management practices among the accounts.
◆ Management team members were receiving reports in different formats and it was hard to get a proper overall picture of all the projects.
◆ Small internal improvement projects were not reported in the same way as the bigger external projects and tended to have more relaxed standards.
◆ There was no overall auditing function for all projects.
◆ There was no early warning system for projects, which made it more difficult for a project to get help if it got into trouble.
◆ The P&PM and resource management (RM) functions were receiving requests for changes to templates or tools that sometimes contradicted each other.

Faced with these problems, the management team asked for a business case to be prepared to establish an enterprise PMO (ePMO).

Our Story

The establishment of the ePMO was to be run as a PRINCE2 project with emphasis on a good business case and strong executive representation on the project board (this is the PRINCE2 equivalent of a project steering committee). From discussions with Fujitsu PMO managers in other countries, we were advised to have the following additional aspects firmly established:

◆ The ePMO must report quite high up in the company hierarchy to ensure information could quickly reach the people who had to make decisions that affected the accounts and to give the new function the appropriate authority.
◆ The ePMO must be able to prove its value to the company by using performance metrics linked to the business case and also help the accounts develop metrics that would help them see problems and take corrective action.

When the ePMO was established, it reported to the newly created Enterprise Business Management Office, which in turn reported to the director of the major accounts.

As shown in Figure S20.1, the first of many things to be established was a set of metrics to be used by each account and the ePMO itself to establish a set of baseline values for various project management metrics. The accounts are responsible for running their projects to a high standard, and the ePMO will check the compliance to that standard. Some of the account key performance indicators (KPIs) are:

- ◆ Budget KPI
  - Measurement: Cost variance at close of project
  - Target: 100% of all projects should be delivered within their agreed budget
- ◆ Customer satisfaction KPI
  - Measurement: Customer satisfaction at the close of the project
  - Target: 75% of all projects should have a customer satisfaction rate of 7 out of 10

Some of the ePMO KPIs are:

- ◆ Account compliance with project highlight reporting deadlines and quality
  - Measurement: Project highlight reports are sent on time (specific due date) by each account and are completed to ePMO standards (according to template specification)
  - Target: 100% of all projects
- ◆ Account compliance with project portfolio and risk reporting deadlines and quality

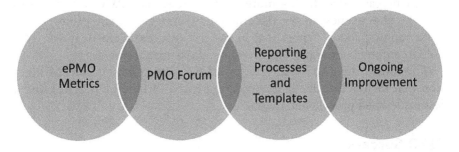

Figure S20.1   Establishing the ePMO

- Measurement: Project portfolio and risk reporting are sent on time (specific due date) by each account and are completed to ePMO standards (according to template specification)
- Target: 100% of all projects

The second thing to be established was a PMO Forum, where all the PMO managers from the different accounts could discuss problems and agree on common solutions. The PMO Forum was also used to consolidate requirements that would then be sent to the P&PM and RM functions as well as a means to reinforce management reporting requirements. At the same time as the PMO Forum was established, we reinforced the usage of the company's time reporting system so that project managers could get the resource costs of their projects more easily rather than tracking hours spent and hourly rates in order to calculate resource costs.

The third thing to be established was a set of reporting templates and reporting processes for individual projects, project portfolios, and risks.

The project reporting template was an improved version of the existing PRINCE2 project highlight report. This new template, which consisted of one PowerPoint slide, was like a mini project plan with a section for cost, risk, issues, overall progress, achievements, and milestones. The goal of this template was to establish a minimum, consistent project management standard for all projects.

The portfolio report template included standard sections on cost and schedule metrics, but also a status history to give an early warning and an additional Excel tab that included a portfolio health check that recorded quality checks for each project along with an overall health rating for each project.

The risk management template contained many standard risk management items with one exception: the degree of control over a risk. Some projects took risk management seriously and had good control of their risks, whereas others took a more relaxed view. Each PMO was asked to rate the effectiveness of the risk mitigation strategies of the projects they were running and to report that in the risk register. In this way we were able to emphasize the importance of good risk management.

The fourth thing that was established was a reestablished P&PM function that included an audit function, improved PRINCE templates, and a lessons learned process and database.

PMO Success

As with all changes in the way a company works, there will be those who will question and oppose the change. Success has come gradually and in steps. Simple things like the wording of various quality checks in the project portfolio quality check has made the difference between causing people to be defensive and people wanting to work with the change.

For example, to say that a business case does not exist for a project can sound a bit harsh for people used to getting away with not creating a business case. Instead we changed the wording to say that we were "unable to verify the existence of a business case." This way, people worked to put together a simple business case in a few weeks and not lose face, as all that we said was that we couldn't find the business case in their project directory.

Other successes have meant that we must make changes ourselves. We have a metric that says that every project must report its risks using the approved risk register template on time. We now have that success, but we need to go deeper and ask questions like "When was the last risk management meeting to review risks on the project?" and "How many new risks have been identified at this meeting?" All the changes we have made so far have been successful as we have defined success, but we must now dig deeper and redefine success in order to drive even more improvement.

Concluding Thoughts and Advice

In conclusion, I am very glad that we developed such a good business case for the ePMO and got the organization anchored quite high up in the company. A good business case and strong executive support have made all the difference between success and failure. In addition, a good project plan and a set of metrics to show the effectiveness of the ePMO and linking those metrics with the business case have also been invaluable. You must be able to prove your value to the organization at all times, no matter how obvious the need for your PMO.

Other advice would be to keep things as simple as possible and add complexity as needed. Watch your language when you are measuring things so you don't cause people to be defensive; remember that you are trying to change their behavior, not punish them. Finally, I would advise that even when you think everything is looking great, keep on pushing for continuous improvement.

PMO Success Story #21: National Insurance Company

Overcoming Challenges in Creating an Enterprise PMO: It All Comes Down to the People

Frank Parth, PMP, MS, MSSM, MBA, President/CEO, Project Auditors LLC

Introduction to the National Insurance Company

The National Insurance Company (NICO)* is one of the largest insurance companies in the United States. It was begun in the 1860s as a basic life insurance company. Since then it has expanded to seven separate divisions incorporating life insurance, annuities, reinsurance, structured settlement annuities, asset management, investment advice to corporations and defined benefit pension plans, and miscellaneous services such as real estate services, aircraft leasing, and other services.

NICO is a very old organization and like virtually all old organizations has become complex as it has grown and evolved. The history of organizations teaches us that growth is difficult to manage effectively. Management gets excited about growing, and their emphasis tends to be on continued and rapid growth and not efficiently managed growth. Business processes grow and become less efficient, and the organization as a whole tends to grow in disparate directions and become increasingly complex.

Business Problems to Be Addressed by the PMO

Until the late 1990s, the central IT group in the organization handled all the IT requirements for corporate as well as for the multiple divisions. As NICO grew, the divisions expanded their offerings and corporate IT

---

*Note: The name of the company was changed, but the facts of the story are accurate.

became less effective for them. They began demanding corporate approval to develop their own IT groups to better satisfy their increasingly complex requirements. The IT needs of real estate services, for example, were quite different from those of the life insurance division. By the late 1990s, corporate management agreed with the divisions and they were given permission to develop their own internal IT groups to more efficiently satisfy their requirements.

Within a few years corporate management realized that giving the divisions carte blanche approval may not have been the most financially beneficial approach. Within five years the life insurance division had spent almost $10M on consulting contracts with a major consulting firm. The annuities division had spent almost as much on a Cray computer for their sole use. Costs were skyrocketing with no end in sight and the cost/benefit analysis had disappeared. The decision was made to integrate all the IT processing back to corporate, a decision that led to a huge outcry from the divisions and refusal to participate in the reintegration effort. (Note: never give something to someone if you think you'll have to take it away later.)

As a compromise, corporate and the divisions agreed that common processing needs such as payroll, taxes, and so on would be performed by the corporate IT department, but the divisions could keep their own IT groups to handle their unique needs. Corporate hired a new CIO for their IT group who was involved in the negotiations process. It was at this point that I was contacted.

Our Story

When I was brought in to develop a PMO for NICO's corporate IT group, the first thing I was told was that we could not call it a PMO. A PMO had been tried before and failed miserably, leaving behind a lot of bad feelings about PMOs. So we called it a PTO—a Project Technology Office. The only difference between a PMO and the PTO was the name.

There were two goals for the PMO. The first was to focus the IT resources on the high-priority projects. Management was paying for roughly 11,000 days of full time equivalent time per month and not seeing their projects getting done. The second goal was to support the reintegration effort. Get concurrence from the divisional CIOs on what would be brought back to corporate and what they could do themselves.

I very quickly realized that this was not going to be a normal PMO effort, not because the organization was unusual, not because they did something really unique, but because of the players involved, particularly because of the new CIO who had been hired a few months earlier. During the discussions about reintegrating IT services, he had angered the divisional CIOs to the point where they were no longer willing to talk to him. The atmosphere had become completely dysfunctional. Getting cooperation from them now became my job.

The new CIO used the same set of *soft skills* in managing the corporate IT department. When I first got there the IT employees were very friendly and it was a good, supportive environment in which to work. The work wasn't getting done as expected, but that was due to a lack of prioritization and unrealistic expectations of management.

The new CIO was a great believer in leadership. He would talk endlessly about leadership. Some weeks we spent over eight hours hearing about good leadership. Unfortunately, the reality of how to become a *leader* did not support what we were being told. The CIO's approach to leadership was to tear into staff members and berate them in all-hands meetings. Humiliation was a common tactic of his. There were many meetings where people who had been there for 20 and 25 years would leave in tears. Within a few months what had been a collegial atmosphere had changed to a purely political, backstabbing environment. Finger-pointing became the daily exercise when things weren't happening.

Despite the difficult environment, the development of the PMO had to continue. The first steps in developing a PMO are:

◆ Identify the goals of the PMO.
◆ Identify the work that's already being done.
◆ Identify the priorities. If there are no prioritization or project selection processes, develop one.
◆ Develop the project management processes that are needed.
◆ Implement the changes.

The goals of the PMO were already determined. The staff I determined I needed was a minimum of five project managers and seven business analysts (BAs), one BA for each division and for corporate. The BA's job was to understand how the divisions operated and what their priorities were. The small number of project managers turned out later to be a resource limitation in getting projects completed, but because of the length of time required to hire personnel, the request was put into HR before the project portfolio was completed.

There was no list of projects that the IT staff was working on. Rather, there were multiple lists that did not agree with each other. When we compiled the full suite of projects, we discovered there were 105 projects in work or waiting to be worked on. There was no project selection process or prioritization process.

Corporate IT was divided into the website team, network operations, mainframe data center, an architecture group, corporate information security office, and my PMO. Because of the lack of timekeeping there was no way to tell what the staff was working on. People were working over 40 hours a week, but the work wasn't getting done as management expected. One of my first steps was to use a programmer to develop a small time tracking app. On Friday afternoons the developers and testers were asked to log on to the internal IT site and input, as well as they could remember it, what they spent their time on in the past week. Very simple, but remember that there was no time tracking before. We asked them to estimate how much time they spent in core maintenance work, project work, bug fixes, and *anything else*. The anything else included vacation, sick time, training, holidays, etc.

After about two months we discovered the availabilities for project work as shown in Figure S21.1. Once we saw these numbers, the reasons why management's projects weren't getting done as expected were immediately obvious. The majority of the projects were done by either the website team or network operations, and most of their time was spent on nonproject work. The PMO was 100% dedicated to project work and the security team's work was done through projects, so 90% of their work was

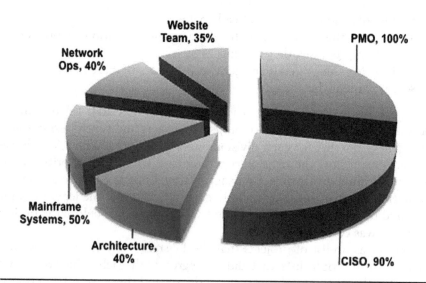

Figure S21.1   Availabilities for project work

project related. For the other teams, most of their work involved all the other activities of a normal IT shop. There were some project management processes in place, but they were very rudimentary. There was no change control board and no consistent approach to planning or documenting.

PMO Success

Despite the serious political and personnel issues involved, the PMO was established by starting slowly and evolving. Once we understood the number of projects in the pipeline, we worked with both corporate and division management to determine the priorities. We then laid out the projects according to the resources available using the average availabilities we found by doing the timekeeping effort. Part of this new process was a formal project selection process involving all the divisional CIOs at a monthly strategic planning meeting. Because of the poor relations the corporate CIO had developed, the PMO led the meeting and presented a list of potential projects to the CIOs to be voted on. The list was created by the BAs based on their work in the divisions.

Not all divisions had equal votes. The different divisions contributed financing to the integration effort depending on their income. Larger divisions had greater influence over the projects selected because they contributed more money to the overall effort.

All projects were scheduled according to the most limited resources. This is similar to the critical chain approach to managing projects. As projects completed and resources became available, we would pick up another project. In order to ensure the project managers within the PMO were not working a hundred hours a week, we limited them to a maximum of no more than four projects at a time depending on project size and complexity. Several times the limited number of project managers was the primary resource limitation.

The next step, once we had determined the priorities, was to develop some basic project management processes such as change management, formal requirements gathering, and so on. This was no more than a CMMI Level 2 capability per the Carnegie Mellon University Software Engineering Institute's Capability Maturity Model Integration process improvement approach, but it was an improvement over what existed before. We implemented the processes on new projects as they arrived at the top of the priority list.

After several years the PMO is still in place and is doing more than the original plan. As a consultant, I left after about a year but kept in touch with the full-time employee who was brought in to manage the PMO on an operational basis. The PMO has outlasted the CIO, who was *released to his destiny*, to use phrasing popularized by Jack Welch when he was CEO of General Electric.

Concluding Thoughts and Advice

Even in difficult political environments it is possible to establish a viable PMO. The PMO itself must be perfectly neutral and focus on what is best for the larger organization. Start by understanding what upper management expects out of the PMO and ensure their expectations are reasonable under the constraints of time and resources. The IT department in any organization exists for the benefit of the organization. After cleaning existing projects, ensure that there is a selection process in place focused on the highest priority projects that can be done given the resources available for projects.

PMOs have attracted lots of attention in the past 10 years. A poorly designed PMO will not last long. It will be taken apart by a stakeholder who always felt it was not worthwhile, or it will simply die of inertia if it becomes too bureaucratic and process driven. A well-designed PMO will become part of the organization's DNA and provide lasting benefits by ensuring that only the most beneficial projects are worked on.

PMO Success Story #22: IBM Branch Office 120

Back to the Future–An Unusual PMO Story

Mark Price Perry, Founder, BOT International

Introduction to IBM Branch Office 120

In the year 1982, Branch Office 120 located in Dallas, Texas, was one of over 200 IBM branch offices peppered about the United States. It was one of the largest branch offices in the IBM Data Processing Division (DPD), and it was responsible for selling and installing large systems hardware and software that companies needed to run their businesses, such as mainframe computers, channel systems and control units, storage devices, magnetic tape subsystems, terminal display devices, operating systems, databases, applications, and a wide variety of industry-specific devices. Back then, we had two mottos: "If it don't drink, it don't think" (a barb intended to discredit the new air-cooled mainframes coming from Japan) and "If God thought distributed computing was a good idea, then He would have put brains in our wrists" (another barb, intended to dismiss the growing interest in minicomputers and the newly announced personal computer). Thank goodness for the progress in the last three decades!

As a rather autonomous business unit, Branch Office 120 was a $250 million operation with over 100 employees, mostly comprised of account marketing representatives, systems engineers, account administrators, and management. The branch office was headed by a seasoned and well-respected branch manager, Doug Potter, who was accustomed to not just making but exceeding his business objectives, mainly revenue, profit, and customer satisfaction. Likewise, the executive management team of IBM expected its branch managers to run their branches as if they were their own company. Yes, headquarters was there to help, but they gave the branch managers full powers and discretion to develop and execute the local branch office plans and strategies. Those branch managers who made their numbers were rewarded, and those who didn't were replaced. Period.

Business Problems to Be Addressed by the PMO

By the start of 1982, IBM had a big looming problem. By way of background, back then a customer couldn't purchase a mainframe computer; rather, it was rented on a monthly basis and you had to place your orders early as there was a two-year waiting period for delivery. For years, this model had served IBM well, providing it with a *cash cow* business in which 80% of the next year's revenue was known in advance and two years of manufacturing backlog was committed to by a highly loyal customer base. So what was the problem? Well, there were two problems actually. One was the growth rate in the consumption of information technology. Simply put, demand was greater than IBM could meet. The other problem was rising competitors, mainly from Japan, that were offering mainframe computers with significant price-performance improvements over the existing IBM mainframes and with delivery schedules and customer availability measured in months, not years.

Imagine a customer that needed new additional computing capacity faced with the decision: go with the $5 million IBM mainframe and wait a year or more for delivery, or go with one of IBM's competitors offering similar capacity but a price of $3 million and a delivery time of four to six months. Now imagine 10,000 of these customers worldwide. Bottom line: IBM needed to tune up its business model and it did. IBM made tremendous investments in raw manufacturing that significantly increased supply and decreased delivery periods. It also moved away from its rental model to a purchase-only model. Hence going forward, IBM's future success would be measured by the introduction and timely delivery of new, leading-edge, competitive products and technologies that customers would purchase as opposed to IBM having a large rental base of increasingly outdated machines with shorter and shorter life expectancies that, oh by the way, customers could walk away from at any time.

All of this change was needed and it was well received by customers, market analysts, and Wall Street, but it did leave a few problems, or, as I had learned in the IBM training program, *opportunities*, that needed to be addressed by each IBM branch manager, such as:

- ◆ How to educate the field sales teams in the new purchase and leasing programs?
- ◆ How to train the field sales teams in the competitive marketing skills that they will need in order to prevail over a growing list of lower priced competitors?
- ◆ How to inform customers of the new pricing structures and financial offerings?

♦ How to perform the new set of operational processes (selling, contracting, and accounting) in support of the change from a rental to a purchase business model?

♦ And lastly, how to get the fair share of the IBMs staff support to help with all the work?

It was the belief of Doug Potter and his management team that the best way for the branch office to address all the required transformational work that had to be done, above and beyond business as usual, was the formation of a *revenue* project office. Internally, we called it the *Revenue War Room*, but in today's parlance it was just another form of a PMO. The business problems to be addressed by the PMO were simple: ensure a successful transformation and make the revenue plan. No excuses, just results.

Our Story

The management team of the branch office decided to have a PMO and I was named to head it. As explained to me by the branch manager, I would be a one-man project office dedicated to solving problems and getting results. I would have no direct report resources, but I had the full support of the management team and an untold number of potentially available resources not only at the local branch level but at the regional and headquarter level as well. And to ensure that the purpose of the PMO and reason for its existence was not lost upon me and to ensure that I would not get distracted with well-intentioned ideas and pursuits, I was given two measurements that served as both my employee performance plan measurements and the measures for which the PMO would be held accountable. The first measure was based upon end results achieved, and this was given to me in the form of a quota that was the branch office revenue plan. If the $250 million revenue plan was met, I would be appraised as "met expectations"; if the revenue plan was not met, I would be appraised as "failed to meet expectations." The second measure was based upon PMO strategy development and execution, and this was based upon the benefit, perceived or real, by the management team of the collective projects that were undertaken over the course of the year. These measurements resulted in a clear, aligned, and unambiguous focus of the PMO. It is important to note that there were no measurements or credit of any kind given for effort. Effort was not viewed as something to be appraised on or paid for; rather, effort was expected and a condition of employment.

As shown in Figure S22.1, the Revenue PMO was placed quite low in the Dallas Branch Office 120 organization and was far beyond visibility

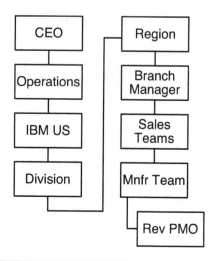

Figure S22.1   Branch Office 120 Revenue PMO

within IBM's executive ranks. I continued to report to the manager of the manufacturing unit, making the placement of the PMO just about as low as it could be. (Author's note: for those who have the view that a PMO is an organization that is either a strategic PMO, enterprise PMO, or IT PMO, this was not that.)

So what did this Revenue PMO do? Well, the first order of business was to meet individually with each of the six sales managers and six of the most senior sales representatives, one from each sales team, to get their input on how the Revenue PMO could help. Immediately, three areas of potential projects emerged that we categorized as knowledge, process improvement, and competitive vitality.

First, in terms of knowledge, we needed customer-grade information that could be used to explain all the new financial acquisition alternatives. That there were data in abundance in the form of a wide variety of announcement letters that arrived at the branch office every Monday was not of debate. That anyone could find and keep up with it all was. As I was told by a number of frustrated managers, data are not the same thing as information and information is not the same thing as knowledge. The field sales teams needed knowledge.

Second, in terms of process improvement, there were a number of administrative considerations with this rental-to-purchase transition that had not been completely thought out. For example, it took an account administrator a minute or two to prepare a purchase quote for a machine that is currently rented. For quoting one $5 million mainframe this was not a big deal, but for quoting a thousand 3278 terminals, the equivalent of a mainframe in terms of revenue, there was not enough time in the day to process the individual quotes. This was just one example of the need to streamline back office accounting functions. There were many others.

Third, in terms of competitive vitality, we needed the ability to more effectively demonstrate the total cost of ownership. In the days of the rental model, this was not an issue since the customer did not own the equipment. Simply comparing the purchase price of a $5 million IBM mainframe to a similar in function competitive mainframe that only cost $3 million would not result in the outcome we wanted. Additional considerations such as end-of-life residual value, upgrade ability, financial terms, service and support, and other areas of IBM *value-add* had to be monetized in a way that was not only fair and accurate but that would pass the scrutiny of the internal IBM business practices advisors, who existed to ensure that IBM maintained the highest level of integrity and accuracy in its competitive marketing.

Armed with a list of projects and more on the way, we converted a 400-square-foot storeroom into what we called the Revenue War Room. It was here that temporary project teams were colocated to work on projects together. We adorned the walls of the war room with our battle plan. On one wall we had the revenue quotas and attainments graphically dashboarded from management down to the individual sales rep level. For this we used a nifty mainframe user application called GDDM—Graphical Data Display Manager. Mind you, this was all pre-PC. On another wall we showed the alignment of the current projects under way and the pipeline of next-in-line projects to the critical success factors required to make the revenue plan of the branch office. And on a third wall, for each active project we showed the high-level project plan in terms of tasks, dates, resources required, costs, and priority, all of which was developed and documented in another mainframe user application called Document Composition Facility or DCF for short.

Throughout the course of the year, the branch office management team met monthly in that Revenue War Room to review revenue performance achieved to date, revenue outlook for the full year, and the list of current and next-in-line projects. In the last month of the year they met weekly in the Revenue War Room and in the last week of the year they met daily. By today's standards we were using stones and axes for tools; no doubt about that. But we were also employing what is now some of the many best practices and principles behind the Agile Manifesto such as colocation, self-organized teams, highly motivated individuals, face-to-face conversations, simple practices, continual reflections and adjustments to become more effective, and a clear focus on the outcome to be achieved in the eyes of the customer.

PMO Success

By the end of the year, this low-level departmental PMO had performed over 75 revenue-enabling projects ranging from customer events to executive fly-ins, development of purchasing quoting tools, internal training events, strategic account analysis workshops, and a wide variety of process improvement activities as well as provided regular control reporting for the annual revenue plan. Far more important however, the PMO exceeded its $250 million goal by 8%, contributing a $20 million surplus in revenue, which earned the branch manager the #1 rank and a trip to the prestigious IBM Golden Circle recognition event in Hawaii, not to mention a handsome year-end bonus. Additionally, the Revenue PMO was recognized as a key driver of revenue performance and a key differentiator between Branch Office 120 and its many branch office peers that had the same set of business conditions, but that did not arrive at the same strategic decision to establish a departmental PMO.

Concluding Thoughts and Advice

There is no limit to the value of a business driven PMO. I would like to think that no one is more passionate about this than I, but I know that is not true. But perhaps what makes my PMO convictions just a little different than others is that all of my PMO-related experiences in my early career were not in the IT department PMO or enterprise PMO or strategic PMO; rather they were in field divisions, departments, and business units and well down the corporate organizational ladder. The Revenue PMO story you have just read was the first of six very successful business unit PMOs that I was a member of, led, or that existed within my organization. The end results achieved by these field business unit PMOs were not only measurable and significant, but in each case they presented direct evidence by way of comparison to other peer business units in the same company that could have had a PMO but for whatever reasons did not think about it or chose not to do it. Bottom line: in my career experiences and observations to date, those field business organizations that had a PMO of some kind outperformed and achieved better results than those that didn't.

PMO Success Story #23: ING Central and the Rest of Europe

A PMO Best Practice

Henny Portman, PMO Head, ING Insurance & Investment Management

Introduction to ING Insurance Central and the Rest of Europe

ING is a global financial institution of Dutch origin, currently offering banking, investments, life insurance, and retirement services to meet the needs of a broad customer base. ING was one of the first Western financial service companies that entered the insurance market in Central Europe after the political turnaround at the end of the 1980s by starting life insurance companies from scratch.

Today, ING is the number one international life insurer and pension provider in Central Europe. It owns life insurance companies in Hungary, Poland, the Czech and Slovak Republics, Romania, and Bulgaria, as well as Greece, Spain, and Turkey and manages pension funds in Poland, Hungary, the Czech and Slovak Republics, Bulgaria, Romania, and Turkey. Together these operations have about 3,500 employees who serve over 9 million clients throughout the region.

ING Insurance Central and the Rest of Europe offers a wide array of individual endowment, term, and whole life insurance policies designed to meet specific customer needs. Its pension funds manage individual retirement accounts for employees. These comprise both mandatory and voluntary retirement savings.

Business Problems to Be Addressed by the PMO

The financial institution where I started in 2008 had developed very fast, but the project structure and culture had not developed at the same pace. Projects were started, changed, or just continued without proper rationale or underlying business case. Oversight was lacking, project progress

289

status of planning, cost, and risk was not available. Control mechanisms to select the right projects or to put projects on hold if needed were not available or were in a very immature stage. Project managers decided on their own how to manage and control their projects. Management team members were asking questions regarding the rationale of projects, but could not control the whole portfolio. On top of this, the geographical footprint of the organization across several countries within Central and Eastern Europe made things even more complicated. Communication regarding project progress between the management of different countries did not occur regularly and was only on an ad hoc basis. Obviously, sharing of ideas, plans, or lessons learned did not happen at all. Reinventing the wheel was more or less the standard.

Our Story

Figure S23.1 gives a visual presentation of the road we followed to become a mature PMO. As you can imagine, these changes required much more than an overnight exercise. It was a heavy and complex transformation process and it took us three years to realize it.

Within the program we used three plateaus (tranches). The first plateau is called *Foundation* and finished by the end of the first year. The second plateau, *Extension*, took the whole second year, and the last plateau, *Deepening*, took the third and final year of the transformation.

Within each plateau we distinguished three focus areas (projects): (1) Organization setup, (2) Training & Education, and (3) Standards, Methods and Tools. Within each focus area we delivered different but coherent products with proven benefits for the organization to direct portfolios and improve execution power of projects. The three plateaus were defined as follows:

◆ Foundation: This plateau delivered an active PMO community with a supporting regional and local PMO model, including clear roles, responsibilities, and job descriptions. PRINCE2® was selected as the project management standard to accommodate a common project management language, including supporting classroom training and certification. During this plateau a first group of project managers became certified PRINCE2 Practitioners. Development and implementation of a regional lean documentation standard based on building blocks to avoid bulky, inaccessible documents (Portman 2009) supported the idea of having a common project management language. A PMO manual became available to transfer all available know-how and decisions for all involved.

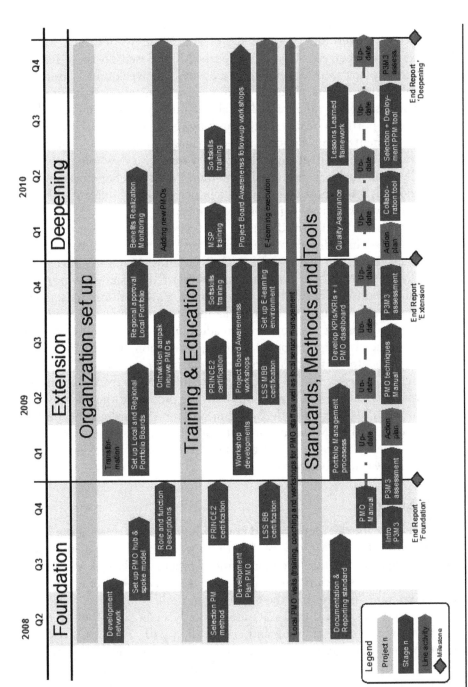

Figure S23.1 Becoming a mature PMO

- Extension: By using the P3M3® model of the United Kingdom Office of Government Commerce of Her Majesty's Treasury, we assessed the current stage of all local PMOs. Based on these results, action plans were developed to improve the weak areas. Some local business units changed their PMO organization structure. All business units implemented local portfolio processes and installed a local portfolio board. An overarching regional portfolio board was implemented too. Besides project manager training, we started to train all project board members. Every quarter a new release of our PMO manual was published, a method that is still being used. On a monthly basis local and regional key performance indicators (KPIs) and key risk indicators (KRIs) are published.
- Deepening: In the third year of the transformation program we introduced, in addition to project and portfolio management, program management. In line with PRINCE2, we chose Managing Successful Programs (MSP®) as our standard. We started to make use of more advanced tools for portfolio management. PMOs offer more services like quality assurance and benefits monitoring. We also moved to a blended learning environment. In addition to classroom training, we introduced computer-based training, simulation, and videos to accommodate continuous learning or *education permanente*. The PMO network was expanded to incorporate new PMOs from the smaller business units. On a continuous basis we promoted the added value of the PMO services, delivered information regarding the performance of the PMOs and project portfolios, and whenever possible we celebrated successes. At the end of this plateau the existence of a PMO was undebatable.

PMO Success

After three years, the moment had come when I had to move away from this initiative. Local PMOs were able to improve the quality of their services as well as their project management process. Relations with their own organizations became more and more a key success factor. A PMO cannot be more mature than the organization itself.

All PMOs of all business units are similarly organized. Project managers follow the same training and certification path. All PMOs use the same project management methodology and use the same documentation standard. Project portfolios are significantly reduced (more than 70% smaller). Projects in the portfolio now have a reasonable chance to become successful. Local and regional portfolio boards drive the priority setting, assess the rationale and feasibility of the projects, and using lessons learned from projects became a common practice.

On a periodic basis progress reports on projects and KPIs and KRIs of PMOs are available. For (new) project board members, project board awareness workshops are available and have been used many times. Yearly PMO assessments, based on P3M3, keep local PMO heads sharp. Our goal "to have more successful projects using fewer resources (people, means, budget)" is more than achieved.

The quality of local PMOs is comparable. PMOs can now focus on projects that are facing *bad weather*. Projects in the portfolio are there to help achieve the business unit's strategy. Priority setting makes embedding of new projects in the portfolio easier. Everyone knows what project has the highest priority. Authorization at the regional level makes leveling between local portfolios possible.

In line with PRINCE2, benefits review plans are available. Local PMOs monitor the realization of those benefits (not yet implemented everywhere). More than 200 staff members are certified PRINCE2 Foundation and more than 70 are certified PRINCE2 Practitioner.

By managing the PRINCE2 training classes by ourselves we reduced the barriers to start with these training classes enormously. Also the blended environment with e-learning facilities helped a lot. Project board members are the key to success; they can create favorable circumstances for project managers to become more successful. Local PMO heads know each other; sharing of knowledge and best practices is generally accepted. More and more project managers start their projects with requests for information and sharing of experience from their colleagues.

Concluding Thoughts and Advice

The importance of a PMO is not in question. We showed more than adequately that the existence of a PMO helps an organization become ready for battle, be effective and efficient, and have the power to execute projects. Whether an international or local organization or a big or small private or public company, every organization is facing the reality of having to realize its programs or projects with scarce resources, time pressures, and changing interests. A PMO can facilitate and support organizations.

Of course, your journey will not be the same as mine. What I envisioned as a difficult problem could be a piece of cake in your situation. There will be problems to overcome. Divide them into smaller parts. You cannot eat an elephant in one bite; you have to chew it bit by bit. I enjoyed my journey and the destination; I hope you will enjoy yours.

Reference

Portman, H. 2009. *PRINCE2 in Practice: A Practical Approach to Create Project Management Documents.* Van Haren Publishing, Zaltbommel, Nederland.

PMO Success Story #24: Consulting for the Pharmaceutical Industry

One Size Does Not Fit All

Patrick Richard, Senior Project/Program Manager, PRGPPM

Introduction to the Company

PRGPPM is my own single-employee project management company, working specifically in IT software development and customization. Previously I worked for a company providing project and program management services in manufacturing IT, mostly for the pharmaceutical industry. That company started as a group of 10 employees in a single office, grew to 150 employees in five offices in Canada and the United States but with projects worldwide, and was finally acquired by the U.S. branch of a multinational engineering and construction company.

Projects ranged from the very simple to the very large and clients from single sites to multinational concerns. This allowed us to witness project management needs from the most basic to those of a whole enterprise. The strengths and weaknesses we witnessed are not those of the pharmaceutical industry in particular; they are present in IT in many industries.

Business Problems to Be Addressed by the PMO

As you would expect from the range of projects and clients, and considering the growth of the company I worked for, the business problems were manyfold. The larger clients needed to instill some semblance of consistency in their project management practices with an aim of having projects end on time and on budget because there was just too much variability for comfort. Some projects had budgets that ballooned to three times the initial estimate whereas others came in under budget. Some technically simple projects had an elapsed duration six to nine times the initial estimate, tying up client resources and their capacity to take on more projects.

The smaller clients needed the same consistency but for different reasons; a single project could kill the company by being late or over budget. Imagine a company fueled by venture capital and in a fiercely competitive environment. It may run out of funds and fail to deliver a new drug that would save or improve the life of many. It may come out too late, which means the company is scooped by its competition and its efforts result in a *me too* drug.

The company I worked for needed to increase the predictability of the execution of projects; many of which were delivered under the worst of the fixed cost forms: time and materials—not to exceed. Growth for us meant that the estimation might be done by one group and the execution by another, and because these groups could have very different levels of experience, the budget or schedule may be compromised from the get-go. This meant that we could face instances where money was left on the table, where the company would be left holding the bag, where personnel would become available earlier than expected, or where personnel could not be freed fast enough. All these are growth limiting for a services company.

Our Story or Stories

As you might expect by now, there is not only one PMO story here. My bigger clients typically had large and multiple PMOs. The medium-size ones might only have an IT PMO. The smaller one typically relied on the project management structure of the company for which I worked.

Interestingly, the bigger clients had more PMO maturity in the construction and plant delivery areas of the business than in the IT or financial areas. Specifically related to IT, in most cases it appeared that PMOs were created more because *you have to have one* than as a result of a need analysis. This resulted in PMOs appearing in companies where project managers typically did not set up and maintain means of tracking schedules and financials. Oftentimes these PMOs were established as overlords to the actual project managers delivering the projects. Most of the time they had reams of procedures that had to be obeyed and were staffed by people well versed in project management theory rather than equipped with practical experience. In one particular instance, we were directed to enter only milestones in the enterprise project management system but we were expected to use the system for earned value calculations. Basically that meant maintaining and synchronizing two sets of schedules. Risk registries, issues registries, etc. were to be maintained outside the enterprise project management system.

Even the company I was working for had its book of project management practices. It can be viewed as a paper-based PMO. It had been written by two very experienced project managers and resulted in a three-ring binder of procedures that was four inches thick. It covered everything from soup to nuts and was, in theory, to be applied to every project, big or small. There were no mentions in there of document management systems or other electronic systems that could aid in managing projects.

PMO Success

I'll start by covering what happened with the variations described above and finish with a minimalist but successful outcome. First, the large-scale enterprise-wide IT PMO failed to take hold for a number of reasons: no real buy-in from the client because it was just a fad, no real buy-in from the project managers because it caused duplication of effort and other issues which made the system too cumbersome, and no buy-in at all from the project teams that just ignored the tasks automatically delivered to their e-mails.

The IT-only implementations failed mostly because they were a case of too much, too soon. They were put in place without the support of a project management culture that existed in the engineering areas.

My previous company's approach failed because, although it was based on valuable experience, it was too cumbersome and manual. There were meetings to decide on every little tweak to a procedure, you had to adhere to way too many procedures regardless of the size of the project, and you had to maintain way too much paper manually when a computer could have done it better and faster. Also, it did not fulfill a need genuinely recognized by the organization.

The very minimalist application that worked for us did so because it had buy-in from the few individuals who worked with it, was mostly automated, allowed anyone to modify it as needed and have the changes propagated automatically, allowed all project managers in the group to be constantly updated on the status of all projects, and promoted peer review of documents and sharing of problem-solving ideas.

Basically, we used the Microsoft tools available to us, although other vendor offerings likely have similar capabilities. We wrote our document in Word, built the schedule in Project, created risk and other lists in Excel, etc. The glue that provided automatic propagation was Workspace over

SharePoint. For example, you would prepare a schedule with Project and Workspace copied it from your computer to the SharePoint server. The other project managers were also part of the Workspace, and any document that they created or modified was sent to SharePoint. A project manager who had been working remotely got synced when his/her computer reached the SharePoint server. This meant that all procedures, all project artifacts, etc. were always synced between participants and that documents existed in multiple, simultaneous exact copies, diminishing the possibility of loss. Of course SharePoint was backed up daily.

Outside the technical approach we used, we made a conscious choice to keep our PMO streamlined by keeping the number of procedures to a minimum and by adjusting their use to the scale of individual projects. I'd like to say it was our collective genius that made it a success, but it was really blind luck.

Concluding Thoughts and Advice

This may seem too simplistic a list of thoughts and advice, but simplicity has virtues.

Walk, don't run. If your organization does not have a project management culture, develop one from the ground up before going to a PMO.

Get the PMO you need, or put another way, think BIG (enough). Maybe you can realize the benefits of a full-featured PMO. Maybe you even need multiple PMOs to address the full range of activities of the company. Maybe what you need can only loosely be called a PMO. Be sure to avoid having the PMO become its own bureaucracy that starts to exist for its own benefit, crushing projects and the company under its weight at the same time.

Use your PMO as a tool to strengthen your project managers, not as a tool to constrain them. This is a variation of the old adage that says that there are more good ideas in multiple heads. If you constrain people, they won't join in and you'll miss out on the opportunity to capture and share their wisdom and experience.

Regardless of the size of PMO you decide to implement, remember that it will not appear fully formed out of thin air. Expect that it will take some time to hit its stride and that there will be successes and mistakes along the way. You can have a slow and boring rollout of a successful PMO or a fast and spectacular failure.

PMO Success Story #25: NAVMISSA

"Finding Balance"

LCDR Andrew Wilson, Director PMO, NAVMISSA
Karen Krause, Deputy Director PMO, NAVMISSA

Introduction to Navy Medicine Information Systems Support Activity

The United States Navy has over 50 medical organizations that span the globe requiring an information management/information technology infrastructure that reliably and securely transfers patient medical information across the world, at sea or on land. These organizations range in size from large medical centers to warships at sea and total over 50,000 users. The Navy Medicine Information Systems Support Activity (NAVMISSA) was established in 2008 to provide the operational management of the many enterprise health care and/or medical business systems used to provide care to our patients. Its mission is to deliver health care value through high-quality information systems and services for military medicine. To support this mission, NAVMISSA utilizes a range of professional and technical services that are provided to the enterprise including project, program, and service management.

Business Problems to Be Addressed by the PMO

NAVMISSA was essentially a start-up in 2008, a clean slate with new staff and few policies and operating procedures in place. Executive management made the assessment that in order for NAVMISSA to be successful, they needed to establish a PMO that would adopt best practice project management tools

---

and templates. Specifically, those tools and templates were to be solely based on the Project Management Institute's (PMI®) *A Guide to the Project Management Body of Knowledge* (*PMBOK® Guide*).

This business problem was seen as urgent and thus NAVMISSA's PMO was immediately established and put into action, answering straight to the Commanding Officer (CO), the Navy's equivalent of a CEO of an organization.

Our Story

Our PMO was initially staffed with a director and a staff of two. Our first task from the CO was to produce a project management book of templates based on PMI best practices. The PMO worked for four months to complete 15 templates and the instructions and training for their use. With a sense of great pride in our accomplishment, we set up a daylong training session with the project managers to introduce the templates and provide instruction on how they should be used. Our CO was delighted because we had produced exactly what was requested, but our project managers were less than enthusiastic. They found that the templates were too restrictive and did not provide them what was needed to assist them in managing their projects. This resulted in every template the PMO produced becoming project management shelfware. The PMO's value to the organization was questioned, and we were deemed unnecessary overhead by most, if not all, of NAVMISSA's staff with the exception of the CO.

Knowing we had missed the mark, we decided to take a look at the lessons we had learned. We found that having the support of our CO was necessary in establishing a PMO. However, we found there were actions we could have taken that would have improved our chances of providing value to the organization:

- ◆ We should have developed a business case/plan. Had we taken the time to develop a business case that addressed the business problems to be solved, and clearly identified our vision, mission, goals, and objectives, we would have been able to communicate with all of our customers better and determine the initiatives required to meet our goals and objectives. This would have given us the ability to show value back to the organization from the beginning.
- ◆ We should have identified all of our customers. By focusing on one customer (our CO) and only gathering the requirements of the CO, we missed an opportunity to understand how the tools would be

used by the project managers and what pain points the tools needed to address.

◆ We should have understood the business needs before attempting to implement best practices by producing tools without the process behind those tools.

To apply the lessons learned, we took a strategic pause in the development of new products and focused instead on our customers. We admitted the first release did not go well and worked specifically on establishing relationships with all of our customer groups. This required formal and informal meetings to understand our customers' pain points, how they do business, and what their requirements were of the PMO.

We created the *Out of Your Seat Policy*, meaning PMO staff needed to be away from their desks and in the trenches alongside their customers. To rebuild credibility, we worked on several small projects that generated some quick wins to demonstrate value and restore confidence in the PMO. Our second release was much different. We attempted to introduce process to support the latest release of project management tools. More importantly, we moved away from a best practices approach where we dictated how a project manager should manage his project to one where the project manager had discretion to use whatever tools and process he wanted and in whatever way he felt was best. The second release, though not entirely successful, was an improvement. Because we had worked so closely with the project managers, we had buy-in prior to the release and were able to restore confidence in the PMO. However, executives had mixed feelings in this release due to the amount of discretion a project manager had in the management of his projects, which resulted in little to no standardization.

We decided to complete another lessons learned session and found the actions we had taken from the prior lessons learned session, such as building relationships at all levels of the organization and gathering requirements from all our customer groups, had generated positive results. These lessons learned also identified areas for improvement.

◆ We realized too much customer discretion had resulted in practically no standardization and no project management processes, which made it very difficult to measure performance and quality. We had basically overcorrected.

We again applied our lessons learned to further refine our approach. This time we looked inward and standardized the way our PMO developed its products. Doing so allowed the PMO to develop products more efficiently and measure the quality of our products. We also moved away from producing tools and focused on developing outcome-based project management processes that are standardized, integrated, and measurable.

Our process development focuses on identifying best practice but tailoring it to the needs of the organization. We accomplish this by assembling small teams of subject matter experts (SMEs) from across the organization to help us develop project management processes. By identifying an applicable best practice and gathering the requirements of the SMEs, we are able to strike a balance between best practice and the needs of our customers. Our process developers lead the SMEs through the design and testing of the process, which is based on best practice and the requirements gathered. Each process has metrics defined that allow the PMO to measure the quality of the process and drive continual process improvement. Process competencies are also defined for each process, providing us valuable insight into training needs.

All together this new development approach provided a holistic view into the health of project and process management, and we had finally found the right balance between the needs of the business, best practice, and the needs of our customers.

PMO Success

Our PMO didn't realize success for quite some time. It took nearly three years for the evolution of our PMO as outlined in the story above. We had successes within that time but most were simply internal measures of the PMO in its ability to successfully develop tools and templates. Unfortunately, these measures of success were inwardly focused and not reflective of the successes of our customers and ultimately our organization.

It was when our PMO finally understood the concept of a business driven PMO that we saw true success (see Figure S25.1).

Our newly adopted motto was "The success of our PMO is underpinned by the successes of its customers." By focusing on the needs of the organization we developed outcome-based process and products that increased maturity and ultimately organizational success. This led to customer acceptance of the PMO as a dependable and well-respected partner in assisting them with their business needs. That truly is our biggest success.

After accepting the PMO as a required element for organizational success, our executive leadership invested more in the PMO. Our staffing was increased to seven employees and our scope of services expanded to include other organizational business functions such as strategic planning, enterprise governance, process and quality management, and IT service management.

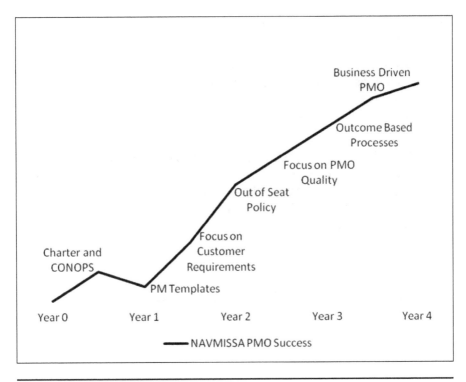

Figure S25.1   NAVMISSA PMO success over time

Concluding Thoughts and Advice

We are occasionally asked to meet with organizations that are starting PMOs. The last two meetings started with "Can we have your templates and tools?" Before we commit to sharing we typically ask a few questions like: What are the needs of the business? What are your leadership's pain points? What is your PMO trying to accomplish? Typically, these questions are answered with blank stares for several moments and then followed by "instill project management best practices." This doesn't answer our questions.

It is our belief that PMOs are initially put in place to be change agents. Change is hard and isn't centered on a set of tools or templates that follow a best practice. Change is truly about people. Through our experiences we have concluded that the following five very basic management principles are instrumental to the success of any PMO and will help facilitate the acceptance of change created by the PMO. Because the principles are elementary in nature they are often overlooked and/or not understood. Don't make that mistake! They are:

1. Know/focus on your customer.
2. Relationship building is paramount.
3. Gather customer requirements.
4. Practice quality management (internal and external to the PMO).
5. Practice what you preach.

The value delivered by a PMO is typically measured by its ability to successfully deliver on the needs of the business or customer. Applying these five principles enables a PMO to fully understand its customers and it ensures that the products the PMO produces meet the needs of the customer and provide value to the business.

PMO Success Story #26: A Global Software and Internet Protocol Networking Product and Service Provider

"Growing Pains"

Troy Youngnickel, PMO Manager, APAC

Introduction to Juniper Networks

Silicon Valley-based Juniper Networks is a global provider of high-performance network infrastructure built on simplicity, security, openness, and scale. As a pure play, high-performance networking company, it offers a broad product portfolio that spans routing, switching, security, application acceleration, identity policy and control, and management designed to provide unmatched performance, greater choice, and true flexibility, while reducing overall total cost of ownership. In addition, through strong industry partnerships, Juniper Networks is fostering a broad ecosystem of innovation across the network. The company has annual revenues in excess of US$4 billion, has offices in 46 countries, and employs more than 9,100 people.

Business Problems to Be Addressed by the PMO

Due to the innovative nature of Juniper's business, a short time to market with new products is imperative to maintain market share and remain at the forefront of customer needs. This necessitates an aligned approach to product development and project delivery. At the outset of this project, the organization had multiple PMOs within the Services organization with minimal project management processes or tools. This, combined with multiple reporting lines and inconsistent project reporting, led Juniper executive management to look for a better way to *steer the ship*. To address this,

305

the team of Professional Services (PS) PMO leaders representing all three theaters was charged with enhancing and developing Juniper's PMO practice. I was included in this team, representing the Asia Pacific PS team.

Our Story

During the fourth quarter of 2010, to determine expectations for the PMO, we requested feedback from executive management as well as theater vice presidents on what specific functions and business needs they expected to be addressed by the PMO. The outcome of this process was a consolidated mandate from our collective management team:

- ◆ Predictable project outcomes
- ◆ Uniform reporting across the globe
- ◆ Methodology that followed recognized standards
- ◆ Scalable processes
- ◆ The most appropriate project documentation management tool selected from those currently available

The global PS PMO team came up with the following prioritized deliverables and priorities:

- ◆ Develop an industry standard project management process and methodology
  - • Predictability in project outcomes
  - • Methodology to follow recognized standards
  - • Project processes must be scalable in line with current and planned projects
  - • Project processes must be aligned with other Juniper business processes
- ◆ Standardize project/portfolio reporting across the globe
  - • Uniform reporting across the globe
  - • Utilize existing project portfolio management (PPM) tools and incorporate into standard templates
  - • Position the new PMO and its tasks with other business functions
  - • Include into Juniper project management methodology (JPMM) suite of processes
- ◆ Adopt a standard project documentation tool and process
  - • Utilize the existing PPM tool (SharePoint) for all project documentation to allow for version control and hierarchical PMO and project filing

- Leverage the knowledge sharing capabilities of MATRIX (Juniper proprietary software for process development) and also individual project knowledge sharing

After much deliberation in the global PMO team due to theater nuances, rather than develop our own methodology, we decided to run with a readily available off-the-shelf project management methodology, which provides a complete methodology that can easily be integrated into current business tools and or processes. Why?

◆ Being a global player and working with many government agencies and large global enterprises, we needed to be able to clearly demonstrate our project management processes are aligned with recognized project management industry standards, in this case PMBOK and PRINCE2®.

◆ There was also no point in reinventing the wheel. Our global team had broad experience with industry standards and it was clear that using base processes rather than developing processes from scratch would save a great deal of time and money.

By the first half of 2011, the target was to take the base processes and load them into existing Juniper tools and formats. This included keeping our JPMM Principles (see Figure S26.1) consistent with the Juniper Way, a set of five values and behaviors all Juniper employees endeavor to follow:

1. We are authentic.
2. We are about trust.
3. We deliver excellence.
4. We pursue bold aspirations.
4. We make a meaningful difference.

With our guiding principles determined, I discovered that—as is common in growing organizations—most members of the global PMO development team were overcommitted on project delivery and unavailable for process development. So I rolled my sleeves up and got into the task of adopting the project management methodology and principles that we purchased and turning them into Juniper documents, making minimal enhancements such as more specific process templates and examples along the way. Reusing some existing process templates and also utilizing input from the rest of the global team meant we were already customizing the base processes into our own methodology. The decision to use *off-the-shelf* base processes was a good one and made it quite easy to take the base documents and transfer them into Juniper templates or directly into our knowledge sharing tool.

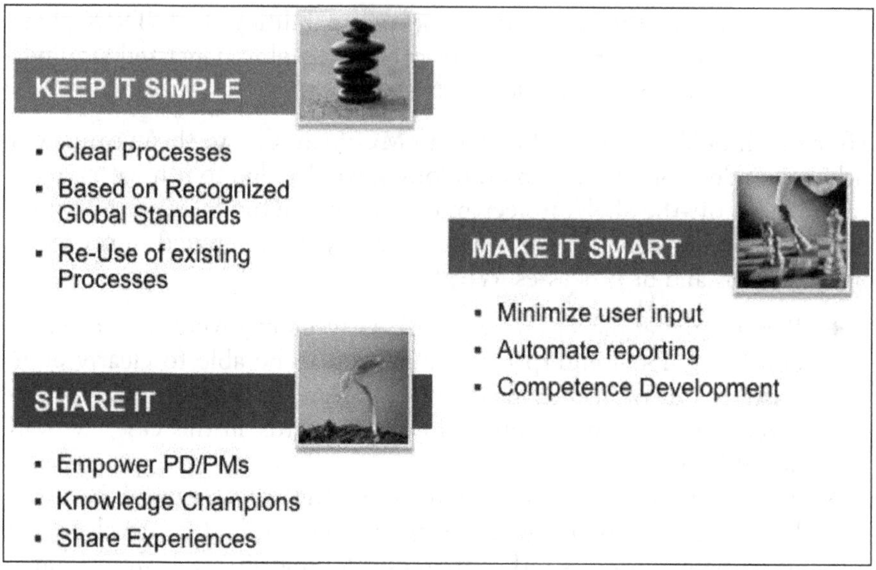

Figure S26.1   JPMM principles

By the second half of 2011, as we went live, wider input from the global team was required, so we asked team members actively running selected programs to provide their feedback on the process. All process development was being done in a knowledge sharing tool, so the extended teams could easily access the processes/templates and provide feedback to me as the administrator of the site for the processing of any updates or changes to the base process documents. This allowed full team visibility with a level of control ensuring we are all operating on the latest version for each document.

The next step was to select strategic *pilot* projects and run them following the JPMM in a controlled environment. This would allow us to further align and enhance the JPMM and allow us to develop the project scaling metrics with real projects while maintaining a globally standard approach. The scaling metrics allow us to scale down on the processes required for low-value/low-risk projects. As a result of the scaling exercise and also some excellent collaboration within the Asia Pacific (APAC) PS team, the *JPMM Umbrella Methodology* consisting of the PM Lite and PM Lite+ was born.

As shown in Figure S26.2, this type of methodology is known as an *umbrella* or singular project management methodology. The approach is not uncommon; it provides flexibility and, more importantly, a business driven project governance toolbox, which very much suits the types of projects we deliver and also accommodates our current business structure. JPMM allows a controlled level of governance across all types of project engagements.

JPMM scales by covering low-risk, one- to two-month consultancies to multiple work streams and very complex and high commercial risk projects or programs. After taking feedback from the project teams running with the strategic *pilot* projects and incorporating best practice industry knowledge, we released JPMM v2, including PM Lite+, which is a subset of JPMM processes. PM Lite targets our consultants and architects, giving them a project management toolbox and enabling them to carry out basic project management activities. Coupled with focused training and theater PMO support, the technical *experts* are now able to manage low-risk projects.

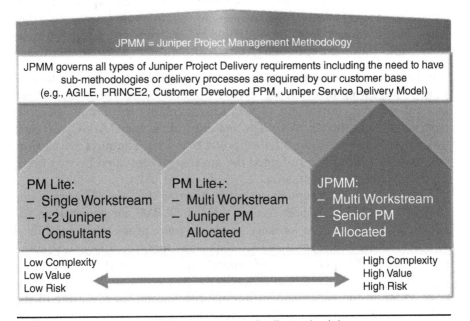

Figure S26.2 Overview of the JPMM v1 *Umbrella Methodology*

We expect to provide new releases of JPMM every six months as new best practice processes come into play, our PMO practice matures, and by continually improving our performance.

PMO Success

After attending a Business Driven PMO workshop conducted by Mark Duddy and Mark Perry in Singapore, my approach to the development and growth of the APAC PMO changed for the better. I was intrigued by a simple question:

> *What does the business need to comply with project management standards and to provide management with what it actually needs?*

This question brought me to other questions:

- ◆ Do I really need to hire project controllers, schedulers, document controllers, and so on?
- ◆ Or should I look at the business requirements and explore more efficient ways of meeting management requirements?
- ◆ Instead of spending on resourcing, can the current team provide the same with a bit of training?

The PM Lite process grew out of this new approach and also the frustrations of a growing professional services business conscious of the bottom line but wanting control and a level of predictability without all the overhead of the traditional PMO. The majority of Juniper (APAC) Services projects are lower-risk consultancy projects and the contracts are all time and materials, which do not need the governance provided by traditional project management processes.

Basic project management training targeting Juniper PS consultants coupled with PMO support has provided the APAC theater with an adequate level of project governance and many more project-savvy technical resources. PM Lite's lower resource requirements save money, too—more than US$250,000 per annum of annual savings versus the classic PMO approach.

In addition, there are signs of internal recognition for the value of the PMO, including approaches from sales teams wanting more project governance. This demand is paving the way for organic growth of the PS Asia Pacific PMO.

Concluding Thoughts and Advice

Having worked within the PMO of a few large organizations over a 15-year project management career, I have noticed that most have a similar emphasis on big beefy processes and adherence to all of them, regardless of the relevance or value to the organization. This adherence is deemed a necessary cost. I grew up as a project management professional thinking that this was *best practice* and the only way to achieve the next level of PMO maturity in the organization. Attending the Business Driven PMO workshop certainly remodeled my thinking and put some hard and relevant facts in front of me for digestion. I recommend that anyone looking to set up or streamline their PMO, large or small, focus on what the company actually expects from the PMO. This approach helps you think outside the box and promotes new and innovative ways to address the PMO.

PMO Success Story #27: PartnerRe

Simple and Adaptable–PMO Success Factors in an Integration Project

Erhard Zingg, Senior Project Manager, and Martin Kuepfer, Head of the Group IT Project Management Office, PartnerRe

"The wise adapt themselves to circumstances as water molds itself
to the pitcher." *—Chinese Proverb*

"Everything should be made as simple as possible, but not simpler."
—Albert Einstein

Introduction to PartnerRe

PartnerRe is a leading global reinsurer, offering risk assumption solutions for the global insurance and capital markets. It provides insurance companies with multiple lines of reinsurance—property and casualty, catastrophe, specialty lines, life, and alternative risk products—through its offices worldwide. Founded in 1993, in response to a market shortage of capacity for catastrophe reinsurance, the company expanded its footprint over the years through the acquisition of two multiline reinsurance operations and subsequent growth of its business.

Business Problem to Be Addressed by the PMO

In 2009, the company decided to acquire another mid-sized reinsurance operation, increasing staff from 1,000 to 1,400 employees. Soon after the undertaking had been announced, both organizations were faced with a challenging road map set forth by executive management to merge the two companies into one. Within five months after the announcement of the acquisition, a new client-facing organization had to be in place, coupled with the establishment of PartnerRe as the sole brand going forward

313

(see Figure S27.1). An additional six months later, all back office functions, processes, and systems were to be integrated, and the newly merged entity was to function as one organization. In this context, many business leaders were appointed to stream leads with project management responsibility. Some time before the acquisition took place, PartnerRe's IT management had decided to install a PMO to mature project management skills and improve project delivery. Hence, executive management turned to it in search of support of the extensive undertaking the company was about to embark upon.

Our Story

When the PMO was established, its first mission was to develop and implement a project management methodology. It was to provide guidance and boundaries with respect to how projects should be managed, but on the other hand was flexible enough that it could be adapted to different types and sizes of projects. All members of the PMO continued to lead and manage projects and did not solely act as a staff function. As a consequence, a concise but practical methodology evolved with a number of tools, templates, and a comprehensive browser-based project management repository, called the PMO Knowledge Center.

When executive management turned to the PMO for support, the decision was quickly made to take what already existed, adapt it as necessary, make it less IT focused, and tailor it to the needs of the business managers who were going to act as project managers. Also, in order to quickly become effective across the two separate operational entities, we provided a common collaboration platform that was both easy to access and intuitive to use. The browser-based platform was used by all project streams. The positive effect was that people of both companies were brought together in a common space where they could work and share information. The structure and functionalities were identical for all, with sufficient flexibility to meet differing requirements. For instance, the legal and HR streams used the platform despite sensitive and confidential topics; we ensured confidentiality by applying restrictive access rights on their respective project sites. An important additional asset was the possibility of bringing everyone onto one platform, even before the IT infrastructures of both companies were merged.

There was only limited time available to ramp up the project organization and make structure and tools available. It was not possible to start offering multiday training blocks to those who were going to take significant

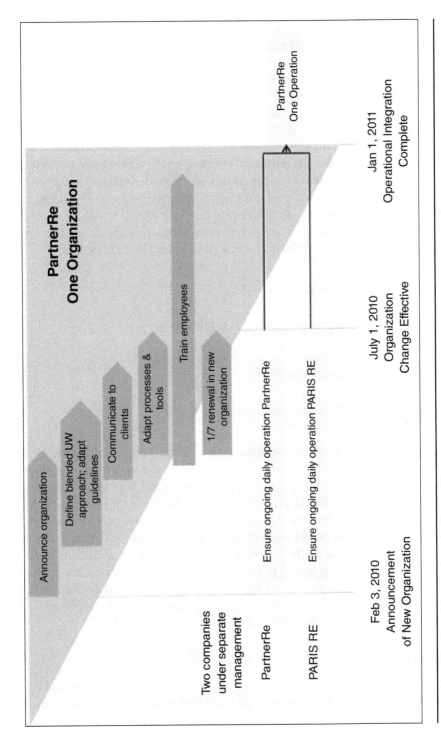

Figure S27.1 Transition to the new PartnerRe

responsibility in this large undertaking. Hence, everything we provided had to be intuitive or self-explanatory and easy to use. This meant, for instance, reducing the complexity of the progress reporting template. Business leaders did not want to be burdened with sophisticated performance indicators and long-winded explanations of how they had to be used or interpreted. What they wanted was a few condensed, concise, and self-explanatory indicators to quickly capture, assess, and challenge the status of each project stream.

It was decided that the business streams would follow a lean project management approach with a minimum set of guidelines, tools, and templates. The IT stream and its subprojects, however, were still obliged to adhere to the full project management methodology because IT project managers had been trained on it and were familiar with its application. The minimum set of project management deliverables included:

- ◆ Project mandate
  - • Project objectives
  - • Project scope
  - • Project milestones and deliverables
  - • Major tasks
  - • Interdependencies to other project streams
- ◆ Project progress report
- ◆ Project budget
- ◆ Project change request(s) as applicable
- ◆ Project completion report

Roles and responsibilities were defined right from the start and made clear to all involved. A comprehensive road map was used to provide the timeline and guidance on the key activities of all streams. A series of recurring status and steering meetings completed the organizational framework. Although some skepticism existed among the professional project managers that the framework would be adequate, experience showed that the lean toolset was sufficient to provide the necessary structure and identify deviations from the plan in a timely manner. The toolset helped the stream leads concentrate on the actual *content* of their stream rather than being perceived as administrative overhead. This would not have happened had the toolset been too time-consuming.

PMO Success

The PMO's most obvious value was certainly the ability to set up and run a dedicated project PMO as quickly as required to drive the integration project forward. The PMO was key in enabling people to start immediately with project work once the green light was given by the executive management. This was greatly owed to the existence of a project management methodology tailored to the needs and the culture of PartnerRe, as well as the fact that the PMO consisted of project managers who were actively leading and managing projects and ready to take on additional responsibilities. The other professional project managers within the organization served as a reservoir to take on coaching and support tasks. Where necessary, business leaders were supported by professional project managers to ensure structure and successful outcome.

The chosen organizational setup resulted in many business leaders being exposed to project-management-related topics with the following effects:

♦ Appreciation for the fact that project management is a discipline
♦ Adaptation of project-management-related tools and techniques that are now more widely accepted in the organization than before

From the very start, all stream leads used the same templates and presentation formats in workshops. The workshop participants could therefore concentrate on content rather than form—and that proved to be very efficient. This was possible because the Project Management Knowledge Center illustrated in Figure S27.2 already existed and all of its content was easy to access. If everything needed to be created from scratch at the initiation of this integration project, it would have been much more painful.

One remarkable example of simplification concerned the project progress report template. Our original template had to be simplified quite a bit to gain acceptance throughout all ranks of management. Some detail was lost, which we as professional project managers had always perceived to be absolutely key for the success of a project. Reality taught us that the simplified version actually served the purpose very well, if not better than our original template, as it forced people to focus on the essentials. Did we lose anything? No. Did we gain something? Yes—acceptance and widespread use of the methodology and tools and a focus on the essential information.

An episode involving status reporting is clear evidence of this. Frequent discussions took place around traffic-light colors to be used for stream status reporting. A tendency, not surprisingly, was to show most of the streams *green*. In one of the reporting cycles one stream lead insisted on reporting an *orange* status because it was felt that this was the right status to show. In the subsequent project steering committee meeting after a significant number of open topics had been discussed, one of the executives observed that all streams but one had reported their status as *green*. This

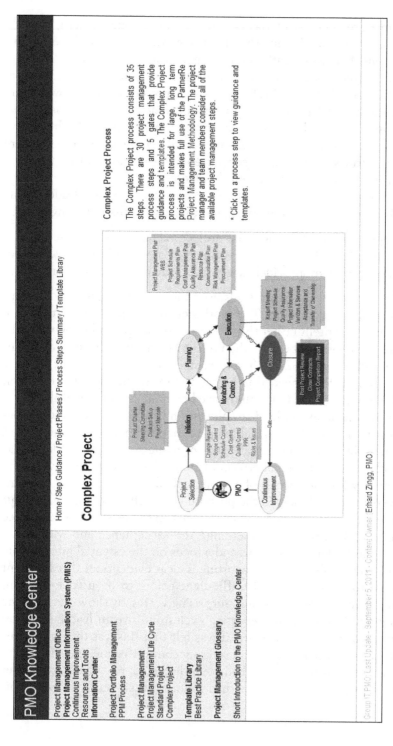

Figure S27.2   PMO Knowledge Center—complex project entry page

did not match his assessment of the overall state of the project having just reviewed all the open topics. The status reports were actually used and interpreted! They were seen as a useful tool due to their relative simplicity. This is in strong contrast to other situations where status reports very often go unnoticed and unread—with the effect that project managers in those situations feel like they are just doing admin when preparing status reports.

Concluding Thoughts and Advice

The bigger and more complex a project looks at the outset, the more one could be tempted to apply rigorous boundaries and rules to keep everything under control. However, this story shows that pragmatism in the application of project management practices sometimes is necessary. Finding the right balance between a prescribed structure and the empowerment to be flexible and creative can make or break an initiative. Adapt to the circumstances and don't overdo it. Policies, guidelines, and standards do not always have to be absolutely perfect, but rather good enough to serve the purpose. In the case described here, a good collaborative platform and a limited set of tools definitely made big contributions to a successful outcome.

People are receptive to using what already exists—provided it is not overengineered but *practical* to use and adds value rather than overhead. This can be achieved through intuitive tools and templates that allow for a short learning curve, quick evidence of productivity, and readily available support from the PMO.

Epilogue

As a young business professional more than three decades ago, I became passionate about PMOs. In my first PMO experience, we decorated the walls of the PMO office with all kinds of dashboards and reports for our leadership team and visiting executives. The mainframe VM/CMS end user computing tools that we accessed from our color CRT terminals were state-of-the-art at the time, now ancient relics more primitive and less useful than stones and axes. Yes, technology and the many ways in which we can use technology have changed rapidly and massively over the years, but what hasn't changed is the business premise under which companies, organizations, and people operate.

Far too often, organizations lose sight of the business premise. Carried away with the latest buzz and hype, organizations jump on the band wagon and implement strategies du jour without first understanding the business context for which that strategy may or may not even be relevant. This putting the cart before the horse is followed by a runaway freight train of good intentions and effort, but rarely followed by end results achieved. It happens all the time.

In a roundtable panel discussion at the 2010 Gartner Group PPM and IT Governance Summit to talk about the topic "The New Normal," it was best put by Mark Langley, the President and CEO of the Project Management Institute, who, after following a number of other panelists who gave their apocalyptic predictions and views of what CIOs must do to keep the world as we know it from ending, said, "If this is the new normal, then I would like to know, what was the old normal?" Mr. Langley's point was not lost on the audience. Businesses have been and will always be faced with change. The answer isn't to quixotically stab at the latest windmill. Rather, the answer is the same as it has always been: to manage the business in the most effective way possible, to seek continual improvement, and to never give up the search for that which is excellent. But where does one learn how to do that?

One approach employed years back by many companies, especially large companies, was the continual rotation of management leaders between line management positions and staff management positions. The premise was that as good as line executives might be, it was important for their professional development and continued advancement to experience first-hand staff management positions and vice versa. The benefits gained with this strategy were enormous. Line executives such as sales and marketing vice presidents and division managers, all too familiar with their objective rich business units that were directly in the supply chain of the company, were exposed to the management challenges of business units somewhat removed from the immediate supply chain. Similarly, leaders of divisions and departments who supported but were not in the immediate supply chain and who typically were not accustomed to the management by objective measurement and compensation system soon learned it. That this approach was effective could not be denied; that it was affordable could not be defended.

At present, few organizations rotate their management and leadership teams. Hence, people develop their business, management, and leadership skills from the organizational silos in which they live. For many departments, this approach to management development is just fine. A steady state of work comes to the department and the department performs that work. Aside from emptying the work in the queue as effectively and efficiently as possible, there is not a great deal of business planning, analysis, goal setting, strategy development, staffing, organizational development, leadership, and accountability for business results in the form of attaining measurable objectives that serve as fulfillment of the business expectation.

Enter the PMO. For most organizations, the PMO is contemplated, approved, and funded by the leadership team in hopes of solving a problem or set of problems for which business as usual is not a viable option. Hence, a PMO is much like a business in a business. The PMO has a problem or set of problems to be solved, it has customers to serve, it assuredly has limited resources, it requires sound planning and management, it needs effective leadership, and it must have an ability to demonstrate that it has met the business need for which it was created to serve. So who is put in charge of the PMO: a skilled manager with years of business management and leadership experience or a subject matter expert who may even hold a certification but who has had minimal business management experience? For most organizations, it is the latter and that is where the problems of most PMOs first start to take root.

It is not that individual contributors, subject matter experts, and trained and certified project managers can't be good PMO managers; they can. In fact, most project managers are inherent servant-leaders, highly competent, and possess many skills that are essential in business management. The problem, however, is that in the absence of years of business planning and management experience, most PMO managers look to the formal project management and PMO community for advice on how to set up and manage their PMOs. And for most PMOs, not all of course, this is the wrong place to look.

The reasons why are many. Although it would not be hard to cite one example after the other ranging from misguided advice to biased perspectives and exploitative behaviors, a kinder assessment would be that the formal project management and PMO community, though proficient in plan driven techniques, inherently focuses too much on the means to the ends and lacks the requisite business acumen and leadership skills and experience needed to establish and preside over an organization that is accountable for the ends to be achieved. And if that sounds too provocative, then at least consider that the formal project management and PMO community is not the only place to look for advice on how to set up and manage an organizational entity within a business.

If I can borrow from a truly great man, Lee Kuan Yew, whose vision, integrity, and resolve led Singapore from a tiny island of differing peoples to a strong vibrant nation, from third world to first, one should ignore the advice from all the quasi-experts who have their pet theories of how to do things, and instead one should be pragmatic and seek to be correct, but not politically correct.

In the context of PMOs, we must seek to be correct. Being correct will never be a cookie-cutter "people, process, tools" strategy and being correct will never be achieved in just six months. We must seek to first understand the very business problems for which the PMO can be created and exist to serve. We must set up and manage our PMOs with the same business acumen and leadership skills expected of all other organizations throughout the enterprise. With rare exception, the PMO is not a Center of Excellence, Community of Practice, country club, or otherwise entitled-to-exist organization; it must earn its keep.

This book and the Business Driven PMO series were intended to fulfill a void in the current literature about how to set up and manage a PMO. The three-book series, *Business Driven PMO Setup*, *Business Driven Project Portfolio Management*, and *Business Driven PMO Success Stories*, has attempted to provide a corrected and balanced perspective to the cacophony of standards, best practices, approaches, and views (means to the ends) that have amassed over the years which though well-intended have contributed to an unacceptably high organizational failure rate. In response to those who in discussions about PMOs lead off with a diatribe of PMO models and all the rest, I have responded that there is no such thing as a PMO model. However, after quite a bit of reflection, and after writing these three books, I have changed my position. There are PMOs models, but only two to be precise. They are PMOs that are driven by the needs of the business and PMOs that aren't.

The future is full of promise. The old hierarchical style of rank and file management has long given way to hybrid organizations driven by goals, enabled by knowledge, and led by highly talented people. There is no better organizational example of the potential for this than the business driven PMO.

Index